ALARM
STARBOARD!

ALARM STARBOARD!

*A remarkable true story
of the war at sea*

by

Geoffrey Brooke

Pen & Sword
MARITIME

To
John Persse, Lieutenant, 7th Rifle Brigade
Edward Egerton, Lieutenant, Royal Navy,
Sandy Buller, Pilot Officer, Royal Air Force

———▸◆◂———

First published in Great Britain in 1982 by Patrick Stephens
Published in this format in 2004 by Pen & Sword Maritime
an imprint of
Pen & Sword Books Ltd
47 Church Street
Barnsley
South Yorkshire
S70 2AS

Copyright © Geoffrey Brooke, 2004

ISBN 1 84415 230 8

The right of Geoffrey Brooke to be identified as Author of this Work has
been asserted by him in accordance with the Copyright,
Designs and Patents Act 1988.

A CIP catalogue record for this book is
available from the British Library

Printed and bound in England by
CPI UK

Pen & Sword Books Ltd incorporates the imprints of Pen & Sword
Aviation, Pen & Sword Maritime, Pen & Sword Military, Wharncliffe
Local History, Pen & Sword Select, Pen & Sword Military Classics
and Leo Cooper.

For a complete list of Pen & Sword titles please contact
PEN & SWORD BOOKS LIMITED
47 Church Street, Barnsley, South Yorkshire, S70 2AS, England
E-mail: enquiries@pen-and-sword.co.uk
Website: www.pen-and-sword.co.uk

Contents

Acknowledgements

My grateful thanks for assistance of various kinds are due to many, but particularly: Captain A.H. Barton, Commander W.T. Blunt, Captain E.H. Cartwright, Admiral Sir Henry Leach, GCB, Mrs M. Luce, Captain C.W. McMullen, DSC, Mr B.A. Passmore, Captain D.G. Roome, Lieutenant Commander P. Snow and Vice Admiral D.B.H. Wildish, CB. In addition the following two books proved invaluable: *Atlantic Meeting*, by A.E.W. Mason, and *Battleship Bismarck*, by Burkhard Von Müllenheim-Riechberg.

Introduction

This is not the story of a famous sailor, even a successful one, so it may be wondered how I have anything to say. In defence I would quote Admiral Sir William James, and a young female acquaintance who exclaimed, after my recounting a somewhat bizarre brush with the police, 'Why *is* it that such odd things are always happening to *you?*'

Strange things *have* happened to me, and this remark, coupled with Admiral James' dictum that every Naval officer has a good story to tell so long as he does not pontificate, started me off. An Irish weakness for a tale has helped but the going—entirely in my spare time—has proved harder than expected.

I am sure to have made mistakes, but have also been lucky. Quite unexpectedly my mother produced most of my letters written home during the period covered (1938-1945) and having always been a magpie I do have a store of contemporary papers. Some of these sources are quoted verbatim (the letters are all to my parents, except where otherwise stated) as they give the atmosphere of the moment better than any subsequent reflection. I must admit that some of them have also proved salutary; it is disconcerting to have dined out on a good story for years only to find that it did not happen quite like that!

The spelling of Indonesian place names may offend some, but I have found them to vary as much as my memories of that fascinating area.

It happens that battleships, carriers, cruisers and destroyers all figure intimately herein, laced with a lot of seasickness, a little sport and a happy home life. Therefore I hope it is not too presumptious to claim that, viewed though it is from a low 'height of eye', this very personal account—though with enough background to set the scene—presents a fair view of the Royal Navy during the traumatic years covered. That is before it was decimated by a feckless country unwilling to read either history or the writing on the wall.

There goes one pontification, but there won't be too many more!

G.A.G. BROOKE
Beech House, Balcombe, Sussex
May 1982

1

Prewar Midshipman

'Alarm starboard! Green seven-0; angle of sight six; engage—engage—engage!' A near-black bomber—though the first ever seen it was clearly a Heinkel 111—had broken through the scudding clouds and was diving on the battleship and the carrier. All three officers in the former's Air Defence Position had seen it at the same moment and we were feverishly pressing buttons and shouting into telephones and voice-pipes; to be acknowledged from far below by staccato orders and the metallic thuds of closing breeches.

Not in time, however, and the enemy aircraft roared down unmolested, straight for us in the *Nelson*. There was nothing more to do. I felt a dastardly desire to take cover and stole a glance at Whitting, the other Midshipman, to see his reaction. As often when tense moments stamp the scene on one's inner eye, I have a clear impression of the sun on his weatherbeaten, snub-nosed features, the eyes narrowed to slits as he gazed upwards with complete unconcern.

At the last moment the plane jinked to its left, steadied up on the *Ark Royal* astern of us and let go what in those days was a huge bomb. It fell deceptively slowly, like a fat cabin trunk, as we stared fascinated. Landing with a huge splash a few yards off the carrier's starboard side, it burst beneath, heaving her bow right out of the sea so that the angular, brown-painted forefoot jutted clear. At the same time a massive cowl of black smoke and dirty water rose up about twice the height of the flight deck and obliterated the entire forward part of the ship. My heart missed a beat and there were gasps from the others. But the *Ark* sank back, the upheaval subsided and we were astonished to see her unscathed. The guns' crews were stood down and the two ships continued their patrol of the unhospitable grey waste of the North Sea.

The clang of feet up the steel ladder to our eyrie forty feet above the bridge heralded reliefs and Johnny Bowles, flushed with the effort, was soon beside me. Ignoring his 'You were all fast asleep, I suppose?' I followed his gaze to the destroyer screen, a dipping, wriggling arrowhead of purposeful little ships, each with its pennant number painted on the side. They were 'E's of the 5th Flotilla and instinctively we scrutinised the *Esk* as she rose and fell, the figures on her bridge occasionally ducking as a sea broke clean over them. Johnny turned to me with a malicious grin. I knew what he was thinking. We had done our three months' destroyer course together in the *Esk* and I had been dreadfully seasick most of the time. I made a rude gesture at him and went below to the welcome fug of the Gunroom.

After wolfing some tea I got out my journal—a mammoth diary we had to write up daily—and recorded the Heinkel's doings while they were still fresh in my mind. The war was two weeks old and the big, ugly bomb—this was it; the real thing that we had been preparing and training for ever since I had joined the ship nearly two years ago.

It did not seem two years since that cold January morning at Portsmouth when the three of us had presented ourselves to the Officer of the Watch ('Midshipman Brooke come aboard to join, Sir!') resplendent in round jacket with its vertical row of brass buttons, 'snotties'' white collar tabs and bright new dirk. I read again, with a patronising smile, the first halting entry in my journal; how it brought it all back.

We new arrivals, directed down to the Gunroom, were being eyed like lepers by the senior Midshipmen when in strode the Sub-Lieutenant. He gave each of us a silent scrutiny and we took stock of him with hardly less interest, a tallish, fresh-faced and—after a few to-the-point remarks—obviously live-wire customer called Hawkins. He saw Johnny Bowles of medium height and very broad, with black hair (usually a bunch of it over his forehead) and dark, lively eyes; 'Pop' Snow, very small but well built and already going bald—hence the nickname— unflappable and phlegmatic; and me, tall, thin, keen (according to my reports!) and maddeningly vague. Because of the latter I sensed trouble with the Sub and was not far wrong. I had been the first cadet of my term to be beaten on arrival at the RN College, Dartmouth, and the last before leaving. Still very much a Gunroom tradition, it looked as if this painful progress—my posterior was poorly upholstered—was going to continue. (As it happens it did not, more a measure of the forbearance of Hawkins, who certainly drove us hard, than of me.)

It should be explained that Midshipmen were found only in cruisers and above. Their mess, the Gunroom, was presided over by a Sub-Lieutenant who had powers of life and death except in the realms of education and leave. These were the responsibility of the 'Snotties' Nurse'—a Lieutenant Commander saddled therewith in addition to his normal duty—who now introduced us to the Captain, W.T. Maceig-Jones, and the Commander. The former was huge—he had been a heavy-weight boxer in his time—and rather intimidating at first, though not on closer acquaintance. The Commander really was intimidating but my morale was restored by the Gunnery Officer who asked whether I'd done any pheasant shooting and said 'I'll give you a pom-pom director—it's much the same thing'.

Boatrunning, in charge of one of the ship's many boats and quarter-deck watchkeeping, as assistant to the hard-pressed Officer of the Watch, started at once. HMS *Nelson* was the Home Fleet flagship and one was constantly coping on the quarterdeck with important visitors to the Commander-in-Chief, Admiral Sir Roger Backhouse. The ceremonial ramifications were at first overpowering; only those of the *Nelson* herself seemed greater. Getting to know the big battleship was a bewildering if fascinating task. Often one would be more than a deck out in one's calculations after emerging from an overalled exploration of engine room, magazine, store room or gun turret. The main armament of 16-in guns (postcards on sale at the canteen showed grinning sailors emerging from their gaping barrels) and all their ancillary machinery, from the loading arrangements that brought the sinister, black projectiles up from their beds, to the delicate fire control table, were laboriously explained to us. (The latter was in fact a huge table, solid to the ground with gears, spindles, cams, electric motors and differentials; all the paraphernalia that enabled one to set data and have it point the guns at the correct spot in the sea so that when the shells arrived 30 seconds later they would, hopefully, find the enemy there too.)

Early in the third week, fallen in so as to line the ship's port side, we heard the tugs ordered to slip. The deck began to vibrate under foot and on the first of umpteen occasions in my naval career the Portsmouth panorama unfolded steadily: the Hard, fronting its railway-bounded lagoon, the stone frigate *Vernon* (home of naval torpedoes) and the ancient quay that Nelson knew. An exchange of salutes with bugle or pipe marked each authority until, with Southsea fading in the drizzle on our side and the Spithead forts looming on the other, 'Disperse—make up wires and fenders' had us guiding the arm-thick hawsers back on to the reels as they had not known for weeks.

*   *   *

The Home Fleet's year was divided into three cruises followed by leave periods, much like school terms, and we were now embarking on the Spring Cruise to the Mediterranean. The main object of this was the Combined Fleet Manoeuvres with the 'Med' Fleet, all of us based on Gibraltar where the ship berthed a few days later. The weather was kind, the band played lively tunes to encourage the hundreds of men painting the ship's side and life was good. It became even better.

My father, a retired Naval Captain, had told me to 'look out for Colonel Sturges, he's an old friend of mine!' Naturally the only steps I took in this direction were to ascertain that he was the Fleet Royal Marine Officer on the Admiral's staff, and it was a surprise to receive a summons to his cabin. He said he had been offered a mount in the amateur 'scurry' at the races on Saturday, would be unable to get away and would I like to take over? Thanking him profusely and accepting the loan of his racing boots I went off in a haze of excitement. It was difficult to contain myself, but at last the owner, a sunburnt young man with sleek black hair and a pencil moustache was inferring that 'Pierrot' had every chance, though he eyed my disproportionate length, attired in 'mauve, grey-silver cross, mauve cap', without enthusiasm. It was a flag start. A paternal dictum had recently come back to me that few people rarely drop a flag cleanly; they always raise it a fraction first in the unconscious effort to get a quick movement.

'Are you ready?' A twitch from the flag and I dug in my heels. It went down all right and I seemed to have pinched half a length. Nobody got it back and an unashamedly excited jockey slid off Pierrot in the winner's enclosure, to be projected into a little circle. A distinguished old gentleman, afterwards revealed as the Governor, handed over a nice cup and asked where I had learned to ride 'short'. 'At Chattis Hill', I said, without a thought that it might mean nothing to him. 'Ah', he said, obviously well informed, 'I call that hardly fair!' (Chattis Hill was the racing stable of my uncle, Atty Persse.) However, any personal kudos was largely evaporated the next Saturday when the process was repeated, the Governor being almost disapproving as he handed over an exact twin, and the jockey's part was still further discounted when Colonel Sturges, pounds overweight, rode the gallant Pierrot to victory the third week. But it was gratifying to be instructed by the Sub to produce the cups on guest nights. They gleamed most satisfactorily in the candlelight and helped to bolster my ego in those early uncertain weeks.

Gunroom guest night was an amusing affair. At least for the hosts. Wardroom guests would be chosen primarily for their gladiatorial ability, to be tested after a more or less set progression of pitfalls (such as mention of a lady's name before passage of the port) had been fixed and fallen into. After replacement of the port stoppers, 'Dogs of war' marked the end of such decorum as remained. A Midshipman would be accused of some misdemeanour and up would go the cry 'Dogs of war on Mr X', the signal for all the others to rise and project him bodily through the door, if possible removing his trousers in the process. In the case of a powerful fellow this took some minutes, he taking advantage of every pillar or post that intervened. Black eyes sprouted fairly freely but as soon as the victim felt the cold passage deck on his behind the mob would disperse and return for more. (On one occasion the victim was Whitting, currently unpopular for continually pronouncing that he wished he had joined the Army. After a struggle we had him outside and as I had been the nearest 'dog' initially I was now on top of him and underneath a dozen other 'dogs'. My nose bleeds fairly easily; it now poured on to poor Whitting's boiled shirt front and it was a very long time before those on top condescended to get off.)

The hitherto omnipotent Sub would be hoist with his own petard and then would come the pièce de résistance—the unfortunate guests, amongst whom the wiser ones would have already slipped out and changed into an older pair of trousers. 'Dogs of war on Commander —!', and the first of several real battles—Wardroom honour being at stake—would begin. One of the better gladiators was Lieutenant Commander A.C.C. Miers, a submariner doing his big ship time. Though short, he was of immensely strong physique. It would take one of us on each limb to keep him down and he would sometimes descend to the Gunroom after an evening game of deck hockey and incite a rough-and-tumble for the fun of it. (He was to demonstrate not only physical toughness when in 1942 he took the submarine *Torbay* into an enemy harbour, to win the VC.) Events would then take a less personal turn—feats of strength, bawdy songs round the piano—until 'lights'; a plea to the Commander for an extension, and then the end of that, with most people ready enough to desist.

Such high-jinks were really but bright interludes to endless exercises in the local Atlantic. Most enjoyable of these was live practice with my pom-pom director, of which I was inordinately proud, usually at red sausage-shaped targets towed behind Gib-based aircraft. Mounted on a projecting sponson high up on the side of the bridge (it had a twin the other side), the director itself was a miniature application of the universal gunnery principle that a gun is better aimed and fired by remote control, away from the 'dust of the battle, the din and the cries'. Though entirely a matter of how far to aim in front of the target, that was about as near to pheasant shooting as it came, there being a cart-wheel sight among the rings and spokes of which one placed the target as accurately as possible. Movement was recorded electrically at the gun, where the layer and trainer followed pointers in dials. It was a considerable thrill to press the trigger and loose a shuddering cacophony of fury as the eight kicking barrels pumped away below, deafening anyone near and living up to their Press nickname of 'Chicago Pianos'. Two shells left each barrel every second and great things were expected of multiple pom-poms (not really fulfilled in the acid test, especially, as will be seen, against Japanese suicide aircraft.)

The time came for the ship to sortie yet again from between the moles, but to turn east for a change. A leisurely week at Malta ensued, welcome breathing space before the manoeuvres. Soon after our arrival the Captain addressed the ship's company; he said the *Nelson* was at last fairly clean and now it was the duty of everyone on board to make her an efficient unit by knowing not only his own job but the next man's as well; that we must be prepared to fight in the not too distant future, and success would only come from hard personal effort. I think this fell on somewhat heedless ears as far as the Midshipmen were concerned. Everyone talked of war but we lived for the moment.

Across the limpid water of Grand Harbour, its glorious blue contrasting with the yellow cascading terraces of ancient Valetta, lay two battleships and two battlecruisers of the Mediterranean Fleet. They were *Warspite*, the flagship, *Malaya, Hood* and *Repulse*. In particular *Hood* and *Repulse* evoked admiration—huge, majestic and beautiful. The symmetry of their stately battlements, shining almost white in the hot sun, was mirrored in the limpid water, broken only by the wash of a picket boat or the more leisurely passage of a high-prowed Maltese dghaisa. They looked unbeatable. Perhaps if I could have had a glimpse into the future to see both of them sink only yards away, the Captain's words might have been more strongly heeded.

The visit to Malta was finally made memorable by a faux pas at the opera, to which I had been bidden by the Marquesa Mattei, a grande dame of Malta (my cousin, Lieutenant Commander John Tothill, had married her daughter Mary). We were promenading sedately in the entr'acte when, to my consternation, there loomed the venerable figure of Admiral Sir Dudley Pound, Commander-in-Chief, Mediterranean, approaching to talk to her. We were both in uniform, he splendid in mess dress and I in my less gilded round jacket. I hid behind her skirts, shifting from one leg to another, until he, obviously aware of my embarrassment, gave me a kindly wink. Without thinking, I winked back and received a very old-fashioned look.

On return to Gibraltar the Home Fleet battleships carried out a main armament shoot at a battle-practice target. The junior Midshipmen were put in a turret on this occasion and it was with a pleasant tingle of apprehension that we watched the three guns' crews go through their preliminary drill. The officer of the turret with his Midshipman and turret Petty Officer sat at the back. Behind and above them was the rangetaker, peering into his 30-foot instrument that spanned the whole gunhouse to protrude, like a pair of ears, each side. The guns' crews, some ten to a gun, wearing white flash-proof balaclavas and gauntlets, stood or sat in bucket seats beside their particular bits of machinery. Orders from the Gunnery Officer in the director came through with staccato precision. The whole place gleamed with hospital whiteness and reflecting metal.

It is not difficult to recall the atmosphere. All is ready; no-one moves and the air is expectant.

Suddenly, 'Follow director! All guns load!', and controlled pandemonium takes charge. The huge breech nearest me swings open with a shrill hiss (compressed air automatically loosed to clear smoking

12

barrels), *clang* goes the loading tray and an ever increasing rumble announces the approach of a shell. 'Salvoes!' *Thud* and the shell cage locks itself on to the rear of the tray. Then a rattling roar as the hammer—a bicycle chain as thick as a man's waist—hurtles up the same path, round a hidden sheave and, its great joints a horizontal blur of speed, punches the black one-ton shell into the gaping barrel. The copper driving band bites into the rifling with an echoing ring. Each action is followed by a report from its originator, yelled with the full force of his lungs but only just audible; each report is the signal for the next man to move his lever, and unleash another mass of hydraulic power. Back rattles the rammer (more gently and not so far) and we just glimpse the white cotton cylinder with its red tip as the first cordite charge is sent in. Another goes in behind it, the rammer disappears, the cage drops, the loading tray leaps back and the breech swings shut. Some of it revolves as precision grooves lock with their static partners. Machinery hums and the whole affair drops down. It wavers gently as the gunlayer picks up the slowly moving pointer from the director eighty feet above him. 'Layer on!' he shouts. 'Right gun ready', yells the breechworker and knocks up a big brass switch with the palm of his hand. This burns a light both in the Transmitting Station and in front of the director layer; when all the guns are seen to be ready he can press his trigger. The breech is deep in the gunwell below us, moving gently on its trunnions, 20 tons of cannon balanced like a child's seesaw as the ship's roll is counteracted and the range increases or decreases according to a dozen varying factors. I find I am holding my breath. One cannot see the barrels, of course, but they are high in the air. 'WOOMF!' goes the gun, leaping six feet backwards; up comes the breech; it opens with a hiss, and all begins again.

The spectacle of huge chunks of metal moving as if they were made of wood, being placed with instant precision and split second timing, the shouted reports, the angry recoil of the guns, the noise, the smell of burnt cordite, and the whole scene being enacted in glistening white triplicate, never failed to thrill. I felt that 'this was what I had joined up for', a phrase more often employed in sarcasm for the unpopular chores of naval life.

The end product was also spectacular. A broadside of nine 16-inch shells would send up a white curtain 200 yards wide and almost as high, to fan out and subside with leisurely grace.

Eventually the day of the Combined Fleet Manoeuvres dawned. The Red (Home) Fleet left harbour to form up eastwards in Algeciras Bay, the *Nelson* slipping last, to glide through an avenue of shrill salutes, to her place at the head of the battle line. With the destroyers in their usual protective formation and beyond them the cruisers, the dark grey armada moved into the Atlantic. Our pale grey opponents, the Blue

(Med) Fleet, were making for their war base—Madeira—and we were out to intercept them on the way. A night action took place between the cruisers and destroyers, the former spread in a ten mile diagonal line before their respective battle fleets. I saw starshell fired for the first time—yellow balls of light that, projected in our case from the high angle 4.7-inch guns, descended gently on their parachutes to turn night into jaundiced day beneath. As with a good firework display a new batch would take over just as its predecessor dropped into the sea. Sometimes they would be behind the enemy who stood out silhouetted, like a model in a bowl of molten brass; at others in front, when every detail of his upper deck could be discerned.

At first light the sky was dotted with *Courageous'* aircraft, waiting to break up a Blue air attack. Later both fleets combined for tactical positioning manoeuvres. Another night encounter after dark, and so it went on. The following year, when increasing familiarity bred a more blasé attitude, I found little to record in my journal, but the combined manoeuvres, 1938, saw a fascinated youth covering page after page of a sketch book as cruisers careered, destroyers darted and battleships bowled along. Destroyer torpedo attacks were the most exciting, usually materialising as dots in line abreast from behind rolling black smoke screens, furious heaving midgets that, rocketing to head us off, would suddenly elongate into sleek grey ships as they turned as one to fire. 'Blue four numeral—down' a voice would yell; 'Starboard twenty' in level tones from the Officer of the Watch on the bridge nearby, and it was our turn to shudder and heel as the battle fleet altered course to 'comb' the tracks, whether real or imaginary, of torpedoes. The destroyers would be away again, probably back into their smoke screen, departure hastened, as in fact their approach had been harassed, by the long accusing fingers of our 6-inch guns.

The danger past, we would alter course back again, the *Rodney, Resolution, Royal Oak, Ramillies* and *Royal Sovereign* (in order of the seniority of their Captains) hauling ponderously round as the flags dropped from the *Nelson*'s yardarm. It was interesting to see how each ship came into her station; a simple enough manoeuvre but requiring only a few seconds delay at the start, slow reaction from a raw quarter-master, or too heavy an application of opposite rudder, for the delinquent to find herself nakedly out of line. On these occasions one could imagine an exasperated Captain growling at a flushed Officer of the Watch, as I had witnessed on our bridge, or perhaps a few words of quiet encouragement as I had also seen. Both would be dreading the dry comment from *Nelson*'s yardarm 'Manoeuvre badly executed' if the Admiral had been looking aft at the crucial moment—as it seemed he always was.

I would study the battleships astern through binoculars (issued strictly for the early detection of attacking aircraft), watching them roll with the slow dignity of their kind; great pyramids of power that looked as if nothing in the world could stop them. I could see the bridge personnel of our next astern and wondered who the Midshipman of the Watch might be; it looked like that chap who robbed us of the hockey final—'Alarm port!' shouts my communication number. *Zeep, zeep, zeep,* goes the alarm buzzer and I am guiltily aware of screaming aero engines. Half a dozen Nimrods are diving down sun and the first three are over and away before we are properly settled. But we reckon to have got two of the remainder. There are white smudges on the fo'c's'le, where bags of flour have arrived, and then it is 'return to lookout bearing'.

Darkness seldom brought abatement. All one saw of the nearest ship was a denser blackness poised over the intermittent glow of her bow wave. With the ship's company closed up at night action stations, the great 16-inch guns trained over the inky water that glided under them, and everyone with binoculars sweeping slowly back and forth, the atmosphere of expectancy was almost tangible. Perched on top of the towerlike bridge stood the main 16-inch director and two smaller 6-inch ones, both with the same basic tasks as my little pom-pom director. Heavy cylindrical towers, mounted on roller paths and ingeniously full of men and machinery, they hummed and groaned away the waiting minutes, training slowly from side to side with grim expectancy.

Suddenly, 'Enemy in sight, bearing 154' from Cartwright, a snottie with gyro-stabilised binoculars. 'Alarm starboard, green four-0' from the Captain, echoed immediately by his communication number at the back of the bridge and then taken up, like 'noises off' by colleagues in various stations around. The groaning of the directors rises to a near scream as they churn themselves on to the bearing indicated. By this time the Captain can see the enemy (if he had not been first to spot them at the outset)—a line of battleships at 6,000 yards. '3BS-160-3-070-20!' The enemy report comes out pat. Click goes a switch and a microphone hums. '3BS-160-3-070-20!' intones the Chief Yeoman of Signals and if the remainder of the fleet do not know already they learn that *Nelson* has three enemy battleships in sight, bearing 160° at three miles range, steering 070° at 20 knots. 'Searchlights on' from Snow. 'Director target' from the Gunnery Officer. 'Battle fleet from C-in-C stand by to alter course 20 degrees to starboard' from a metallic voice. 'Battle fleet from . . .' 'Yes, I heard it' from the Captain. 'Ready to open fire!' from the Gunnery Officer. 'Open fire!' from the Captain, 'Shoot' from the Gunnery Officer, and then 'Illuminate!' *Ting-ting* from the fire gong and *clang*, a fat pencil of white light has shot out from half way up our only funnel to reveal the *Queen Elizabeth* about 4,000 yards away and the suggestion of her consorts astern. We have just time to see that

15

we are looking down the barrels of her guns before she disappears in a ball of brightness, her searchlight on us.

'Stand by to alter 30 degrees to port together, Sir!' 'Stand by; EXECUTIVE SIGNAL!' 'Port twenty', says the Officer of the Watch, almost confidentially, bending over a voice pipe. His eyes, lit from the side, are strangely translucent. 'Twenty of port wheel on, Sir' reports the Quartermaster, 90 feet below. *Ting-ting* from the fire gong again, warning of an impending salvo. It looks as if we beat the *QE* to the punch, a first class example of where seconds count. 'Midships' from the Officer of the Watch. 'Ready to fire torpedoes' from the Torpedo Officer at the wing of the bridge. *Ting-ting*. 'Battle fleet from C-in-C, stand by to resume previous course together.' 'Torpedoes fired, Sir.' 'Switch off.' 'Stand by . . . executive signal.' 'Starboard twenty.' *Ting-Ting*. 'Cease firing!' And then all is blackness and comparative calm. Soon the signal 'Exercise completed' arrives, guns come slowly fore and aft, canvas covers are put over exposed instruments, ladders clang with feet eager for hammocks and I join the queue outside the gunnery office where recorders are handing in their columns of words, deeds and split seconds.

Night firings at battle practice targets, if more deliberate, were just as exciting. If those in exposed positions did not shut their eyes at the warning *ting-ting* of the 16-inch fire gong, the great orange wall of flame that belched out of the muzzles would leave them blind for 30 seconds. A hot pressure wave would surge over one but the sound, more of a majestic roar than a bang, was not as unpleasant as that of the 6-inch secondary armament.

★   ★   ★

When Gibraltar finally faded astern, most of us were sorry to see the last, for a year, of this hectic work-and-play ground. Soon after our return the Commander-in-Chief left (to become First Sea Lord) and all the officers were introduced to the new one, Admiral Sir Charles Forbes. A small, well-built man with a lined face, heavy jaw and inquisitive eyes, he was to take on Jellicoe's mantle and with it the ability to 'lose the war in an afternoon' as Churchill had put it.

The idea that such a thing was not impossible had begun to dawn on some, but by no means all. Just before the ship sailed on the second cruise of the year, the area was blacked out, or was supposed to be, for trial. The C-in-C, Portsmouth, flew over the city and expressed himself dissatisfied with what he saw. No doubt the man in the street's attitude was the same as that of the average junior officer: a definite apprehension, not without its tinge of excitement, fed by political speeches from both Hitler and our side, but the whole under an umbrella on which was painted 'It can't happen to us'. Chamberlain's visit to Munich was just four months off as ships of the Home Fleet began to leave their respective bases for assembly at Portland.

Fitted into the heavy programme of firings and exercises there, was training for the Battle Squadron pulling regatta. Dovetailed might be a better word. On entering harbour, boats descended immediately from davit and derrick, returning to an exact timetable for fresh crews, the process continuing till supper. In all some 50 crews trained in cutters, gigs and whalers of which less than a quarter would represent the ship. A regatta training news sheet was printed daily with the times of the various trials; challenges were made and accepted and interest fanned to fever pitch. Though the accolade of the Gunroom 'A' crew passed me by, a fair share of hand and bottom blisters did not. With each ship putting so much into it, the result would be a fair reflection of the general spirit of all concerned. Came the day and race after race peeled off to non-stop cheers, a tight organisation of picket boats and launches towing fresh crews to the start as the gladiators of the hour struggled for the line, muscles straining, heads rolling and coxswains bellowing the stroke. At the end of it all we had come third—a considerable disappointment—beaten by *Royal Oak* and *Rodney*.

Morale was shortly restored, however, when the *Nelson*'s 4.7-inch battery shot down a pilotless, wireless-controlled Queen Bee aircraft. (As it happens, I was to marry the niece of the officer who developed the Queen Bees, Commander The Hon Henry Cecil, a charming and most talented man.) The satisfactory splash made by this plummeting plane seemed a healthy augury for the great event, now only a fortnight off, that was everyone's dateline from the staff completing plans for three days' demonstrations to boys sewing chinstays into new caps. King George VI was to visit the fleet.

It was late one evening when His Majesty's sleek blue barge came in sight, planing out to the Royal Yacht, *Victoria and Albert*, with an escort of fast motor boats. The whole fleet, anchored in Weymouth Bay, was spread seawards of 'The Yacht', their ships' companies paraded. The Royal Standard billowed out from the masthead as the King stepped on board the *Nelson* at 09:30 next morning (and with such a bevy of VIPs that, half way through the day, when a signal boy was told 'Look out! There's someone important comin'' I saw him glance down from the flagdeck and say 'Oh, its only the C-in-C'.)

We put to sea immediately for a demonstration programme to unfold with clockwork precision. The 2nd Cruiser Squadron (*Southampton* Class) came past at 25 knots, catapulting their aircraft; these formed up and dipped over the flagship in salute; by this time the 4th and 6th Destroyer Flotillas, led by Rear Admiral (D) in his cruiser *Aurora*, were already coming in with a massed torpedo attack; the close screen (5th

Destroyer Flotilla) counter-attacked; they were not back in station before aircraft from *Courageous* swooped down, thunderous dive bombing runs being synchronised with the bubbling tracks of torpedoes as several passed right under our keel; the air was no sooner clear than *Newcastle* launched a Queen Bee to be shot at by the cruisers, *Southampton* bringing it down.

The King then walked round the upper deck, watching the boys at field training and the normal work of the ship in progress. It was on his return to the Admiral's bridge that, on my way down, I nearly disgraced myself. Passage was via many steep ladders in the enclosed structure and one's usual method of descent was to slide down with hands on the rails and feet in advance, well up. I was launched into this manoeuvre when the landing spot was suddenly filled by a gold-braided cap and body to match. With a great effort I managed to land short and scramble back. The cap, now followed by another, looked up. It was Captain Lord Louis Mountbatten and Rear-Admiral the Duke of Kent. They were both chuckling over something and as they continued past (I was pressed hard against the bulkhead) the Duke of Kent said 'And the killing thing is they've forgotten to pack the monarch's dinner jacket. There *will* be a row!'

Momentarily marvelling that such a homely error could be made in such exalted circles, I realised that someone else was coming and then, by the hum of voices, many more. First was the Master at Arms, looking important fit to burst. He was holding his black handled sword clear of the steps in front of him like a bishop's crook. We exchanged horrified glances but flight for me was out of the question; I was in a royal sandwich and must stand my ground. The King came next. He gave me an inquisitive glance and I tried hard to look composed. He passed a few inches in front of me, turning to the foot of the next ladder and continuing up. I studied him as carefully as I dared; he was a little shorter than photographs had led one to expect and looked incredibly healthy with frank, clear eyes and a bronze skin. Then followed most of the retinue but, in common with the earlier signal boy, I had lost interest in mere Admirals and they passed in a blur.

Just before returning to harbour three flights of bombers dropped live bombs in the sea just in front of the *Nelson*, who steamed through their discoloured aftermath. The next day was spent going round shore establishments, during which all available boats were sent away under sail, a considerable armada. Having ordered 'Splice the Mainbrace', the King finally left through lines of ships crowded with cheering men.

The *Nelson* sailed the following morning for the Clyde, reached after intensive exercises with four submarines. The new carrier *Ark Royal*, passed at anchor, was the subject of keen scrutinies; she looked massive and rather ugly, I thought. A gale was blowing when we anchored and the weather continued thus, on and off, for the whole of the fortnight there.

One night in my launch (a 40-foot mostly open boat) it was too rough to secure her to the boom and I decided to go inshore. There was no response when I hailed the Officer of the Watch on the quarterdeck; obviously the blighter was sheltering so I vented my midnight spleen with six energetic but successful wrenches on the klaxon horn. Return next morning, stiff and miserable, was enlivened by the Snotties' Nurse: I had woken up the Admiral and my leave was stopped for a month. Bored with nothing to do in the ensuing dog watches (off-duty evening hours) I took over my friends' boats so that they could go ashore. The weather continued atrocious, keeping me permanently soaked and the day we sailed for a social visit to Kristiansand in Norway I reported sick.

Having taken no interest in the following week it was with great surprise that I awoke in a large brass bed. My surroundings were so much more civilised than anything experienced since the last leave that it seemed at first I must be in a hotel. But if so it had a gently throbbing undertone, round brass windows and a heavy footed gentleman exercising outside with a 'squeak-thump' that was curiously familiar. I raised the telephone by the bed, at which there was an unusually quick response, and asked where I was. An incredulous pause, then 'You're in the Captain's cabin, Sir!' Even though he had a separate sea-cabin, this was particularly nice of Captain Maceig-Jones. Apparently I had been dangerously ill with pneumonia and he had cabled my parents daily bulletins. There would seem to be two or three morals to this story, but 'Let sleeping Admirals lie' must be the chief.

⋆   ⋆   ⋆

The *Nelson* went into dock shortly after return to Portsmouth and it was instructive to walk under the immense hull, now green with weed, and gaze up at the 20-ft propellers that had churned their way many thousands of miles even since I had joined. The Commander was relieved by Commander T.K.W. Atkinson, who proved most approachable with a cheery charm. He was very neat and won our early approval, shoregoing, by affecting a silver tie with a dark blue shirt. Moreover, he could see us all off on the hockey field.

By now Bowles, Snow and myself could be trusted to break our boats up only in exceptional circumstances, we were of some assistance to the Officer of the Watch in harbour and could at least make good cocoa at sea. Hawkins had even eased up a little, possibly a sign that we were getting into the groove. Instructions arrived for us to join destroyers for the prescribed three months' experience and Johnny Bowles and I found ourselves on board HMS *Esk* of the 5th Flotilla, in the trot (a line of buoys at the inner end of Portsmouth harbour, thick with destroyers, two by two). Within minutes I was correcting charts under the dapper navigator (Lieutenant R.H. Fanshawe) and Bowles had disappeared in the opposite direction. More time was to be spent in charge of some small operation than being lectured about it, and one learnt, often after scathing comment, the hard way.

We messed in the Wardroom, slinging our hammocks in the officers' cabin flat. A very young Gunner (T), (torpedo specialisation, which included electrics), just promoted from the lower deck, joined on the same day; all his uniform was, of course, brand new and I remember helping him that first evening with an unco-operative bow tie. The Wardroom lay athwartships at the bottom of a small steel ladder from the after superstructure. The heavily built, ruddy faced Captain, Lieutenant Commander R.H. Peters, who never seemed to miss a trick, had his day and night cabins just forward. Next came the engine and boiler rooms which were not connected for passage and extended below the 'iron deck'. This was the long waist of the ship, where revolving quadruple torpedo tubes—each side of the after conning platform— were mounted on the centre line. With two 4.7-inch guns forward and two aft, a box-like bridge and two funnels, the 'E' Class destroyers, built about 1933, epitomised the current British destroyer shape.

The ship went out for local exercises at once. I had been sick in the *Nelson* in really rough weather but so had many other people. The *Esk* had hardly begun to raise and dip her sharp bow in a Solent sea that would not have moved the *Nelson* at all, when I began to feel bad. Amid amused glances from the sailors on watch, all rudely healthy with chin stays pressed into blue chins, I descended a deck to the bridge 'heads'. This continued all day. Johnny Bowles looked on also amused and quite unaffected, which made it worse. When the welcome shelter of Portsmouth harbour was regained I had kept down nothing. Fanshawe said of course I'd get over it after a few days; but this did not happen. When the flotilla finally sailed for Scottish waters it was blowing hard. He and I had the middle watch (midnight to 04:00) and I felt that this four hours with not a lot to occupy the mind would be the acid test. Called at 07:15 with no recollection of the middle I found it was still blowing a gale and the kind hearted 'Pilot' had countermanded my shake. Having determined that seasickness would never be allowed to interfere with duty I was very put out; the issue was, of course, only postponed and I soon discovered to my considerable distress that I was indeed a chronic sufferer. This was to colour my entire career in the Navy, as can be imagined, the knowledge that Nelson had been similarly cursed being small compensation! Life in the *Esk* therefore became a turbulent mixture of pleasing responsibility and this depressing cloud that lowered at sea.

She formed a sub-division with *Express*, often working in concert and securing alongside whenever ships paired off. The two First Lieutenants, inscrutable and ageing officers (of about 26!) invariably went ashore together; hers had chromium-plated the handrails and other brass fittings on *Express'* quarterdeck out of his own pocket and very good they looked.

Both ships were capable of minelaying and the Munich crisis saw us back in the Clyde where the deck rails and ugly black mines sitting on box-like sinkers were kept. The rails were being bolted on aft, warheads shipped on torpedoes and shells fuzed, so that the upper deck looked like an open-air machine shop, when I came out of the charthouse and into the hearing of a large and presumably unflappable, West Country signalman who was oiling the shutter of his 10-inch light. 'Zaturdaie', he growled, 'Oi was going to Glasgow Exhibition [with rising indignation] but now this ruddy warr cum alarng and Oi can't go!' Three days later he went; Chamberlain had come back from Munich, and naval war preparations were cancelled.

Mine rails discarded, the *Esk* sped to rejoin the Home Fleet on the east coast of Scotland where a pleasant personal interlude occurred at Invergordon. The Captain had an understanding with one of the local farmers and sent me ashore to enquire whether we could shoot partridges (no one else seemed to have a gun on board). The farmer said the shooting was let to the Captain of a battleship but had no objection if the latter was at sea! I semaphored this back, the skipper's answer was in the affirmative and we had a fairly fruitful day. The usual, more strenuous shooting went on all the time. With eight rivals the competitive element was always strong, as indeed it was in everything the destroyers did from streaming anti-mine equipment to simply hoisting the red and white pennant, to signify that the signal fluttering at *Exmouth*'s yardarm was understood. Though the *Nelson*'s signal staff were well drilled I wondered if they were as quick as these men who ripped flags out of their cubbyholes, clipped them together and seemed to have them shooting into the air all in one movement. Understaffed when things were really humming, occasion often arose for Bowles and I to give a hand, sometimes with success and sometimes overwhelmed with the speed of flashed letter or fluttering flag. At bursts of speed over 30 knots the little ship seemed to hurl herself from wave to wave, vibrating with a thrilling urgency and heeling over like a yacht when under helm. The stern would sink as the screws bit deep, the sea was a blur past the iron deck and a white highway frothed for a mile behind. This was the life I thought, and then when it began to blow, was not so sure!

21

Attacks on the battlefleet presented the reverse of the recent Mediterranean picture. We saw half a dozen heavy, relatively motionless ships, occasionally obscured by a shimmering wall as our downward plunge shattered an oncoming wave into glittering fragments. The Torpedo Control Officer, squinting along his brass sight, would begin to intone 'Ten degrees to go—five degrees to go' as the target ship grew. 'Flotilla stand by to alter course . . . 45 degrees to port together' from the Yeoman, watching *Exmouth*. We were in quarterline and a glance to port showed a diagonal view of the next ahead, 300 yards away, an occasional puff of brown smoke streaming horizontally from her funnels; over one's right shoulder the heaving bow of the next astern.

'Two degrees to go.' 'Stand by.' The Control Officer's right hand felt for the first of eight small levers, set in groups of four. 'Executive signal. Stand by to fire torpedoes' from the Yeoman and the Captain brought the ship round. 'Fire one', said the Control Officer methodically, moving the first lever. 'Fire one', repeated his communication number, a sailor in contact with the tubes' crew who also fired as an insurance. There was a slight *whoosh* and those with nothing to do saw the long silver cylinder with orange head leap out of its tube to dwell a second over the waves and then disappear with a splash. 'Fire two'— *whoosh—splash*—'Fire three', 'Fire four' and so on until, the swing of the ship imparting a fan shaped pattern, an eight-fold area of potential menace was spread towards the enemy. As we surged upright on the getaway course the target ships changed silhouette. They were combing the tracks that would soon trace thin green lines among them. Our new course had put the flotilla in line ahead and opened the range quickly. Nine navigating officers were feverishly plotting the torpedoes' final resting—or rather, floating—places. At the end of their run the practice heads automatically filled with compressed air and the great 'fish' would, it was hoped, await recovery, orange nose up and exuding bad-smelling smoke to assist recovery.

Incessant exercises with submarines, when we would sometimes take on the adversary solo, but more often in pairs, provided an introduction to the magic Asdic. A small cabinet in the corner of the bridge, just holding one man—though by bending over his shoulder one could see what was going on—emitted the intriguing *pong-wong, pong-wong*, amplified from the bottom of the ship. The second syllable was the echo off the submarine. It rose in pitch and frequency as the range closed, until, when the two sounds had almost run together, there was a stream of *ping-ping, ping-pings*. It was uncanny to hear the desultory *pong, pong*, feeling its unhurried way through the sea ahead, the direction altered by a steering wheel in the little cabinet. Then, suddenly, a faint but unmistakeable echo. 'Sub echo 102°' from the operator. *Pong-wong, pong-wong.* Sometimes it was not a submarine—bits of wreckage, fish, and even eddies often playing games with inexperienced hands.

The standard form of attack was for one ship, stopped, to hold the echo whilst radioing details of the target's movements to her consort. The latter, coming in at an angle and in receipt of information from her own Asdic, was in a good position to pinpoint the target. The last seconds of the attack would rely greatly on the watching ship since very close range shortened the echo time to an impracticable extent. The submarine would tow floats in the early stages of training to save time when she got lost but the hunter's Asdic team were not, of course, allowed to look at them. When proficiency became high the submarine Captain could try everything he knew (such as stopping bow on, diving to the bottom, last minute bursts of speed) and with all concerned from our skipper downwards straining every nerve, the contest of skill and guile had a fascination that turned hours into minutes.

One could imagine the white-sweatered submarine officers, icy, olive green fathoms between them and the sunlight, listening, calculating, listening. Reports of our movements would be coming from their own operators, and then as likely as not their Captain would act, breaking the tension with a getaway under full rudder perhaps, just before (or if Peters had been one move ahead—just as . . .) the token charge exploded nearby.

★   ★   ★

The end of our destroyer time came all too soon even if my innards were ready for it. Return to Gunroom life was anti-climax but there were compensations to come; the 1939 Spring Cruise in the Med more than lived up to its predecessor, providing delights equestrian, bibulous and aerial, to name only three. Poor Pierrot was sick but I soon got a line on another horse, owned and trained—most conveniently—by a taxi-driver. Mecaliff would call for me at 06:00 in a huge Buick and amidst much speculation among the quarterdeck staff as to my influential friend, I would be swept away to his stables at the North Front. There is nothing like a gallop before breakfast unless it is the taste of bacon and eggs to follow.

Rocambole, as the horse was named, turned out to be a miniature mass of near unstoppable energy and I would end a gallop gasping for breath; he would snort indignantly and paw the ground while Mecaliff sat, grinning, 50 yards behind. We came second in our first scurry and won the next, prompting entry in a pukka race of, I think, a mile; it was disappointing to lose this by a short head, especially when the rider of the winner received a gold cigarette case.

23

Sandwiched between these came an extended visit by some French cruisers. Being somewhat of a linguist I was told off as interpreter and lived during the day in their flagship *Algérie*.

Life on board was most enjoyable when one was not wrestling with the translation of technical terms in British signals. The French officers did themselves well and on the last evening there was a full-scale dinner. A new wine appeared with every course. When there were five glasses in front of me, most of them empty and one was then plied, as the British thing to do, with whisky, I suddenly remembered the few yards back along the jetty. The story ends there as I have no recollection of returning to the *Nelson* where I woke up fully dressed in my hammock the next morning. Presumably an understanding Officer of the Watch had done his stuff.

My head must have cleared quickly because following hard on this was our air course, a fortnight's hectic familiarisation with the Fleet Air Arm in HMS *Ark Royal*. Though 'Pop' Snow was the only one to be seduced into eventual specialisation as a pilot, we all had the time of our teenage lives, going up as passengers during the Combined Fleet Manoeuvres, usually in a 'Stringbag', the now famous old Fairey Swordfish biplane that did everything: dive bomb, torpedo, reconnoitre and fight when it had to. With two open cockpits and a top speed of 120 knots it was very manoeuvrable but in fact hardly out of the First World War tradition. I had never flown before and whether waiting my turn to roar down the deck, gallivanting about the sky or approaching to land on an undulating grey strip that looked far too small, it was all one big thrill, as described in a letter home:

HMS *Ark Royal*
10/6/39

We did a torpedo attack on the battle fleet diving from 11,000' to 0' and having dropped the torpedo were attacked by squadrons of enemy fighters which had been waiting in the clouds. We spent about fifteen minutes twisting and diving and banking about trying to shake them off which had the most super Wembley sideshows absolutely flat. I did not feel in the least sick. Once the pilot outmanoeuvred a fighter and sat on his tail for about a mile going all out. During which I took photos of him in line with the gun sights which the pilot, Sub. Lt. Cooper, is rather keen to have!

It was certainly strange that I did not feel sick; not so everyone. Another Midshipman found in the pocket of his loaned flying suit a note from a pilot to his observer—'The next time you are sick, lean further out of the cockpit!'

HMS *Ark Royal* (cont)

I did a dive bombing attack on Cousin John which means dropping vertically from about 3,000 feet at over 200 mph and boy was it a thrill or was it a thrill?

24

In fact I was scared stiff! Whether the aircraft really dived vertically I do not know but I did look down the funnel of the *Royal Sovereign* (in which John Tothill was serving). Just before going was the worst moment. Our sub-flight of three, of which my pilot was the most junior, was in formation above wispy cloud. The leader spotted battleships through a hole and jerked his thumb backwards. With a slight check on the throttle and rocking of wings we were in line astern. One could see the four heads in front taking quick glances over the side. Suddenly the leading pilot raised his hand and tipped it over forwards. There was hardly time to gasp before his tail reared up in front of us, showing the red, white and blue bands, and then vanished. Seconds later No 2 followed suit right in front of our noses. We were alone. I knew a moment of intense fear. But nothing could be done about it, especially when there was a terrific lurch, an unseen hand pressed me into the back of the seat and another squeezed my stomach into an excruciating knot.

A second later we burst into the sunlight and I found myself suspended, body almost horizontal, over a wonderful scene. The other two aircraft were in line in front of us again, and beyond them a huge grey and cream lozenge, dotted with black. Its background of blue was broken at its blunter end by turbulent white lines that moved slowly outwards to disappear.

All three of us were dropping like stones on to an 'R' Class battleship. She was growing with fascinating urgency. I realised with pleasure that the stomach pain had gone and forced open the flap of the camera that was round my neck. As I got it up to my eye the foremost aircraft changed from a thin silhouette to fat silver wings and fuselage as it pulled out of the dive; then the second one too. Heavens we were close! The battleship seemed to fill one's entire view—there was the black oblong of its single funnel, hot air shimmering aft. I was just about to click the shutter for the picture of a lifetime when a blurred stream of rushing sea replaced the target, followed by white sky, and the giant hand returned to force me down on to the floor of the cockpit. I resisted for a moment, during which the unspeakable knot again twisted my vitals, and then, almost crying with frustration, did a knees' bend out of view. The resulting photograph—of out of focus instruments—was at least good for a laugh.

By good luck a great friend of mine, Edward Egerton,* who was a Midshipman in the newish cruiser *Sheffield*, also did his air course in the *Ark* at the same time. His parents—his father was another Naval Captain—were my honorary uncle and aunt and Ed and I had done lessons together at the age of seven before going to the same prep school

---

*E.G.E. of my dedication.

and then Dartmouth, affording each other mutual support as each advance brought its difficulties to be surmounted. Having a better brain than myself, a very strong physique that brought success at most team games, and a pleasant but determined personality, Ed appeared destined for great things. Another keen horseman, he was too heavy for the Gibraltar racing scene and had to content himself with vocal encouragement of me. One day, with both fleets in, we climbed the Rock to gasp at the view into Spain and across the straits to Tangier; immediately below I counted nine battleships, two battlecruisers, three carriers, 14 cruisers and about 30 destroyers, an array that seemed as normal and permanent as the Rock itself.

The *Sheffield* was known to be fitted with a revolutionary device. Our sister ship *Rodney* had just been similarly equipped, but there were no others. It was very secret, the details being known only to those closely concerned, and even its presence not discussable. I was in fact slightly nettled when, under pressure, Ed would not volunteer a word. This of course was radar (to be known at first as RDF) awaiting at this time the major advance which was to come from Birmingham University in 1940 and put the British version well ahead of competition.

The Combined Fleet manoeuvres continued to unfold much as the year before but with an even greater urgency. Munich was behind us and I think that by now everyone knew what was before. As destroyers dashed and aircraft dived there was the uncomfortable feeling that soon these things would happen in earnest.

Almost before one realised it the Rock was shrinking astern for the second year and the Home Fleet making for its own chillier waters. The end of the Easter leave period came two days before my 19th birthday and four months before what my particular vintage were to know as the end of an era. The next and final cruise before the war was standard in content but marked by the ever-deepening atmosphere of foreboding. Exercises, the Regatta again and Scottish ports shaped the content and Hitler the atmosphere; most weeks saw a move of some significance by the ranting German Chancellor.

The Regatta came and went though to dismiss it thus is heresy. The whole energy of the ship went into it and this time, probably assisted by the fact that we had been longer in commission and were therefore capable of fanatical rather than merely ferocious effort, we won. *Rodney* was second and *Royal Oak* third. Great were the celebrations, culminating in a triumphal tour of the fleet by our drifter—unrecognisable in carnival rig and crewed by 'pirates'. At the masthead was a passable imitation of the cock—traditional trophy of the whole affair. The real cock, a beautiful, lifesize, silver specimen, was presented to Captain Maceig-Jones by the Commander-in-Chief on the following Saturday. We cheered ourselves hoarse as the burly skipper approached the dais to collect it, the springy step that often accompanies a heavy man and wide smile denoting his obvious pleasure. It was indeed a fitting culmination to his appointment, due to end with the cruise.

Next stop was Rosyth whence we sailed in time for a social visit to the Firth of Forth by the French battlecruisers *Dunkerque* and *Strasbourg*, and three cruisers. Edinburgh was Johnny Bowles' main stamping ground and I came in for a lot of pleasant poodle faking (Service slang for social pursuit of the female) as his willing accomplice. The ship passed Portsmouth breakwater on the morning of June 28 and steamed up harbour. Only a clairvoyant could have known it but the next time she was to do this was not so far off and with a 'coach and horse' hole in her bottom. The new Captain (G.J.A. Miles), relieved Captain Maceig-Jones at the end of July and shortly afterwards we sailed for Invergordon, Scapa Flow and World War 2.

★   ★   ★

HMS *Nelson*
Invergordon 24/8

It seems there will be a war as we are all pushing off to Scapa. This is doubtless secret, so don't expect letters at my usual daily rate! Am in training for the battleships' cross-country which is now off I suppose—very annoying. Was third in the ship's race yesterday. I have just been showing round some of the Admiral's guests and got them covered in paint! Had a row with a new Mid yesterday and got him six cuts.

I was now Senior Midshipman, a somewhat thankless position with a good deal of chivvying to do but little extra authority. The Sub who had relieved Hawkins had been too easygoing but had given place to another—H.R. Wykeham-Martin, a cheery, down-to-earth disciplinarian.

HMS *Nelson*
Scapa Flow 30/8

I hear from an official source that the one thing that delays Hilter's hand is fear of the British Women's Land Army, particularly the Amazon Battalion recruited from Chailey district! We are right on the top line for anything now and the latest signal is permission to fire on hostile aircraft, which must be the last straw I am afraid. We have done nothing since my last p.c. but sit here and do occasional shoots. The fellow I got beaten just refused to do something I told him—writing out a list of Gunroom orders which he did not know. Some of the new Midshipmen are rather bolshie as they don't seem to have had much discipline before.

The reference to the Land Army was a dig at my mother who had just taken over responsibility for our patch of Sussex. The following extracts from 'Pop' Snow's journal (kindly lent following the demise of my own) chronicle the last days of peace:

26/8 Secured 'A' buoy, Scapa. Conference of all Admirals. 'G' dept fuzing shell all day.

27/8 Reserve officers join.

28/8 Ambassador Sir N. Henderson flew back to Berlin with the reply to Hitler's peace plan.

29/8 Mediterranean closed to all British shipping. Merchant vessels ordered to leave Italian and Baltic ports.

30/8 Arrangements made to evacuate children from London. Many more reservists called up. Country—on paper—prepared for war. Ships in harbour raised steam for full speed. To sea 1715. Several German ships reported leaving Wilhelmshaven and large number of submarines in the Skaggerak. Steamed 040° throughout the night—*Rodney, Ark Royal, Hood, Repulse*, 6th Flotilla, etc.

A handful of discoloured naval signal forms, from among my papers, keeps the momentum going:

31/8 Fire may be opened on hostile aircraft. 1427.

31/8 Complete fuzing of all shell. Ship all warheads. Prepare for war. 1529.

1/9 Hostilities between Germany and Poland have begun so it is probable we shall be at war shortly. 1258.

From journal:

1/9 Turned south in forenoon and during the night passed through Channel Orkneys—Shetlands. German fleet is somewhere off Iceland as far as we know—1 battleship, 2 pocket battleships, 2 cruisers. Action stations 0530 and all day. Rendezvous made with 'D' and 'C' Class cruisers at 0630. These are now spread out on A-K line eight miles apart. So far we have not declared war though it was expected we should do so last night.

(From C in C Home Fleet):

3/9 Authoritatively learned in London Henderson saw Ribbentrop 0900 BST. Gave him till 1100 BST to answer Britain's ultimatum. (No time of origin.)

A popular pastime was the painting of weird designs on our 'battle-bowlers'. I do not think that the lighthearted tone of my letters about then was put on for the alleviation of maternal anxiety; the prospect of a war was undoubtedly exciting and when it was given out over the broadcast system that an ultimatum had been delivered to Germany that we would declare war if they had not retired across the Polish frontier by 11:00 there is no doubt that (in the Gunroom at any rate) there would have been disappointment at such a retreat.

Those of us off watch sat around the clock. At 11:15 with, I suppose, a sense of history, I took a photograph of it; we received the expected signal 'Total, repeat total, Germany' and that, as someone said, was that.

*   *   *

HMS Nelson
6/9

Will you please send my sheep-lined gloves that may be in the hall chest. We are of course at war since starting this. It sounds rather stupid to hear Belisha and people promising that no one under 19 will be called up when there are boys of 15 and 16 serving here. When the declaration of war was broadcast one boy did not even trouble to stop reading his book. An old hand said 'Doesn't this mean anything to you?' At which he looked up and said 'Well, we won the last one, didn't we?' and went on reading.

I think we expected a sudden holocaust but the only obvious signs of hostilities were propaganda broadcasts from Germany, news of heavy losses in an RAF raid on Kiel and censorship of mail by Wardroom officers. Life became tedious at sea. Some wit has said that war is long periods of boredom punctuated by moments of intense fear and we soon learned the aptness of the first part. What had been experienced only during exercises now became part of our lives. The ship went about with most of the massive steel doors in bulkheads, hatches in decks and so on closed, which made movement awkward; 'darken ship' became a nightly occurrence with its corollary in the morning and the ship's company—at reduced defence stations all day—closed up at action stations at dawn and dusk. Being called 15 minutes before first light, not long after a night watch, was hardly popular and the Gunroom began to lose its glamorous ideas of war rather quickly. The long periods of boredom returned perpetually to mind, as nothing seemed to happen. Until at last it did.

The *Ark Royal* was astern on a blustery, grey day and the destroyer screen a tortured chevron in front when 'Alarm starboard! Green seven-0; angle of sight six; engage—engage—engage!' set the ball rolling.

Which is where we came in.

Our Heinkel became notorious. The optimistic pilot (one Francke) had seen only the initial eruption and within hours, the first of many '*Ark Royal* sunk' stories was given out by 'Lord Haw-Haw', the loathsome but somehow difficult-to-ignore British traitor who had begun to whine at the UK on Berlin radio.

HMS Nelson
22/9

There is no repeatable news of course. The binoculars are very useful. I do hope poor old Captain M-Jones is alright, though we very much doubt it. What

29

luck for little Larcom that it was not him. With the Russians in it we will certainly have a hard time as far as I can see.

W. Churchill was on board yesterday and gave us a very good speech.

The carrier *Courageous* had been sunk by a U-boat in the Western Approaches on September 17. This was the first loss of a capital ship, something uncomfortably like first blood to the Germans. Captain Maceig-Jones had gone from *Nelson* to her (relieving Captain Charles Larcom, who had in turn become Ed's CO in the *Sheffield*). My fears proved sadly true. Captain Maceig-Jones was lost insisting, so we shortly heard, on going down with his ship. His brave end was very much felt on board; we knew he and Commander Atkinson had made the ship efficient and what was more done it with a minimum of pain. The question of Captains going down with their ships, still a strong sea tradition, became a talking point. I think it true to say that as losses mounted the tradition became outdated and died. Many Captains were to be lost simply because a sense of duty delayed their efforts at self-preservation until too late, but I only had personal experience of one other officer who seemed determined not to survive.

Stalin had just concluded a non-agression pact with Hitler and the outlook was grim. Churchill had returned to the government as First Lord of the Admiralty (the news was flashed around the Navy by the signal 'Winston is back') on the outbreak of war. What he said on this occasion to a representative gathering from the Fleet I do not remember, but no doubt it was a rousing harangue in what was to become the best tradition.

Shortly after this there was a high-level bombing attack on Scapa Flow and an enterprising U-boat got in and torpedoed the *Royal Oak*, with heavy loss, including her Admiral. Until satisfactory counter-measures could be completed the Home Fleet's base was transferred to Loch Ewe, a sea-loch entered by a single gap, on the west coast opposite Skye. Its existence was supposed to be secret, reference always being made to Port 'A', but as far as the *Nelson* was concerned any trust in secrecy was misplaced.

At 07:00 one morning the communal Gunroom bathroom was its usual noisy self, four baths and several wash basins accommodating singing, whistling or merely splashing Midshipmen. I was lying back and thinking of nothing in particular, when there was an almighty *CRUMP* and my bath leapt about a foot, almost throwing me out. It continued to shake in a series of minor convulsions that coincided with an ominous rumbling sound. Some of the lights went out and the place became a shambles of spilt water and slithering bodies scrambling for clothes. It seemed obvious that the ship had been torpedoed and of course we were down in the chest flat and dressed in seconds.

Up on deck no-one seemed to know exactly what had happened but the ship was heavily damaged right forward, being down by the bow with a list to starboard. I was guiltily shocked to find the shores of Loch Ewe close around us; the boom had been passed some minutes earlier and the ship was stopped in the main anchorage. Guilty because I knew that the Cable Party must be on the fo'c's'le. As the First Lieutenant's 'doggie' (aide), which I then was, I should be there too. Presumably the return to harbour had been unexpected and I had missed the relevant bugle call. It was an even greater shock when my boss was carried past me, white-faced on a stretcher, the first of a steady stream of wounded. The explosion had caused the fo'c's'le deck to whip about four feet, the whole of the Cable Party, two officers and some 30 men, being thrown several times into the air. None escaped with less than a broken leg but even worse were the casualties on the deck below. This housed the long line of lavatory cubicles, all full, it being shortly after breakfast. The unfortunate men came down again and again on the jagged edges of broken pans and some of the wounds were very serious. As I surveyed the rows of stretchers I realised that I would have been on one of them had it not been for a lucky failure to hear the Cable Party call. 'Didn't hear the pipe' is a frequent but never accepted naval excuse—the broadcasting system being theoretically infallible—and my feelings were an uncomfortable mixture of shame and relief.

One made oneself useful here and there and was thus oblivious of the tension that gripped the bridge. The Fleet Navigating Officer was of the opinion that the *Nelson* had been torpedoed by a submarine that had 'done a *Royal Oak*' and got in. We could therefore expect another three or four torpedoes at any moment. Even if it was a mine it must have been laid by a submarine which might still be lurking. But nothing further occurred. It eventually transpired that we had passed over a submarine-laid magnetic mine, the enterprising U-boat having got in when the boom had been opened for the entry of a ship and similarly out again. Magnetic mines were set off by the magnetic field of a vessel passing overhead and this was one of the first successes of this new menace.

Shipwrights of the damage control parties were already hard at it, shoring up bulkheads against the sea that now filled several compartments. Even when the status quo was comparatively restored, there were many hundred tons of water in the ship and she remained permanently down by the bow. We were allowed into compartments adjacent to the damage and one of these was the torpedo body room. It presented an astonishing sight; the 20-ft torpedoes, normally clamped in orderly rows and overhead racks, were jumbled like cigars in a half empty box that had been shaken by a madman.

The hole in the ship's bottom, not seen of course until the *Nelson* docked at Portsmouth many weeks later, proved big enough to accept a double-decker bus. The damage was kept very secret as the immobilisation of a battleship for several months was serious. The Germans never got to know.

Meanwhile, my Midshipman's time was drawing to a close; promotion to acting Sub-Lieutenant with courses at Portsmouth to follow would round off a packed two years.

HMS *Nelson*
3/12

We have one of *Royal Oak*'s Mids of my 'pub'* group on board having had six weeks' leave. He hardly moves without his Gieves waistcoat poor devil.

Gieves had produced a serge waistcoat with an inflatable lifebelt incorporated, more comfortable than the regulation rubber ring with supporting straps which we were all supposed to wear at sea. My next contact with the firm was infinitely happier. For Johnny Bowles, 'Pop' Snow and myself, the end of the month brought exams, farewell parties and then the train south for leave and Sub's courses. We paused only to pick up our best reefer jackets in the Bond Street Gieves, the sleeves ego-inflatingly gilded with a single stripe. How every arm movement caught the unaccustomed eye!

*Public school entry.

2

Destroyer 'Sub'

Subs' courses—compressed from the normal nine into three months—
were hard work but of course we made the most of weekends to catch
up with contemporaries, male as well as female. Three in particular as
far as I was concerned. John Persse* was my first cousin; his father was
the well known trainer and character 'Atty' Persse, his mother—my
father's eldest sister—had had a short but brilliant career on the stage
and John, their only son, had received all their talents plus some more.
Popular and gregarious, he was a natural comic who could take off
anyone after the briefest observation. I was also an only son and we
were very close, closer than brothers I sometimes think; though I stayed
at Chattis Hill, on the Stockbridge downs, every leave we never saw
enough of each other to take things too much for granted. A sojourn
there had all the ingredients of a wonderful time—horses galore,
considerable opulence (my uncle was usually near the top of the
trainers' list), glamorous personalities from the racing scene, and above
all, the happiest of family atmospheres. Now in his last term at
Winchester, John was clearly destined for a career on the Turf.

Another great friend from earliest days whom I was more than glad to
see was Sandy Buller†. His family—he was the eldest of three brothers
and a sister—lived near us in Sussex. Being the same age exactly he and
I had always paired off and a wonderful mixture of thoughtfulness,
sensitivity and physical toughness he was. Neither being very
boisterous unless roused, we hit it off well and any time we met there
were notes to be compared. I had learnt to shoot at Netherwood, their
place, more than anywhere else and when there I do not have to close
my eyes to see the 12-year-old Sandy and myself setting out with the
cocker Rufus. (A ruling that only one .410 was to be loaded at a time
was somewhat loosely observed and once, when his Admiral father
heard four shots in quick succession, there was a mini court-martial.)
Sandy had just become a Pilot Officer in the RAF.

Edward Egerton, also doing courses, completed the trio of contacts
pregnant with thoughts of happier days.

With the end of this brief interlude came my appointment to the

*J.H.P. of my dedication.   †A.J.S.B. of my dedication.

destroyer *Douglas* at Portsmouth. I had never heard of her and was agreeably surprised to find her large, if old. She was to be based at Gibraltar. The officers were a cheery welcoming bunch, especially the thickset Captain, Commander J.G. Crossley, and a saturnine young Gunner (T) with whom I was soon to become fast friends, called W.B. Harvey. I found myself navigator, Asdic Control Officer and responsible for the CO's paperwork.

In general layout—she had four 4.7-inch guns and two triple torpedo tubes—the *Douglas* was not dissimilar to the *Esk*, but it was soon discovered that, launched in 1918, she rolled like the proverbial barrel in spite of the removal of a fifth 4.7-inch gun. However, the balmy wiles of the Western Mediterranean beckoned and her worst antics were not unloosed for some months. After a few days we sailed for Gibraltar, suffered the expected upheaval in 'The Bay' and duly arrived under the pleasant shadow of the Rock, only to be sent out again as soon as refuelled. Anti-submarine patrol was the order of the day and seemingly every day—meaning that one followed a set of predetermined red ink diagrams on the chart with boring regularity.

The races were still in operation and I took the Captain along on the first opportunity, winning him £15 and myself considerable kudos. The next meeting was the last as the racecourse was to become an airport. It was a sad day for many naval horsemen, spread now over every sea in the world, when the cheers came for the last winner on that sunlit Saturday evening and the Gibraltar Jockey Club closed down.

The 'phoney war' had come to an end with the German attack through the Low Countries, the Allied advance to meet them, and the French collapse, which had meant retirement all along the line. A big *Times* map of the fighting was pinned up in the Wardroom with a ribbon—joining coloured flags—to mark the front line. This needed depressing adjustment westward every day, culminating in the German break through at Sedan, where a bulge in the ribbon dashed one's most optimistic hopes. The news of Dunkirk came through, first to appal and then to uplift as one realised how successful the evacuation was.

HMS *Douglas*
2/6/40

Those something Belgians fairly landed us. I hear there were 28 destroyers in and out of Dunkirk taking the soldiers off. It must have been a show and a half. (Still is I suppose.) I wish I was in an HF destroyer instead of piddling along with nothing but a German submarine on the news. I think the Italians are coming in all right though, and we expect to give them a good finishing.

Was sick again at the beginning of this trip when there was a heavy swell, but we are running with it now. The number of miles we have done this month is equal to father's age x mine x the number of brothers and sisters he has, so at a slow average speed you can see how much we have been in harbour.

(This works out at 8,430 miles. At 14 knots, a likely average, 25 days at sea per month are indicated; about right!)

In the evening of June 23 we were to-ing and fro-ing in the Straits as usual, with Apes Hill behind Tangier alternating with the Rock's mottled crags, when the ship was suddenly recalled. There was no indication why but as soon as we had refuelled Admiral Sir Dudley North (Flag Officer Gibraltar) and a small staff embarked. France had just collapsed and the future of the French Navy—most important for the balance of Naval power—had become a vital issue. Most of it was at Oran in Algeria, some 250 miles east across the Mediterranean. Admiral North had decided that a man-to-man talk with his French opposite number might tip the scales and so course was set for Oran at 20 knots.

Currents round Alboran, an island in our path, dictated a 50° alteration of course, the gyro compass chose this of all moments to break down and the prospect of running a full Admiral on the rocks was one that did not exactly sooth my 19-year-old nerves; but the expected land loomed through intermittent rain at 06:00 and when the western point of Oran Bay was identified the situation became interesting. The terms of France's capitulation were unknown and it was with some concern that we searched with our binoculars to see whether we should be met by French patrol or Italian torpedo. The former it was, a destroyer leading us to the harbour mouth. On arrival off the berth indicated, a gap between a submarine and the destroyer *Tornade*, we turned 180°, let go an anchor and 'made a sternboard' on it a hundred yards to the jetty, watched in curious silence by dejected sailors on all sides. There was always the possibility of being caught by an enemy force coming to take over, but at least we would be ready for a smart getaway.

Admiral North was soon being piped over the side on his way to Admiral Gensoul in the battlecruiser *Dunkerque*. With her sister *Strasbourg* and two cruisers she was visible in the adjoining anchorage of Mers-el-Kebir and I was thinking of the junketings on board her the previous summer when, as Officer of the Day, I was confronted by the British vice-consul. He had with him a Belgian flying officer, very spruce in RAF-like uniform but with a silver tassle dangling from his forage cap. He said there were 400 Belgian airmen ashore willing to ship with us and fight for England. This offer was eventually refused, though I do not know why; 400 trained airmen would have been invaluable in the coming months.

The Admiral was back in an hour, his mission sadly unsuccessful, followed a few minutes later by Admiral Ferry (Admiral Superintendant of Oran) who ran down the ladder to North with tears streaming down his face. Apparently he impressed on the latter that had he been free to do so he would gladly have come away, but he had to obey orders. On departure the poor man was still in tears. Just before sailing we received a signal from *Dunkerque* that there was an Italian U-boat outside, but the passage back was uneventful.

Some days later the *Douglas* was out in the Atlantic with a convoy. There was a concentration of heavy ships in the Gibraltar area and increased W/T activity indicated that something big was afoot. Then the following startling signal (of which I still have the original) was intercepted:

'Oran Base from British Warship.

'Je ouvre le feu encore sauf que je voi que vos batiment coule.' (I will open fire again unless I see that your ships are sinking.)

The originator's French had rusted since his Dartmouth days but obviously the French were being attacked at Oran or just outside, and very soon one knew that HMSs *Hood, Valiant, Resolution* and *Ark Royal* had opened fire on the French ships at Mers-el-Kebir, only the *Strasbourg* and five destroyers escaping. This was, of course, an awful thing to do to an erstwhile ally, and embittered relations with the French Navy for a long time. But the French had failed to respond, first to Admiral North and then to Vice Admiral Somerville (of Force H, the ships concerned) and Churchill had decided there was no alternative. North (among others) disagreed and it is understood that this was at the heart of his subsequent removal, a cause célèbre which rocked the Navy and is still debated.

Gibraltar has nothing but pleasant associations for me, except one. This now came about. The mail arrived one evening, the sailor postman placing a bunch of letters on the red baize Wardroom table. We jostled round good humouredly and there was one from my mother. But when I began to read I could not get past the first few lines. I went up on to the darkened quarterdeck where a cool breeze blew. All round was blackness except where two dim lights by the coal shed had escaped attention. The calm water lapped gently against the ship's side and someone coughed in the shadows.

So Sandy was dead. I repeated the fact to myself but at first seemed incapable of taking it in. A number of my friends had already been killed but no one so close. Suddenly memories crowded in haphazard, and with them a gradual awakening: the incident of the loaded gun; mixed hockey on the lawn with always Sandy the star; long discussions into the night when adolescent dreams were all, and in the background a favourite record, 'Oh you! You're driving me crazy!' Then a sudden, clear picture of a tall Sandy in knickerbockers, weight on the forward foot, peering into the Netherwood undergrowth to see whether a rabbit had got away, blue gun smoke drifting across the autumn air. I wondered what he had looked like in RAF uniform; it must have suited the fair hair and almost girlish complexion that were the basis of his astonishing good looks. The two lights swam and I cried unashamedly in the darkness.

In a dozen words the war was suddenly stripped for me of its cloak of glory and adventure, to emerge for what it was—the purveyor of tragedies one would never forget. I thought of Sandy's younger brother Robin, about to go straight to sea from Dartmouth, and of the rest of the family with whom I had spent so many happy days and who must now be numb with shock. I did not write to any of them simply because I felt no words could be adequate or indeed of any help—but later much regretted this.

In the meantime here was I in the sunny Mediterranean, where we had not even had occasion to load our guns. Until at last a signal told *Douglas* to form part of the destroyer screen for Force H and we found ourselves bowling along on the port bow of *Renown, Malaya* and *Ark Royal*. Italy's entry into the war on June 10 had produced little beyond the odd reconnaissance aircraft, though strategically their considerable Navy spelt the end of the Mediterranean as a British preserve and I think the operation was a coat-trailing sweep to attract attention away from Malta and the eastern end.

Suddenly it was flag A (Aircraft in sight) from *Renown* and 'Alarm starboard!' from the Captain as a large formation of Italian bombers was sighted high on the starboard beam. The unfamiliar red and green markings on the three-engined aircraft seemed strangely hypnotic as, coming on relentlessly, they seemed contemptuous of the black puffs that signified fairly accurate shooting by the big ships. All were banging away at full rate, the destroyers remaining impotently silent. Gun muzzles were vertical when the air was suddenly rent by a ripple of detonations and the sea rose up in a series of gigantic brown pillars; soon forming one solid mass of smoke and water, it covered completely the three capital ships. For a second or two nothing happened. We watched, horrified, across half a mile of water. Then came a brave sight. The dense, ugly mass, for all the world like a wood of dark trees, was still suspended, hardly diminishing, when a sharp grey bow parted the left hand edge like a knife coming through brown wool. Bit by bit the *Renown* appeared, the sun glinting on her pale grey paint. She was untouched. A small cheer went up. Then followed the battleship and then the carrier, all without damage. By now the forest of bomb splashes had subsided into huge round pools that studded each side of the squadron's twisting wake, witness to some very near misses.

The enemy were, in fact, plain unlucky not to have hit at least one ship and all present revised their previous low opinions of Italian airmen. From our point of view the only nasty moment was provided by 'friendly' spent pom-pom shells that, dispatched originally by some super-optimist, boiled the sea all round into a stew of ugly little bangs and splashes.

This was a rare interlude and the ship was soon back on A/S patrol.

HMS Douglas
15/7/40

We had a vague air raid yesterday and one was shot down. At least it went down behind the Rock in spirals and looked like it. Davies, in my term, is out here now as second sub of a Gunroom, poor devil. Jolly good show Bill Tennant getting the CB, wasn't it? Your airmail letter took 23 days to get here so I presume it did not go by air!

Bill Tennant was Captain W.G. Tennant, a very old friend of my father's, whom I had known as Uncle Bill for years. He lived near and they had been sharing a small rough shoot at the outbreak of war. One evening recently my father had left the Admiralty and was sitting in a carriage at Victoria station when the door opened and a dishevelled Bill Tennant stumbled in, to immediately fall asleep. He had come straight from Dunkirk. Sent over by Admiral Ramsay (at Dover), he had been Beachmaster. His opposite number was General (Field Marshal to be) Alexander, and B.T. later told us that when they were walking up and down the beach together before the embarkation he was much amused by Alexander saying in typical guardee lackadaisical tone 'I'm told we may have to capitulate. I wonder how one capitulates. Never done it before myself!'

Very soon after this we sailed for home. I think the excessive sea-time had dictated a major overhaul of the old *Douglas*' engines. The Battle of Britain began in earnest just after we arrived at Portsmouth in mid-August and, on leave for two weeks in September, I have several clear memories. Linking them all is a permanent blue sky, criss-crossed with white vapour trails like a modernistic cobweb.

One morning, from the back of a friend's horse on the downs above Firle, I heard the sound of an aircraft and picked out the small dot of a fighter. It came straight for me, losing height, the engine firing irregularly and just before the black swastika became discernible I recognised the square wing-tips of a Messerschmitt 109. Imagination insisted that it was determined to pick off the lone horseman, but the plane passed just overhead in a crescendo of sound. It reappeared to the right, flying away, and with a coughing fit that ended in silence, glided into the valley like a stricken pheasant. I marked it down behind a wood and set off at speed in search.

A small crowd stood round the fearsome little plane that had churned its way, wheels up, through a maze of corn stooks, propeller tips bent back like the petals of a black flower. The wounded pilot—there was a lot of blood in the cockpit—had already been removed. Someone took a very good photograph of this particular Me 109 that subsequently appeared in many accounts of the Battle of Britain.

During a visit to the Brighton Hippodrome (it was 'Lambeth Walk' time and the star picked out my red-haired consort to dance in the aisle with him) the show was suddenly stopped by the manager coming on with a blackboard and writing 'R.A.F. Score: 156. A record!' Everyone cheered.

I was lucky to be asked out partridge shooting at Glyndebourne, General Beale-Browne (a very special friend though he was 40 years my senior) having taken on the shoot in order to show sport to young officers on leave. One day there was a very low sea-mist. Two fighters, presumably a Messerschmitt chased by a Spitfire or Hurricane, came over our heads unseen though at '0' feet, the sound being quite indescribable and the second plane firing continuously in long bursts. Later that day we were walking through kale at a point where the road does a right-angle bend between Glyndebourne and Glynde. A black car drew up and out got a police inspector. He began to walk through the kale towards us and we stopped to see what he wanted. He asked for Major Harry Sturgis and then went over to say that his younger son had been killed in action. Of course we went straight home. Toby, another boyhood crony whom I had known since we were seven, was in the RAF. He had his beautiful mother's charm and there were many who missed him sadly. Even now I never pass that field without recalling the melancholy message.

But it was back at Portsmouth that the Battle of Britain put on, for me, its most impressive display. My Aunt Emily Persse and her younger sister drove over to see me and we went up to picnic on the Portsdown hills that rise steeply behind the town. It is always a fine view to seaward on a clear day: Cosham and Porchester's Norman castle in the foreground with Portsmouth, Southsea and Gosport all stretching away in a mauve smear of roofs to the sea beyond. The dockyard was clear before us, wisps of smoke rose from lean grey ships in the harbour and only the barrage balloons lent a bellicose air. Suddenly all was changed by the wailing of sirens, that banshee sound that chilled one's heart in the safest surroundings. We decided we were not in much danger, got into the car and waited.

In seconds the air over the town was filled with twisting, diving planes as a score of fighters, appearing as from nowhere, set to. I had not seen a real dogfight before and it was certainly gripping; the roar of engines coming and going, the *rattatat* of the guns, the sun glinting on turning wings, some 'ours', some 'theirs', and above all the realisation that before our eyes men were fighting for their lives. Either a new wave of enemy aircraft came in or they had managed to shake off the defending Spitfires, for the fighting tailed off and then, one after another, the German 109s dived on to the barrage balloons. It was shooting 'sitters'; *rattatat—whoosh!* A ball of flame and the crumpled silver bag floated earthwards trailing dense black smoke. At one moment three or four were ablaze together. Immediately this was over, larger, twin-engined aircraft which looked to be Junkers 88s dived down, released their bombs and climbed away over rising mushrooms of debris. They seemed to have the arena to themselves and it was a grim business watching them, about two dozen criss-crossing from different sides in almost leisurely fashion. The last one let go, set course for home, and all was over. The timing of the whole operation had been entirely admirable.

Several fires were sending columns of smoke skywards and one imagined the dockyard to be badly damaged. After a few moments the steady drone of the 'All clear' sounded and we reckoned that my aunt from neutral Ireland had had her money's worth! Curiously enough it was found on return that the dockyard had suffered little; most of the bombs had landed among the small workers' houses around, which presumably had been the intention.

The Chief Engineer's son was a fighter pilot at a nearby air station and often came on board during his time off. We listened breathlessly to his accounts, graphically illustrated with both hands, of the day's fighting. Though the German effort was clearly very formidable and the probable prelude to invasion, I do not think we realised that these would turn out to be the most crucial months of the whole war. The enemy's huge daily losses (in fact somewhat exaggerated, as one knows with hindsight) were a great fillip and one felt they just could *not* keep it up.

A letter from Johnny Bowles, who had gone to the destroyer *Wolsey*, described the unpleasantness of inshore convoy escort duties on what I knew was the East Coast, and made me feel uncomfortably out of things. It also gave depressing news of several Subs of our vintage.

HMS *Wolsey*
1/8/40

I'm so glad your ship is at least reasonable, but presumably life is not now all free and easy, and you are getting your fair share of this most unpleasant bombing business.

We are, as you know, convoying, which is very dull as you just go up and down splitting the day into Heinkel time, Junkers time and Messerschmitt time. We do get one day in per week, two other bits of day per week and a boiler clean of four days (no leave though) every three or so weeks. We were detached to Dover to take part in all the operations from the Hague (skipper got DSC) to Le Havre inclusive, eventually ending up with a big hole in our bows, guns worn out, no Asdics, no Degausser, and holes in deck from bullets at the end of Dunkirk. So were retired gracefully to Pompey for three weeks.

Just before I end I suppose you know Wood, Read, Davies, Robertson, have been killed.

Although such experiences did not come the way of *Douglas*, the rhythm of our peaceful existence soon deteriorated with a change of scenery to the low braes of Scapa Flow and the non-stop duties of a fleet destroyer. Presumably the losses in Norway and Dunkirk had not yet been made good because the usual shortage of destroyers was particularly acute. Echoing Johnny's, the routine was three or four days out (screening the big ships) half a day in to oil and provision, followed by another three or four days out and so on. 'Fuel remaining', signalled to the senior officer daily, was about the only regulator of sea-time and the occasional longer period in for boiler cleaning, when officers could get ashore for walks and the men their football, was a treat indeed.

As the winter came on the weather became permanently bad. One's memory is of ceaseless gales. The old *Douglas* was certainly a terrible sea boat; worst of all I seldom kept anything down at sea, brandy and soda and ship's biscuits becoming standard diet from the first day out. A child's bucket was kept at the back of the heaving bridge for my sole use and some wag painted it dark blue with a single gold stripe! I never let seasickness interfere with duty and in a way did get used to the actual sensation, but after, say, three days with nothing kept down one's whole being starts to sag. Several trips later there was no change and the question naturally arose as to whether I could go on like this, the dreadful spectre of having to apply for a big ship looming and receding in direct relation to the proximity of land.

HMS *Douglas*
1/11

At the moment it is literally icy cold. Everything is caked with a thin layer of frozen snow, and it is snowing hard. I have my fur-lined boots on with Mother's excellent sea boot stockings, sweater, waistcoat, fawn tweed coat and new sort of lammy coat they've issued. Have been pretty frightfully sick and am wondering whether to put in for a big ship or not. I want to try and hang on. We had a ghastly trip the other day when it was really rough. We picked up the survivors of a torpedoed merchant ship; I don't think that can be censorable. They had three biscuits each for three days (eleven of them) and when picked up had nothing. However, that's not terrific as I frequently keep nothing down for three days, which makes one pretty queer at the end. I haven't seen Robin yet though dare say I will. In harbour eating and sleeping are the pleasures that count. When we go to the cinema (which there sometimes is in a big ship) it's like a school outing. Our food is quite good; Harvey took over catering from the Maltese messman but the messing has gone up to £4*. One hasn't got any other expenses, however, except laundry, so it doesn't make much difference.

Robin Buller, Sandy's younger brother, was now a snottie in the brand new battleship *King George V*.

*A month!

41

We are in for a bit at last . . . I haven't put in for a big ship and will try and hold on . . . Bertie Harvey and I keep watch together (we sometimes work in pairs). He is the most incredible person for an ex-AB being able to recite anything from Shakespeare to Rupert Brooke (he calls me Rupert!). It was pretty good getting the three Italian battleships, wasn't it? With a foothold for us in Greece I think the Italians may not have it all their own way. We have seen no excitement though expect it. I must stop now and eat something. I hear there's fresh milk which I haven't had since last at home.

PS. I don't suffer too badly from lack of sleep thanks as we are one in three. We have had more b . . . . y awful weather. We rolled over to about 70° at one moment and all thought we were going right over. The doctor had his arm broken, the messman his behind cracked and another officer nearly dislocated his shoulder. A man got washed over the side and back again! I was standing with my feet braced against a vertical surface and found myself *standing* on it! Lots of things are bust.

Some of my letters were spread over a considerable period, and posted when the chance arose. Also events were not always related in the right sequence. Taking what some will consider an exaggeration of rolling 70°: one day I was on watch in a full gale with really frightening seas. We were on the starboard side of the screen escorting the *Nelson* and other ships and occasionally, wedged into a corner of the bridge for support, I imagined the comfortable scene in the Gunroom I knew so well, as the battleship rolled predictably from side to side. The Captain and I were soaked to the skin in spite of towels round our necks and in my case, waders over fur-lined boots. Every so often the sea came solidly over us so that we had to duck to avoid receiving it full in the face. Of course I was being as sick as a cat, though the task of keeping our station on the screen—that is, the right compass bearing and distance from the lead ship—took all one's attention. The necessarily slow speed of the fleet and the difficult task for the hard-working helmsman just beneath us in keeping a reasonably straight course, with the bow being thrown bodily sideways one moment and the ship corkscrewing back in retaliation the next, made station keeping an approximate matter at best. I suspect the Captain had come on to the bridge—he would normally spend most of the time in his sea cabin just aft of the wheelhouse—because he smelt danger with the sixth sense that destroyer skippers acquire.

We had taken on a particularly vicious roll, thanks to several seas coming at rhythmic intervals when a freak sequence occurred. A particularly heavy wave pushed us right over to port and then—before we had begun to come back—a second, following immediately, broke over the ship again. She heeled right over so that the end of the yard, two thirds of the way up the foremast, was only just out of the water. She stayed there, trembling, for what must have been about ten seconds. The Captain, the signalman and I were peeling off our oilskins the better to swim and I found myself standing on the side, normally vertical, of the Asdic cabinet. From below came a constant clamour of breaking crockery and the dislodging of every minor movable item that had not been secured against a near 90° list. It seemed like minutes that the old *Douglas* leaned over, shaking like an animal in its death throes. Then the sea appeared to relent and she slowly but surely came upright.

The *Nelson*'s ten-inch light began to wink. '*Nelson* to *Douglas*' shouted the signalman above the howling wind; 'I thought you were gone that time!' 'Make "so did I"' yelled the Captain, buttoning up his oilskin.

It is probable that we would have rolled over with total loss—no ship could have lowered a boat in that sea—if the fifth gun, originally high up amidships, had not been removed. Minor damage below was complete and my cabin was no exception when I got aft via well-judged rushes from refuge to refuge down the iron deck. There was a minor and untraced leak in the vicinity and in bad weather it took in something like an inch a day. This necessitated wooden duckboards to keep my feet dry and these were jumbled up one end while everything else that had broken loose swilled from side to side in several inches of filthy water. It transpired that there was also a large number of minor human fractures in addition to those related. The apparent phenomenon of a man being washed overboard and back again was not really unusual; it was to be met again.

For some weeks I kept up the struggle against seasickness, retaining nothing and making up for it in harbour. Each time the question of giving in seemed to resolve itself in the affirmative, but on return the life was so much more worthwhile that I could not bring myself to throw it over. But I surrendered in the end. One day, in the usual rough weather when I was bracing myself against the continuous motion with a hand on each of the metal balls of the binnacle, I felt for the first time so weak—having kept nothing down for days—that if an emergency arose I knew I would not be equal to it. So I wrote an official letter requesting to be transferred to a big ship. It was a sad moment as most naval officers and men will appreciate.

*   *   *

HMS *Douglas*
18/12

. . . to make life more gloomy I'm rather a cripple at the moment having had a narrow escape from worse injury yesterday. I was sitting in the Wardroom on a settee along the side of the ship when she suddenly lurched over to about 40°.

I got hold of an armchair and its inmate on the way, but its lashing broke and we both went for 6. The next thing I knew was a terrible blow on the head and then the doctor bending over me on the same settee, looking under my eyelids and feeling my bones! They say I described one cartwheel across the room and hit the bulkhead with my head, being knocked well and truly out. Luckily I've now got nothing worse than a badly bruised thigh that got me off two night watches as I can only just walk, and a headache and stiff neck! Also a cut hand which makes writing difficult and a black eye. However, I'm lucky not to be worse.

They said my antics were something marvellous to behold. The chap in the armchair was the doctor who finished up on top of me. I only hope I don't arrive in harbour to find my appointment to another ship and have to go like this. Will you send me a tin or two of Oxo or Bovril cubes that can be dropped into boiling water. I've just got your cake and mince pies thanks, grand. Just off again.

There is still a scar on my thigh, where it caught the corner of a bookcase, to remind of the incident and particularly of our Irish doctor trying to stem the blood from a gash in my head. He was fairly efficient at this, short-term, slapping pieces of sticking plaster on to my matted hair, intoning the while 'Elasthoplasst, Elasthoplasst; God's greatest gift to the medicil profess'n!' Long-term this was a failure; the difficulty of removing a tangled mixture of hair, plaster and dried blood can be imagined.

It was certainly a reprieve to leave Scapa—if not my friends in the *Douglas*—when eventually relieved and sent home to await appointment. Crossing London I struck up a close acquaintanceship—not the misnomer it sounds—with one of the lions in Trafalgar Square (which has been seldom passed since without a nod). A heavy air raid was in progress when the train arrived at Kings Cross with not a soul to be seen, no porters, no ticket collectors and no taxis or other transport. Rather foolhardily—I had not been in a major raid before—and much against the wishes of an ARP warden in his white helmet, I set out on foot for Victoria.

There were, of course, no lights, but searchlights weaved continually, groping for their droning quarry. Bombs, though plentiful, did not seem to be close and good progress was made in the eerily deserted metropolis. I had just entered Trafalgar Square when a shrill whistling, followed by flashes and bangs, erupted all round. Not very confident now, I kept on and was right in the open when there was a series of screeches and explosions that lit up all the surrounding buildings. Running for the nearest of Nelson's lions I lay down alongside it, heartily thankful for the reassuring bulk, even if it trembled repeatedly.

Setting off again in a lull I met a policeman who said there would be no trains until this was over and recommended the Strand Palace Hotel.

Wolfing a late supper there I was astonished to see the large doors at the far end of the dining room burst open to disgorge an avalanche of variegated humanity—everyone carrying pillows or rugs—which immediately bedded itself down between the tables. The waiter, when he had succeedced in getting back, explained that they were from a Polish ship anchored in the Thames, and allowed to do this at 22:00. As it happened, a vision of blonde pulchritude, not wearing much, stretched out alongside my chair and concentration on dead meat was difficult to come by thereafter.

The rumblings and shakings were still going on, when entering the lift I said I hoped the hotel was solid. 'Oh yes', said the attendant 'It's safe enough, below the top few floors that is. Which one for you Sir?' 'The top floor.' For some reason I thought I would shave, probably for a quick getaway next morning, and had the razor poised when the screech of a really near one stayed my hand. It rose to a crescendo while I remained motionless and then exploded with a crash that shook everything. My hand jumped and drew a long red line across my cheek. The bombardment went on most of the night and I was thankful to catch an early train to Lewes; it was all much more peaceful at sea!

As the Downs appeared and my home approached, I could not help thinking of the Snaffles picture there, of a First War destroyer officer on the bridge in filthy weather, called 'T.B.D.s—the beef convoy'. I knew that on the back was: 'To Lieutenant John Brooke R.N., H.M.S. *Ettrick*, from Commdr. Quentin Crauford R.N.—a souvenir of the winter of 1914/15 from his Divisional Leader', and that the *Ettrick* was but the first of several of my father's wartime commands in the Dover Patrol. Once carried off the bridge frozen stiff, he was awarded the DSC and French Legion of Honour and later, as the crack CO of the flotilla, was usually chosen to take Lloyd George, the Prime Minister, Field Marshal Kitchener* and other VIPs to and from France.

I felt a considerable failure, even if I had done my best. It was therefore a fillip to receive an appointment to HMS *Prince of Wales*. Though I had hoped for a cruiser, this was the Navy's latest battleship, not even in commission as far as I knew, and I felt my stocks could not be as low as feared. The job would be Sub of the Gunroom and I felt I knew, for what it was worth, a bit about that.

---

*On one occasion Kitchener was standing beside him when he was bringing the ship alongside at Dover in a full gale. A single bright light on the jetty was blazing down on the ship, which did not help. A voice behind it began to give instructions and my father shouted up to mind his own bloody business, he was not in command of the ship. The voice stopped and a little later Kitchener said 'Do you usually speak to your Admiral like that?'. It was Admiral Sir Reginald Bacon—in command at Dover—who, when my father shortly apologised, was very good about it (as he should have been!).

3

Bismarck and Churchill

A shipyard is a cheerless place at the best of times; Messrs Cammell Laird under four inches of snow in the half-light of 06:30 was no exception, but it could not suppress my thrill at first sight of HMS *Prince of Wales*, dark grey and menacing against the surrounding white. The tall superstructure that loomed to my left seemed to merge with the sky as, still stiff and cold from the night train to Birkenhead, I climbed the brow to her vast quarterdeck. The *Nelson*'s had been small, recently I was used to a few square yards, but the expanse now before me took in an immense four-gun turret with no trouble at all.

From a heavily muffled Bo's'n's Mate who was stamping about in the slush, I learnt that the ship would not commission for some weeks and that I should take my taxi on to the digs where the dozen unmarried officers 'standing by' her were accommodated.

Back on board later, I did a quick tour of the upper deck while awaiting a summons to the Captain. *Prince of Wales*, of 36,000 tons displacement, was a somewhat masculine sister to *King George V*, with three more of the class still to come. Having been on board the latter briefly at Scapa, the general arrangement was familiar: two 14-inch turrets forward (the lower of four and the upper of two guns), one turret aft, a massive box-like bridge superstructure that included aircraft hangars each side of the foremost funnel and then a clear-cut gap (out of which the aircraft would be catapulted) and the after superstructure. This contained the boat deck and second funnel. The masses on each side of the gap included secondary armament batteries at deck level (eight 5.25-inch turrets in all) and the usual director control towers on top. Distinctly unusual was the intriguing array of radar aerials that crowned these in turn. The curved prow, cowled single funnel and pyramid upperworks of our German adversaries certainly looked better, but the solid bridge, tall funnels and general uprightness of the *Prince of Wales* did have a foursquare effect of dignity and power.

The Captain—L.K. 'Turtle' Hamilton—proved to be a very small, fair-haired bachelor who clearly stood no nonsense but there was a humorous twinkle in the eyes that studied me from under bushy brows and he gave the impression of being ridiculously young. Asking after my father, he told me that they had commanded sister destroyers in the Dover Patrol. I knew this—in fact they were still close friends—and I also knew that Lieutenant Commander Hamilton had run his ship aground and the two of them had sat up all night concocting the best possible 'Report of Collision or Grounding' which was unfortunately required of him. It had obviously been well done! 'I didn't ask for you' he said, 'I merely requested a disciplinarian.' I hope he, or rather his successor, got one. I only beat two snotties in the ensuing year (one came up to me much later and thanked me, rather embarrassingly, saying it had done him a lot of good). But this is to anticipate. There were as yet no 'young gentlemen' to crowd the pristine Gunroom, which smelt of new leather, new corticene and fresh paint and, apart from getting on the right side of important people like the Foreman of Joiners for the clandestine production of brass telescope racks and other Gunroom embellishmens, there was nothing much for me to do but clamber about the ship.

Among other intriguing discoveries was the fact that the new-fangled radar extended even to pom-pom directors (shades of my old *Nelson* device). I was fascinated but the two Gunnery Officers, Lieutenant Commander C.W. McMullen ('Guns') and Lieutenant R.C. Beckwith, were far too busy to explain anything in detail. Although below the waterline, my cabin was an improvement on the *Douglas'* especially as it was unlikely to leak. Dick Beckwith heard me bemoan the lack of daylight for watercolour purposes—painting being my principal hobby—and straightaway offered the use of his when not wanted, a kind gesture indeed. He was engaged to a charming and very pretty little girl called Yvonne Pridham whom he would introduce—most inappropriately we thought—as his 'fiasco'.

Other officers joined, including Lieutenant Commander A.H. Terry who, among his various duties, was Snotties' Nurse. It was important that we should see eye to eye and fortunately we always did, in fact becoming good friends. A recent survivor from three sinkings, including the *Royal Oak* and one of the destroyers lost in the Norwegian campaign, he had seen a lot of action. A slightly hesitant manner hid a determined personality. A fine practical seaman and keen fly fisherman, he looked like the 'jack tar' who used to be on Wills Navy Cut cigarettes, with a very powerful frame and thick, light brown beard framing strong features. Another who one noted at once as a most congenial character was Lieutenant Commander George Ferguson, RNVR, a florid bright blue-eyed officer who did everything with great gusto and friendliness.

Commissioning day came and HMS *Prince of Wales* breathed with real life for the first time. Midshipmen joined in ones and twos from then on, until total Gunroom strength was about 25. Few had been to sea and all were roughly of the same seniority. Thus there was no hierarchy of senior Midshipmen to help knock the others into shape and everything from straight discipline and routine to watchkeeping, boat-running and the various mess administrative duties had to start from scratch. My inactivity of recent weeks became very much a thing of the past.

The *Prince of Wales* left Birkenhead on January 28 1941, sailing northabout to anchor off Rosyth in the Firth of Forth, for ammunitioning and storing. I remember being rather rough with the wheel and engine revolutions and the Captain cautioning 'This isn't a destroyer you know!'

Rosyth became the scene of much inter-mess entertainment—the first Gunroom guest night, with Wardroom guests, featured a haggis—and we decided that ordinary cocktails were too hard on a Midshipman's wine bill. Accordingly a special meeting of the mess committee (myself as President and half a dozen others) was convened and the wine steward instructed to produce a bottle of every type we possessed. There followed an orgy of concoction which put the Macbeth witches to shame. Few knew what they were drinking at the end, but the winner was 'Seaweed'—half gin, nearly half the dregs of fruit tins specially kept over the last week, a touch of crème de menthe to give colour and a drop of angostura to counteract its taste!

'Turtle' Hamilton—who had been promoted to Rear-Admiral—was relieved by Captain J.C. Leach and simultaneously another Commander, H.F. Lawson, was appointed. As fine a pair as you could wish for, they had both been Gunnery Officers (the former was not a little deaf in the best Whale Island tradition) but were as unalike in appearance as could be imagined. Captain Leach was very tall and athletic—I believe an ace squash player—with rather boney features, blue eyes, grey hair and a ruddy complexion. He had a wonderful sense of humour and, though to prove a tight disciplinarian, was fair and transparently decent. One took to him at once. Commander 'Tarzan' Lawson was very short and broad with a long, narrow face, prominent jaw and black hair. He had a long, supple stride and his black eyes darted sparks. Otherwise, the same could be said and one took to him at once too.

The battlecruiser *Hood* was in a nearby dock. In mid-March she moved out to anchor in the stream and a few days later the *Prince of Wales* followed suit, to weigh and proceed to Scapa Flow on the 24th. As the Forth Bridge passed overhead, with little enough room to spare, there was many a wistful glance—at least among those who knew their Flow—at receding civilisation (I was even inspired to write a poem, the full extent of which was 'Sad to see—the last tree!'). Gliding up to our buoy off Flotta, with the usual shrill salutes to and from the ships at hand, followed by a flurry of official calls, was a bit like returning after the school holidays: to feel one had never been away. But I do not think I was ever to be seasick in the *Prince of Wales* and henceforth that made all the difference!

A terrific programme of gunnery exercises began almost at once and lasted for seven weeks. All day, and latterly most nights, we carried out drills, shoots and more shoots. Many became fed up with the 'gunnery octopus' as some wag dubbed our tormentor from whose tentacles none could escape, but I thoroughly enjoyed this period, having always found teamwork on a large scale a satisfactory business.

There was particularly good reason for us to become worked up, ie, ready for battle, as soon as possible. The new and formidable German battleship *Bismarck*, rather larger than *Prince of Wales* and thoroughly efficient after much exercising in the Baltic, could be expected to break out at any moment and the Home Fleet at this time had few capital ships fast enough to catch her. If the *Bismarck* evaded our patrolling cruisers, not difficult to do in bad weather, the fat would be in the fire; if she could then evade superior forces for long enough she could be joined by her new sister *Tirpitz* (known to be working up like we were) or by the battlecruisers *Scharnhorst* and *Gneisenau*, or all three. The idea of this quartet loose in the Atlantic was too awful to think about: they could starve out the entire United Kingdom.

The Flow was busy with ships of all sizes, including the *Hood*, but *Prince of Wales* was 'out of routine' acting independently at the will of St Barbara, Patron Saint of Gunnery. Our 14-inch guns, only the second examples to be built, gave a lot of trouble. In particular the loading machinery was entirely new, including the innovation of a 'vehicle' that ran on rails round the bottom of the turret, receiving shells from the fixed structure and locking itself on to the revolving part for transfer. The 5.25-inch secondary armament was newish too; the barrels elevated to nearly 90°, obviating the need for separate heavy AA guns. Lastly, there were six multiple pom-poms, four of which had the new, sophisticated directors to be mastered (a Bofors and several 20 mm Oerlikons were added later). With all this to contend with and a large proportion of untried manpower to boot, the task of welding the ship's company into a fit state to fight for its life would have taken at least eight months in peacetime.

My action station was Spotting Officer in the standby 14-inch director. Mounted on top of the after superstructure, it was a complete replica of the one above the bridge, whence Guns would normally control the main armament. If anything prevented his doing this it was only necessary to move a big switch and all the circuits were transferred to us. Until this happened, however, we had nothing to do except spot the fall of shot. Three officers sat at the top of a compact pile of men and machinery, the Control Officer—Dick Beckwith—slightly raised in the middle, with the Rate Officer (Lieutenant T. Baker-Creswell, RM) on his left and me on his right. Dick had an all-round view through thick glass ports; 'B-C' and I could only see forward, unless we stood up. All of us had huge binoculars supported on pedestals* and the two flanking officers each had three brass knobs. In my case they indicated 'over', 'straddle' (shells each side of the target), or 'short'. B-C's referred to 'left', 'straddle', or 'right'. When one of the knobs was pressed a pin perforated a rolling chart in front of the Gunner in the Transmitting Station (TS) 100 feet below. We had a rangetaker who pressed a foot pedal with the same result, as did each turret, and our radar aerials fed a display in the TS. Strange things can happen in the heat of action, as we were to find out (for instance, one of the directors might be on the wrong target), but the TS Gunner with all this information, was well placed to advise the Gunnery Officer if necessary. When the stand-by director was controlling the shoot, B-C's and my findings had more direct parts to play. Our Control Officer ordered corrections of range and deflection according to a set plan, and as a result of the fall of shot which he saw himself, accepting our verbal reports or not as he thought fit.

The Director Gunner (Mr J. White) was below us and in front, keeping the crosswires of his telescope on the target for elevation, the Director Trainer beside him doing the same in the horizontal plane. As the No 2 of each gun closed his interceptor switch, the last act in the loading sequence, a light burnt in the TS. As soon as all—or in dire straits the majority—of the lights had come on, the fire gong would be pressed. This, sounding throughout the gunnery octopus, told the Director Layer he could press his trigger (providing the Control Officer had ordered 'Shoot') and also warned the rest of us; as learnt in the *Nelson* it is best to shut one's eyes and imperative to do so at night.†

The circuits carrying the director's instructions to the guns (the turrets trained in similar response to the Director Trainer's movements) passed through the TS where additions or subtractions were made by settings applied to the fire control table. These took into account the arc described by the shells for different ranges, temperature, one's own and the enemy's estimated course and speed, and such finer points as barrel wear. The Control Officer's corrections— also applied in the TS— would be superimposed on these. It can be seen how one weak link could upset the whole delicate apple-cart, and how not only the need for

*The three binoculars could be moved within the limits of ports about 18 × 12 inches. The glass of these soon became caked with salt and they were normally left open.

†One normally fired by salvoes, ie, only half the guns in each turret firing at a time. This doubled the rate of fire.

initial training, but constant practice thereafter, was very great.

The secondary armament needed nearly as much attention and the new pom-pom systems claimed their share. Each of the four 5.25-inch batteries had its own director, fairly light contraptions open to the sky. They stuck out like ears fore and aft, switching arrangements allowing any director to control any group of turrets, a considerable insurance against surprise. When a threat from the air only was anticipated, some of us had alternative Air Defence Stations, mine being as a pom-pom Direction Officer on the starboard side of the Air Defence Positions which was as high as one could go on the main bulk of the bridge structure. The pom-pom director was on a lower level and, armed with a long cane, I would lean over and attract the control Petty Officer's attention with a tap on his shoulder. Though it sounds primitive, the idea was to pick out his next target while he concentrated on the threat in hand, and it worked well enough.

My 21st birthday came and went on April 25, unmarked unless a voluntary turn-out at 04:00 counts. A drifter from the mainland arrived then with stores, among which I knew there was a crate containing a large Peter Scott print. Noted by me in Edinburgh when equipping the Gunroom with similar prints, it had been ordered by an old friend. The hoisting in of this delicate package was not entrusted to anyone else.

At last, on May 21, Captain Leach reported to Admiral Tovey, the Commander-in-Chief, that HMS *Prince of Wales* was fit to join the Fleet. This was less than two months after leaving Rosyth.

Only hours later the very same day, *Hood* (flying the flag of the Second in Command, Home Fleet, Vice Admiral L.E. Holland) and *Prince of Wales* were ordered to two hours' notice for steam. Excitement and speculation ran high. Rumour—usually well founded—gets round a ship in an uncanny way and somehow one felt this was no routine exodus. The signal to sail followed and then the Captain spoke over the broadcast system. He said that air reconnaissance had revealed that the *Bismarck* and an 8-inch cruiser were in a Norwegian fjord near Bergen. They were probably about to make a dash into the Atlantic to attack convoys and the Home Fleet was moving to strategic positions to prevent this. Our destination was an area west of Iceland.

Midnight saw us falling in astern of the big black shape that was the *Hood*. Six destroyers, including *Echo* and *Electra* of the old 5th Flotilla, were awaiting us outside and after they had formed screen we settled down to butt into the weather on a north-westerly course. This was the first time we had been in company and with hindsight I would hazard a guess that the date of the *Prince of Wales* officially joining the fleet had been optimistically advanced on account of recent events.

The bad weather, with periods of very low visibility, that was experienced on the two-day steam to our appointed station also precluded air reconnaissance off Norway and it was not until the evening of May 23 that a very enterprising flight (of a Navy-manned target-towing bomber) returned with the news that the fjord was empty. If he was making for the Atlantic, the enemy had a choice of four routes, the most likely being the Denmark Strait, between Iceland and Greenland. Running roughly NE to SW, this was narrowed at one point to some 24 miles by ice to the north and a British minefield to the south. It was to the westward end of the Denmark Strait that *Hood* and *Prince of Wales* were presently steaming at about 25 knots.

Suffolk and *Norfolk* (flying the flag of RA 2nd Cruiser Squadron, Rear-Admiral W.F. Wake-Walker) were already at the narrowest part of the Strait. The former, with a newer and much superior radar, was patrolling to and fro to the north, *Norfolk* doing the same a few miles to the south.

All day *Hood* and *Prince of Wales* ploughed on. The weather moderated a little and some gunnery control exercises were carried out, *Hood* signalling that if the ships were together when fire was opened they would concentrate (on one target). Guessing that we would go to action stations at dusk and stay there all night, with a good chance of a fight, I made the usual preparations of changing into clean underclothes. (This habit has been described as an old naval rite but is simply to ensure that any wounds would not be contaminated by dirty material.)

Suddenly it came—out of the blue, about 19:30—an enemy report from *Suffolk*: 'One battleship, one cruiser, bearing 330° distant 6 miles, course 240. My position so and so'. This was relayed over the broadcast system with the added information that it put the enemy about 300 miles north of us and if all concerned held on as they were, contact could be expected next morning. Half an hour later speed was increased to 27 knots and course altered slightly to the northward (to 295°, 25° north of west) which was calculated to advance the time of meeting. 27 knots was only two short of our maximum (it probably was the *Hood*'s maximum, at this stage of the 20-year-old ship's life) and the after part of the ship vibrated with a continuous and uncomfortable urgency as it rose and fell to a beam sea.

By midnight the *Bismarck* and her consort were 120 miles away and we went to action stations. Climbing through the small door in the back of the director, settling myself into the familiar padded seat, laying out anti-flash gear (long gloves and balaclava of special white flame-resistant cloth) and adjusting one's headphones was no different to the hundred other times one had done it, except for two things. These were thundering at us somewhere out in the murk, and the drill of lining up pointers, checking receivers and testing communications was carried out with unusual care. The order came through to sleep at our stations.

Though the odd catnap on folded arms was possible for the three Director Officers it was difficult to relax physically and impossible mentally. The near-certainty that we would be hard at it a specific number of hours ahead had a finality that made one's mouth dry. I kept thinking of our opposite numbers in the *Bismarck,* sitting there with nothing to do either as they rushed towards us in the darkness. What were they thinking about? Not for the first time I cursed a fertile imagination. The hell of a fight was inescapable, not that one wanted to escape it (the hollow feeling in the pit of my stomach, reminiscent of the ring, was for some strange reason not wholly unpleasant), but the inexorable approach of this big test was awesome. There were sure to be casualties. If I had to be one I hoped it would not be too painful. I shifted my headphones for the hundredth time—they numbed one's ears after a period—and so the night wore on.

The destroyer screen dropped astern during the night, having been detached to effect a search for the enemy. Sporadic reports from *Norfolk*—she had contacted the *Bismarck* shortly after *Suffolk* and both cruisers were now shadowing from astern—indicated that the enemy was on much the same course, about south-west. Ours, adjusted occasionally in response, was such as to converge at a fine angle, meaning that the action would start around 06:00. It would be broad daylight in these northern waters long before this. The weather improved; the visibility was going to be good. The *Hood* was four cables (800 yards) ahead. Suddenly, 'Lookout bearing green seven-0', and the director swung round. The time was 05:10. The light increased. It was to be a grey day with a strong north wind (Force 6) in our faces and a moderate sea. I studied the horizon again and again as the minutes passed.

'Alarm starboard! Enemy in sight. Battleship bearing green five-0. Follow director. All guns with armour-piercing *load.*' Click went the loudspeaker: 'This is your Captain speaking. The two enemy ships are in sight and we shall be opening fire any minute now. Good luck to you all.'

I could see nothing except the unbroken straight line of the horizon but, of course, the forward director was a good deal higher than ours and so could see further. The records say the time was 05:38. The loudspeaker came on the air again. 'This is the padre speaking. I am going to read a short prayer.' This he did. Though by no means irreligious, I must admit I found this distracting. But not for long. Something suddenly came up over the horizon to grow slowly but distinctly; the top of a mast. Then a little to its left something else. I shall never forget the thrill of that moment. A squat grey lump on a stalk, with bars protruding each side—the *Bismarck*'s main armament director. 'Director Target' said Mr White evenly. It grew by the second like a serpent rearing up while our rangetaker spun his wheel, trying to converge his two half-images in the face of driving spume. After widening out into a fighting top of some sort one saw that the stalk was really the top of a tower; other excrescences appeared and between these and the mast, the pointed cowl then the full width of a massive funnel. Guns began again 'Range two seven. Inclination one—two—0 left. Speed three—0'. Down below in the Transmitting Station they would be winding handwheels and pressing buttons as the details came down to them. Mesmerised, I watched the *Bismarck*'s superstructure swell as more and more of its pyramid shape—seen so often in diagrams—came into view. She was just before our beam, steaming from right to left at an angle about 30° this side of right angles.

All our Control Officers' headsets were interconnected and I heard a discussion forward about another ship. Shifting my binoculars a little I picked up a second director a good way to the left and then the performance repeated itself—stalk, lump, tower, pyramid—but on a smaller scale. Surely it must be the *Tirpitz*, only further off, ie, on the far bow of the *Bismarck*. I swallowed hard. If it *was* the *Tirpitz* we were certainly in for something. But Guns decided it was a cruiser, reaffirming the right-hand ship as target.*

We heeled to port a little, the *Bismarck* sliding a fraction to the left before the director caught up, as we altered 40° towards the enemy. It was a turn by Blue Pennant, the two ships—still only 800 yards apart—turning at the same moment so that the flagship finished up 40° on *Prince of Wales'* port bow, both steering to cut the enemy's advance at a sharper angle and so close the range much more quickly.

'"Y" turret will not bear' repeated the communication number, indicating that the turret on the quarterdeck had come up against its safety stops. I imagined Captain Aylwin, RM (the whole turret was manned by marines), fuming impotently. Though the enemy was within range, we were presumably conserving ammunition. For some time we kept on with only the usual sounds of the sea and the voice of the Gunnery Officer as he updated his calculations.

'Ready to open fire Sir!' This was to the Captain and one could not hear the reply. Surely it was yes and why weren't we firing? The whole of the *Bismarck* was now visible and I could not restrain a gasp of admiration, tinged with awe. Long and rakish with undeniably majestic lines, she was a fawnish grey, not bluish like our ships—or it may just have been the light. I noticed with a pang that all her 15-inch guns were pointing in our direction.

There was a *boom* from not far off. The *Hood* had opened fire.

Bismarck was 823 feet long, *Prinz Eugen* 655 (*Hood* 860 and *Prince of Wales* 700); I cannot be sure but think my two colleagues also considered it was the *Tirpitz*.

Seconds later 'Shoot!' said Guns. *Ting-ting* went the fire gong and I shut my eyes. *BAROOM!* The *Prince of Wales'* first salvo was away from 'A' and 'B' turrets. The slight concussion and the brown smoke that drifted aft (the wind dispersed it fairly quickly) brought welcome relief from inaction. My fingers moved up and down the three knobs. Suddenly a rippling yellow flash played in front of the *Bismarck*, followed by a dark cloud that, nearly blotting her out, hung for an appreciable time. She had fired. At whom? The range was 25,600 yards (nearly 13 miles) and it would take almost a minute to find out. There was a hoarse croak from a box on the bulkhead, heralding the fall of our shot, and a cluster of white columns rose to form a wall behind the *Bismarck* (and I think to the right, but that was B-C's pigeon). I pressed 'over'. *BAROOM!* went another salvo, following one from the *Hood*. Another flash from the *Bismarck*. More smoke. Wait. Croak. Splash. Press for another 'over'. *BAROOM!* Flash. On it went, Guns ordering corrections ('Left one. Down ladder shoot') in a level voice as each salvo landed, each time nearer. So far nothing seen of the enemy's shells. Presumably she was firing at the *Hood*. (The cruiser was also firing at the *Hood* but she was so far to the left that I could not see her without taking my glasses off the *Bismarck* and after the initial scrutiny I never saw her again during the action.)

BAROOM! again. Wait. Croak, splash, 'over'. *BAROOM!*—'short'. We must have been firing for nearly three minutes, it was the sixth salvo, when there was the welcome sight of the great white wall partly in front and partly behind the *Bismarck*. Straddle! By all the laws we should have hit her. She did not look any different, but I did not expect her to as armour-piercing shells burst inside, normally unseen. Three more salvoes, one of which was another straddle. We were making very creditable shooting, though I had not taken in that one of our guns was not working.

Another salvo had just gone when I heard Guns warn his director layer 'Stand by to alter course to port'. This long-awaited move— presumably we were going back to the original heading so that 'Y' turret could bear for the first time—had begun to take place, in that we heeled to starboard and it became temporarily more difficult to hold the *Bismarck* steady in one's glasses, when the ship suddenly rolled upright again and then continued to heel over the opposite way; moreover, with the urgency and excessive vibration that comes only from violent rudder movement. We were going hard-a-starboard. Back towards the enemy again. What the hell was going on? There was a momentary lull. Probably the director gunner had been put off his aim, and in the comparative quiet I realised that hitherto there had been an intermittent background noise.

The ship steadied up and then began to come back to port. Dick

Beckwith said 'My God! The *Hood*'s gone!'

I shot a glance up at him. He was staring horrified over his left shoulder, through his rear port. We both looked back into our glasses. Though I heard the words quite distinctly they meant nothing at that moment. It was as if that part of my brain not concerned with the long grey shape that belched flame and smoke simply was not working. I could have stood up and had a quick look (afterwards wishing I had) but it did not occur to me.

Seconds later we were just about steady, with all turrets bearing at last, when the sea erupted a few hundred yards in front, a great curtain of water going up for 200 feet over a wide area. *CRASH!* went 'Y' turret about twenty yards to our right. Distracted, I had failed to shut my eyes at the fire gong and was momentarily dazzled by the big orange flash. The director shook as a warm glow enveloped us and then everything was blotted out by the usual mass of pungent chocolate smoke. Their very forward bearing had brought the muzzles of the guns about in line with our director (never experienced in practice shoots) and at each succeeding salvo we received a considerable shake-up. The smoke had hardly cleared when another, smaller fountain shot up to the left—that must be the cruiser I thought—and then our shells landed and I pressed 'short'. There was a staccato, rippling bang followed by drifting smoke, our 5.25 armament joining in. *CRASH!* went 'Y' turret. A second huge splash in front, much nearer this time and then several smaller ones, some to the left and some to the right. There were more frequent flashes from the *Bismarck*, accompanied by less smoke. Of course the range was coming down fast and she was firing her secondary armament too. Croak. Straddle! That was good, our third.

The whole ship shook, or so it seemed, and a stream of red hot fragments shot past my port from left to right. They were followed by smoke and the distinctive acrid smell of burning. There was another shudder. Obviously we were being hit. The smell of burning continued though the smoke began to thin. More huge splashes and then a positive hail of smaller ones. The range was down to 13,800 yards, ideal for a cruiser action, almost point-blank for battleships. The sea was a turmoil, columns of water shooting up as others subsided and the noise was continuous, with bangs from our 5.25s every ten seconds, the *CRASH* of our 14-inches every twenty, the occasional crunch of something arriving onboard and a continuous background row from the hiss of falling spray and the roar of shells overhead. The *Bismarck* was now very large in my field of view; every detail of her was plain.*

I believe we had two more straddles. Just after our 14th or 15th salvo

---

*An account by an officer in the *Prinz Eugen* says: 'The *Prince of Wales* now suffered heavily under the now concentrated fire of eight 38-cm, eight 20.3-cm, six 15-cm and at times six 10.5-cm'.

there was an almighty *splosh* as a number of 15-inch shells (either four or eight) landed only a few yards short, plumb in front of us. I was conscious of a slight but distinct jolt and then the entire scene was obliterated by a mountain of green and white water that rose up mast high and, helped by the wind behind it, cascaded down on the rear part of the ship. For a few seconds even the fury outside our small steel world was drowned by the splatter of hundreds of tons of water tumbling all round, pouring down vertical surfaces, splashing and bouncing off others. The three of us were drenched through our small open ports and our binoculars covered in water. As this happened the ship heeled violently towards the enemy and again vibrated heavily to the wheel as she altered course to port. We had our binoculars reversed and were feverishly wiping the lenses dry with our handkerchiefs when the cry we had secretly prayed for rang in our headsets: 'After director take over. After director take over'. Guns and his team were clearly obscured as the stern swung round towards the target. But we were temporarily blind too (though probably not for more than 15 seconds) and Claude Aylwin in 'Y' turret, not receiving the expected control orders, assumed we were hors de combat and switched to local control. Each turret was equipped with rudimentary fire control gear for just this emergency and he now used his to get off—rather wildly as was to be expected—three or four salvoes over the starboard quarter. Clouds of black smoke now began to billow out of our funnels—the Captain had ordered a smoke screen—and as the turn continued, the *Prince of Wales* began to come round behind it.

When a warship alters course she pivots about the bridge, her stern skidding outwards. We were ready for action in the after director before the 180° turn was completed and just as I bent to the eyepieces—the *Bismarck* was now on our port quarter—a 15-inch salvo (or it may· well have been a broadside, ie, all guns firing together) landed about 20 yards short of the quarterdeck. It fell in the smooth 'slick' made by the skidding stern, exactly where that stern had been about three seconds before. Even in the heat of the moment I realised it was a good thing the Captain had not delayed that much longer. We got our binoculars on to the enemy just before she was hidden by the smoke, only to see her—not without a sense of relief—alter course away too. Thus the range opened quickly, and the cease-fire gong put an end to 'Y' turret's spirited effort. The *Bismarck* fired a couple more salvoes—probably by radar—and then a strange silence descended.

We sat dazed for a time, saying nothing. My ears sang and my eyes felt sore. It was 06:10. Was it really only 35 minutes before that that mast had first reared out of the sea? Everybody began stretching and taking off their anti-flash gear. Excited conversation broke out. It was all about the *Hood*. Then I remembered. 'My God! The *Hood*'s gone', and the full awfulness of it flowed over me. Where for days before there had been the reassuring sight of 'the mighty *Hood*' thrusting onwards there was nothing now but the lonely sea and the sky. Dick Beckwith was the only one to have seen anything, and then fleetingly, as we altered course to avoid what was left. He said her bow was sticking up vertically, with what looked like her stern, which disappeared quickly, a little way away. It was just impossible that a 42,000 ton ship with 1,400 men could disappear in two minutes, but she had. It was learnt that our destroyer screen, 30 miles astern, had been sent to pick up survivors, of whom there were only three.

Commander A.C. Luce*, who was Executive Officer of the *Norfolk*, was to put in a letter to his wife:

We had a front row of the stalls of the action between the *Hood* and the *Prince of Wales* and the German forces on Saturday morning, and saw the terrible sight of the *Hood* blowing up. It was quite appalling. You know the size of those ships, the splashes from the shells were twice the height of her mast. They had a mercifully quick release, it was all over in five minutes. It seemed absolutely incredible. The sight of the *Prince of Wales* steaming through the smoke and wreckage firing with all her guns, and with fountains of splashes all round her, was a never-to-be-forgotten one. *Bismarck* was hard hit at this time and turned away with troubles of her own.

His ship, which had in fact joined in with a few shots at long range, now appeared and Rear Admiral Wake-Walker, so traumatically elevated to senior officer present, took the *Prince of Wales* under his command. The *Suffolk* was again shadowing the *Bismarck* and *Prinz Eugen* (her identity was not actually established until later), both now back on a southerly course, and for the time being we could relax. The bugle sounded for Defence Stations, and this meant that the after director's crew could fall out.

I climbed stiffly out of the door at the back and down the vertical iron ladder, curious to see what damage the ship had sustained. To get forward without descending to the upper deck it was best to go along the boat deck via a small structure that housed a radar office, stores, heads and the like. I entered this and went down its short central passage. The lights were out and as all the scuttles had their deadlights (thick metal covers) in place it was hard to see. The last compartment on the left was a radar 'office', the forward end of which looked out on to the boat deck. There were jagged holes in its inner bulkhead and the door was either open or blown away. I went inside. There was a smell of cordite, or something like it, and the only illumination came from more jagged holes in the outer bulkhead. The air was full of dust, so that thin

*Sadly killed shortly afterwards in a firefighting exercise at Scapa.

beams of light from the larger holes played up and down as the ship rolled. There was something on the deck and I went over for a closer look. After a bit one of the beams fell slowly across it to reveal the upper half of a man, severed at the waist. It was a young leading seaman I recognised at once. His eyes were open but his white face looked utterly peaceful. I remember thinking 'so people do smile when they're dead'. My eyes had grown accustomed to the gloom and I saw another object in the corner. Going over I found it was a boot with a few gory inches of leg sticking out of the top. This suddenly turned my stomach and I rushed out to the nearby heads with my hand over my mouth. Bracing myself against the bulkhead with one arm I leant over the pan, saying to myself 'I won't be sick. I won't be sick', because I knew instinctively that I must control such nausea now or never.

After a while my stomach subsided and I forced myself to go back and look at the grim sights again. It then dawned on me that I should do something about the poor fellow and so went out in to the welcome fresh air of the boat deck. The charred remains of most of several boats—it was this fire I had smelt—lay all around smouldering. The Master at Arms appeared with two sick berth attendants and a stretcher and I indicated the radar office. He told me that a shell had hit the compass platform, killing or wounding everyone there except the Captain and Chief Yeoman of Signals, both of whom had been knocked down. The two Midshipmen there had been killed. This was a terrible shock. They were Dreyer and Ince, I think Midshipman of the Watch and Navigator's doggie respectively.

There were a few lumps of engineered metal on the boat deck and on the catapult deck below, where twisted steel and blackened paint marked another hit. At first I could not think what the lumps were— they looked like brass castings from an engine room or turret machinery—and then realised that they were from the *Hood*. I picked up a solid fragment of steel with one smooth surface, the curve of which denoted its German origin, and what was clearly a large rivet from the *Hood*'s plating. The latter had just gone in to my pocket when the Captain's messenger saluted and said I was wanted on the bridge.

The Captain, whom I found on the lower (Admiral's) bridge under the compass platform, was his normal self and said he was about to write his report on the action. He wanted me to do a sketch of the last moment of the *Hood* as he had seen it and proceeded to describe this in detail. Basically it was what Beckwith had seen but with a lot of minor debris in the water and a cloud of smoke overall.

The compass platform was a sorry sight. It was being cleaned up. There was a ragged but generally circular hole several feet across on each side (the starboard one higher than the port) where the 15-inch shell had gone through side plating and panels of dials, telephones, switches, indicators and all the usual paraphernalia of a battleship's bridge. It was instructive that some standard naval telephones, which I had always considered unnecessarily robust, were still on their hooks right at the edge of the hole. But Gun's telephone line to the Captain had been broken; he had sent his boy messenger down to tell the Captain that the main armament was all right (he did not know it but at that moment there were five guns out of action), the poor fellow returning very green about the gills at what he had seen.

The Navigating Officer* had had a large splinter of wood through his mouth so that it stuck out of his cheek, but had only just agreed to go below for attention. The two Midshipmen were apparently standing together on the port side right in the path of the shell, which did not burst until through and clear of the ship. The only recognisable sign of either was one cap, which I destroyed. Sub-Lieutenant Knight, RNVR†, one of the several casualties on the Air Defence Position, was knocked unconscious and blinded (though eventually recovering some sight). This was presumably by the 15-inch shell that hit the supporting structure of the two secondary armament directors nearby, putting the starboard one out of action. Our total casualties were two officers and eleven men killed, one officer and eight men wounded.

Not surprisingly, the Captain had been temporarily dazed. It was indeed fortunate that he escaped unhurt. He now went to the microphone at the back of the bridge and spoke to the ship's company. He said it had been a very hard decision to break off the action as no British Naval officer likes to retreat, but he had decided to do so because of the poor state of the ship's guns; the *Bismarck* was clearly at the peak of efficiency; and he did not think it worth continuing to pit the ship against such odds when she was by no means the last card the Commander-in-Chief had to play—*King George V*, *Repulse* and the carrier *Victorious* being only a few hours' steaming away.

If the *Prince of Wales* had stood on much longer things would certainly have gone hard for her. Though Colin McMullen was disappointed when the action was broken off—as any gunnery officer who was straddling the enemy would be—he knew in his heart of hearts that the Captain was right. After the first salvo there had always been one or more guns adrift though the Vickers technicians, who were still on board, had done sterling work, first on one, then on another. In fact there was not really a soul on board who did not agree with the skipper, but I expect he went through a trying time until first Rear Admiral Wake-Walker and then Admiral Tovey confirmed the correctness of his

---

*Lieutenant Commander C.G. Rowell (later lost in the same aircraft crash that killed Admiral Ramsay).
†Now the famous actor.

decision. The latter showed true understanding when he eventually sent the following signal:

P.O.W. (R) C.S.1 From C. in C. HF
1858B/2.

I wish to congratulate you on the very efficient and effective part you took in the recent operation against the *Bismarck*. Knowing your Captain as I do, I was always confident that he would take, as he did, exactly the action I would have wished had I been in company at the time. It is a very fine start to what I am sure will be a very great commission.

On going below to do the sketch I found to my alarm that the whole of the middle deck cabin flat aft, which contained my cabin, was submerged as a result of damge on the waterline. In fact there were nearly 2,000 tons of water in the ship, all adjacent watertight doors were closed and there would be no access until we returned to harbour. However, it was a small personal price to pay. Having completed the sketch to the Captain's satisfaction I joined the little knots of officers who were swapping experiences here and there.

If we in the after 14-inch director had had a rough time, poor Terry and the crew of his 5.25-inch director had fared much worse, both from the blast of 'Y' turret and shell splinters, though luckily there was only one casualty. Luckier still were the shell handing room crew—and one man in particular—of a 5.25-inch turret. An 8-inch shell from the *Prinz Eugen* came in, ricocheted up and went round and round the cylindrical wall of the barbette without exploding. It came to rest on the deck and, weighing nearly 200 lb, was manhandled over the side with some difficulty. I heard that in the course of its gyration it passed close behind the head of one man, taking off a clean swathe of hair in the process. Not believing this I went to see and found an admiring collection of similar enquirers to whom he was showing himself off with a resigned grin. Sure enough, the whole of his scalp at the back was a delicate pink without a hair on it! A 15-inch shell had hit the aircraft crane, as I had seen, wrecking the radar office and causing a fire on the boat deck, but considering its size did not do a great deal of damage. A Walrus was about to be catapulted to spot our fall of shot when a shell exploded nearby. The catapult officer was just 'winding-up'—the circular movements of his flag being acknowledged by the pilot with full revs—when the explosion knocked him down. Getting up he saw that the aircraft was full of holes, so ordering the crew out, he catapuled the petrol-laden remains into the sea. But perhaps the most dramatic tale came from 'Schoolie', the Instructor Lieutenant in the plot, whose job was to keep a graphic record of everyone's positions. After the shell had hit the compass platform he called up the voice-pipe but received no answer. Then to his horror, blood began to drip from its brass

61

mouth on to the white paper in front of him.

Those who had seen the *Hood* actually hit said there was first of all a fire on her boat deck, at the base of the mainmast (Captain Leach is on record as describing it as like a vast blow-lamp), after which she was straddled by a broadside. Immediately a towering column of flame shot up from about the same place to several times the height of the mainmast, and as large bits of the ship flew through the air, her two ends reared up. The flame gave way to a pall of black smoke and they soon disappeared. Terry said he thought he could see the *Hood*'s internal frames exposed as she rolled over and that the after part of the ship appeared to be a mass of twisted metal. Claude Aylwin could only see, through his turret periscope, hundreds of bits and pieces flying through the air and wondered if they were from the *Prince of Wales!**

The ship had heeled over so violently at the moment that I had seen the salvo land alongside the quarterdeck, that 'Y' turret shell ring slid over and jammed (it was part of the new system containing the 'vehicle' mentioned earlier) leaving Aylwin with only two more rounds per gun. He thought for a moment we were capsizing as his binoculars showed only water at close range and Rear Admiral Wake-Walker later said he too thought we were going over.

He now stationed us on the *Norfolk*'s port quarter. As she was already on the *Bismarck*'s port quarter (the *Suffolk* was on the other side) the three of us were virtually steaming in 'quarterline disposed to port', if at widely spaced intervals. Sometime after breakfast *Suffolk* reported that the quarry was leaving a broad trail of oil and this was eventually confirmed by a Sunderland flying boat. Clearly the *Bismarck* had suffered damage, possibly serious. The two enemy ships, having been steering SW, turned south about tea-time. What would they do next? Was the *Bismarck*'s damage serious enough to make her seek shelter and if so would it be Norway or France? A gigantic chess game, or perhaps it was more like 'fox and geese', developed. If all went well the Commander-in-Chief could expect to engage the Germans at about 09:00 the next day (May 25) but, as insurance, the Admiralty had been filling the rear squares of the board, in particular by summoning Vice Admiral Somerville's Force H from Gibraltar—*Ark Royal*, the battlecruiser *Renown* and Ed's recent ship *Sheffield*.

---

*As seen from the *Bismarck*:—'I heard a shout, "She's blowing up!" The sight I then saw was something I shall never forget. At first the *Hood* was nowhere to be seen; in her place was a colossal pillar of black smoke reaching into the sky. Gradually at the foot of the pillar, I made out the bow of the battle cruiser projecting upwards at an angle, a sure sign that she had broken in two. Then I saw something that I could hardly believe: a flash of orange coming from her forward guns! Although her fighting days had ended, the Hood was giving a last salvo. I felt great respect for those men over there'. (Kapitänleutnant Baron von Müllenheim-Riechberg, who was Control Officer in the *Bismarck*'s after director, ie, Beckwith's opposite number. From *Battleship Bismarck*.)

In our particular square, Rear Admiral Wake-Walker was faced with the same agonising decision that Captain Leach had been. Though his squadron was superior on paper he had seen for himself how the decisive battleship element was unequal and in spite of a goading query as to his intentions from the Admiralty, continued to shadow.

It was about 19:30 when the urgent bugle call 'Action Stations' sent those off watch scrambling to our places. The *Bismarck*, taking advantage of low visibility, had rounded suddenly on the *Suffolk* and fired nine salvoes. Warned by her radar and helped by the enemy's surprising inaccuracy, *Suffolk* was able to escape behind a smokescreen. This brought them both in our direction and *Prince of Wales* opened fire at about 30,000 yards. No straddles were seen and after half a dozen salvoes, during which two of our guns went out of action, *Bismarck* turned away and went off westward at high speed. The three British ships were then ordered into line ahead better to repulse sudden attacks, *Prince of Wales* in the middle with *Suffolk* leading. This was because of her superior radar which soon discovered that *Prinz Eugen* was no longer there. She had taken advantage of the distraction set up by *Bismarck* to accelerate over the horizon and out of the entire operation (to arrive without incident at Brest a week later).

Meanwhile, Admiral Tovey had detached *Victorious* with a view to her torpedo striking force flying off as soon as in range. *Bismarck*'s jink to the westward delayed this moment and the aircraft were not launched until 22:30. However, we were still only a little south of the latitude of Scapa Flow and sunset was not until a good time later. I cannot remember if we were expecting them but it was a stirring sight as three sub-flights of the old Swordfish aircraft flew past the ship, having received the enemy's bearing from *Norfolk*. Nine aircraft was all the *Victorious* could muster, she being in a similar unseasoned state to the *Prince of Wales*. We learnt later they pressed home their attack with gallantry—local rain squalls helping—and scored one hit without loss; but it burst on the *Bismarck*'s armoured side with very little effect.

Almost immediately: 'Alarm starboard! Enemy in sight . . .' On anti-flash gear. Round came the director. A quick sweep with the glasses. Yes, there was something. It must be the *Bismarck*. What else? *Norfolk* had a flag 5 up—'Open fire'—but Guns, who had completed his liturgy and only needed to say 'Shoot', was instead carrying out a quick-fire dialogue, presumably with the Captain. Guns thought it was not the *Bismarck*. Evidently the Captain agreed. Personally—though the visibility was bad— I was sure it *was* the *Bismarck* (and was in good company as apparently the Admiral was in a state of exasperation that a precious chance of firing at the enemy was being thrown away). No doubt, as so often happens in war, what you want or expect to see you *do* see. Nothing was done and the spectral ship disappeared. She turned out—I have forgotten how—to have been the US Coastguard cutter *Modoc*, a sort of militarised merchant vessel that had been searching for survivors from a convoy. Plumb on the right bearing for the *Bismarck*, she was one of the luckiest ships afloat, lucky at least in the cool-headedness of our Gunnery Officer.

Not long after this there were flashes of gunfire in the distant darkness but we saw no splashes. We then fired two salvoes by radar at long range before the cease-fire gong put an end to further expenditure of ammunition. Night at last descended on Empire Day 1941, a very full 24 hours.

At 04:00, *Suffolk*, who had continued to shadow independently, signalled the news—to prove so nearly fateful—that contact had been lost with the *Bismarck*. She *(Suffolk)* had been zigzagging to confuse both the quarry and U-boats that could be expected, and the former had timed a quick getaway to coincide with the beginning of a starboard 'leg'. The *Suffolk* had lost contact several times before at the same juncture and initially thought little of it. But the radar screen stayed clear. *Bismarck* had gone.

To every player on the British board this was a terrible blow. All calculations were now in the melting pot. There was a reshuffle of the nearest pieces into searching rather than heading-off roles. *Norfolk* and *Suffolk* were sent to investigate different possibilities and *Prince of Wales* directed south to join the Commander-in-Chief (a useful addition as *Victorious* had parted company so that her aircraft could search in the Greenland area and *Repulse* was about to leave for lack of fuel). The strangest pair of incidents—more like accidents—then occurred which nearly brought success to the hunted and did bring very bad luck to the *Prince of Wales*, now nearly in sight of Admiral Tovey in *King George V*. An enemy vessel—correctly guessed to be the *Bismarck*—made a long wireless signal which was picked up by our shore stations. This was extraordinary because no warship breaks 'W/T silence' unless she has to, for fear of giving away her presence (and if there is more than one listener for obtaining cross bearings—her position). In the present circumstances the *Bismarck* would be particularly cautious, but we now know that she made the signal because Admiral Lutjens did not realise that the *Suffolk*, his tormentor for 30 long hours, had been given the slip! The other accident then occurred, levelling the score. The *Bismarck*'s bearings, received in the *King George V*, were incorrectly plotted and her new position placed to the north of the last one known.

The immediate effect of this was, of course, to move all the pieces in that direction. The *Prince of Wales* turned right round to head back for the Denmark Strait, and, like the *Prinz Eugen*, out of the entire operation. This was because, seven hours later the plotting error was discovered, the *Bismarck* placed well to the south, and everyone's

Right *J.H.P. (Lieutenant J.H. Persse, 7th Rifle Brigade).*

Below *E.G.E. (Lieutenant E.G. Egerton, RN).*

Right *A.J.S.B. (Pilot Officer A.J.S. Buller, RAF).*

Main armament of nine 16-in guns aboard HMS Nelson.

Top left *Nelson having won the Home Fleet Battle Squadron regatta, 1939, Captain W.T. Makeig-Jones receives the silver cock from Admiral Forbes.*

Top right *Regatta supporters – Pay-Midshipman Crawley, foreground, and Lieutenant Commander A.C.C. Miers (later Rear Admiral Sir Anthony Miers, VC, KCB).*

Above left *Racing at Gibraltar, author nearest camera.*

Above *HMS Ark Royal after take-off.*

Left *The intrepid aviator.*

Above *HMS* Douglas *looking aft from crow's nest.*

Above right *On patrol: the port waist of* Douglas.

Right *Destroyers in the pens, Gibraltar.*

Below *Italian bombs around Force H.*

courses reversed again. Poor *Prince of Wales* was by now too far to the north even to try and we set course for Hvalfjord in Iceland, for what would now be called do-it-yourself repairs. Several other ships had to desist for shortage of fuel, a serious consideration that now loomed very large indeed.

The ground lost going north was almost decisive and presumably would have been if the *Bismarck*'s progress had not also been hampered by her own lack of fuel. Of this we knew nothing, but even so the situation in the early morning of May 26 was not quite hopeless, with Somerville's squadron and the 8-inch cruiser *Dorsetshire* closing from the south, the battleship *Rodney* better placed than expected, because Captain Dalrymple-Hamilton (who had been my Captain at Dartmouth) had Nelsonically ignored the order to go north, and a flotilla of our most powerful destroyers under Captain Vian coming in fast from an Atlantic convoy. It was simply a question of whether the *Bismarck* could be slowed up and brought to action before she came under a Luftwaffe umbrella, or the British ships cried off for lack of fuel.

The key to all this was the *Ark Royal*'s aircraft and they were not found wanting. Sighted both by one of her reconnaisance Swordfish and a Catalina flying boat in mid-morning, the *Bismarck* was clearly making for Brest or St Nazaire. The chase continued all day. At 19:00 *Ark Royal* flew off 15 torpedo planes. In bad visibility they first attacked the *Sheffield* by mistake, which was fortunately unharmed (due to malfunction of the torpedoes' magnetic pistols); a second attack, armed with contact pistols, reporting no hits. At this Admiral Tovey, still 120 miles to the north-west, prepared to admit defeat. He had already decided to leave the area—for lack of fuel—the next morning. But one of the torpedoes had in fact jammed the *Bismarck*'s starboard rudder (there were two) and she began to circle to port out of control. Captain Vian's Tribal Class destroyers carried out individual, bitterly opposed torpedo attacks all night—claiming hits—but daylight did not reveal any damage. When the big ships closed in the *Bismarck*'s gunnery was initially good, *Rodney* being lucky not to be hit. Her accuracy soon fell off, however (due to both main directors being put out of action) and by 10:15—pounded by *King George V, Rodney, Dorsetshire* and *Norfolk*—the *Bismarck* was a pulverised hulk, on fire internally from end to end. Another extract from Commander Luce's letter reads:

Our battleships ran in and started the ball rolling, and she was being hit with the colossal explosions of our heavy shell; the explosions were indescribable; huge flashes all over her and she was burning everywhere. She fought back magnificently, but to no effect, and one by one her guns were silenced. We pounded away, and our little shells could be seen bursting all over her, looking ridiculously small on her huge structure. Every time we hit, the troops cheered like mad. By this time she was silenced, but still looked an impregnable fortress, despite the hammering she had had.

Then started the most fantastic phase of all, which made the most blood-thirsty feel rather sick. We simply could not sink her, and we expected large scale air attack at any moment.

Two battleships and two cruisers steamed around her at close range pumping all they had into her. It was quite appalling. You would never believe the frightful effect of our heavy shell. Colossal flashes inside her, which must have been a shambles long before this, and wretched men running hither and thither on her deck, but she would neither sink nor surrender.

It is simply incredible that any ship could stand half the hammering she took. Our heaviest shell sent water up nearly three times her height, and great chunks of her upper works were blown away. She was finally despatched with torpedoes. A most dangerous and incomparably powerful ship. Her company were subjected to the long drawn-out sufferings of four days . . . chase and incessant attacks, and finally had 2½ hours' agony of what must have been hell on earth.

As Admiral Tovey left for home, the *Dorsetshire* hit the *Bismarck* with torpedoes from both sides and at about the same time her internal shuttling cocks were opened. At 10:40 she sank, a little over 100 survivors being picked up.

HMS *Prince of Wales* anchored in Hvalfjord, Iceland, even as these final moves were being played against the cornered, desperate fox. There were only 50 tons of fuel remaining, a veritable cupful. It was good when we heard that the *Hood* and our little band of dead, who had been buried at sea with simple ceremony, were avenged; but we were also full of admiration for a gallant foe. How the fortunes of war had swayed first one way and then the other, culminating in that luckiest-ever torpedo hit on the *Bismarck*'s one vital spot!

★   ★   ★

I discovered later that the slight delay in our opening fire was because the *Hood* had signalled for concentration on the leading ship. As known, Guns had recognised this as a cruiser and stuck to his right-hand target. Admiral Holland, who could expect the battleship to be in front, obviously realised his mistake soon after, because he made 'Shift target right' before opening fire. This does not seem to have reached the *Hood*'s gunnery officer, because the *Hood* fired at the *Prinz Eugen* throughout. We in the *Prince of Wales*' two directors were sure of this because none of the former's splashes were seen. (The Captain of the *Prinz Eugen* later confirmed that the *Hood* was firing at his ship, which was narrowly missed by 15-inch shells 'on all sides'★). Guns, who had been '2nd G' in the *Hood*, said that with ordinary binoculars (they did

*★Told to me by Captain Russel Grenfell, author of *The Bismarck Episode*.*

not have our very large ones) and the constant spray in their faces, the mistake was only too understandable. Initially, all our range takers except one had been defeated by this spray and fire had been opened soley on information from the 15-ft rangefmder in the forward director (unfortunately, calibrations on the gunnery radar screen ended short of 26,000 yards, so radar was not initially available).

Admiral Holland's end-on advance, with eight out of eighteen guns unable to bear, was much debated. No doubt he desired to close the range so that the poorly protected *Hood* would not be exposed to plunging fire for longer than necessary. We were not to know that this was also the tactic propounded by Admiral Tovey, whose theory was that a smaller target is presented in the more important lateral dimension. Again in Admiral Holland's favour, one could not help feeling it was part of a laudable desire to get to grips as soon as possible; after all, the *Bismarck* had a couple of knots in hand on both of us and awkward questions might well have been asked if she had been allowed to decline action. What all agreed was unfortunate was the failure to station us wide apart, as were the enemy. A mere four cables meant that anything over and left of *Hood* came unnecessarily close to *Prince of Wales* (the reverse could also have applied) and even more important, the enemy control teams had the minimum corrections to make when they shifted target. In fact they were hitting the *Prince of Wales* with hardly any delay.

Regarding awkward questions, one knows now that when the dust had settled, the First Sea Lord told Admiral Tovey that he wanted Rear Admiral Wake-Walker and Captain Leach court-martialled for failing to re-attack the *Bismarck*. Tovey replied that if this was to be so he would haul down his flag and act as 'Prisoner's Friend'. No more was heard of it!

The entire *Bismarck* operation was a classic in naval warfare in that about every weapon and technique was employed. As an epilogue to the action in which the *Hood* was sunk it may be of interest to record the damage the *Bismarck* sustained from the *Prince of Wales*, not of course known until after the war. One 14-inch shell hit on the waterline well forward, obviously beyond the limit of armour plating because it passed right through the ship without exploding. On the way it penetrated two oil tanks and destroyed the control valves of others, so that not only was oil lost straight into the sea but the engines were cut off from a further 1,000 tons. There was also considerable flooding which put her two or three degrees down by the bow. For some reason *Bismarck* had started out lacking several hundred tons of oil and the shortage that now accumulated not only forced the decision to abandon the Atlantic foray for a return to France, but dictated progress at an economical speed, where a full-power dash would probably have carried her beyond the range of *Ark Royal*'s aircraft. A second hit struck amidships beneath the armour belt, destroying an electric generator, putting two boilers out of action and causing more flooding, so that she had a list of nine degrees to port and the starboard outer propeller was coming out of the water. A third carried away a motorboat amidships and damaged the aircraft launching gear, before going over the side without exploding.

Though there were other important incidents during that eventful week, the first hit undoubtedly takes its place alongside the aircraft torpedo as one of the two really vital factors in the entire operation. It is a little hard—particularly on Captain Leach—that the fact was not properly appreciated until too late. Regarding the *Hood*'s gunnery there was an element of *de mortuis nil nisi bonum* in the aftermath of the action, so little was said and even a generation later accounts do not always give credit squarely where it is due. However, at the time there was at least satisfaction at having acquitted ourselves rather better than could have been expected, especially when Admiral Tovey made the following general signal to the Home Fleet:

'. . . What was particularly satisfactory to me was the almost uncanny way in which all ships and commands operated exactly as I wished them, without the necessity for any signalled instructions from me . . . The *Prince of Wales* must have done considerable damage to the enemy, very creditable for a new ship which had completed a short working up only a few days before.'

It is true that our performance not only reflected credit on the officers concerned but indicated a high standard throughout the ship. Nor was this attributable only to the seaman side. The engine room department performed wonders in keeping the ship's new machinery running at full power for hours, and coping with damage. In due time both Captain Leach and Commander (E) L.J. Goudy received a DSO and the Gunnery Officer a (to my mind meagre) Mention in Despatches. On the subject of our seven-week work-up, it is interesting that the *Bismarck* had been working up for many months and at this time her sister *Tirpitz* had been doing so for four months and was not going to be considered ready for another four!

★   ★   ★

We were hardly at rest, with the bleak Icelandic snow-capped hills close in on either side, before the ship was listed to port by transferring oil fuel. Though local steering connections and a good deal of electrical cabling on the compass platform had been shot away, the most immediate job to be tackled was the flooding aft. As the starboard side came out of the water (one was reminded of Nelsonic wooden walls being beached and careened to plug shot holes or scrape away weed) two 8-inch hits were laid bare; they had burst on the 'turtle-back' armour protecting the propeller shafts. The water inside was pumped out and the twisted hull plates smoothed off and blanked over with metal patches. One of the shells appeared to have burst in a cabin adjacent to mine. Several had been gutted, the flat was blackened and what the shell did not accomplish the sea had mostly finished off. There was little woodwork left and most of my belongings were just a soggy, jumbled mass. Curiously enough the precious Peter Scott print, though totally submerged, was not irredeemable. A shell splinter had gone straight through my best poodle-faking reefer (I subsequently lost nothing in pointing out the repairs to admiring female acquaintances, most of whom thought I had been in it at the time) and my Midshipman's journals, over which I had laboured for so many tedious hours, dripped like porridge through my fingers.

Two of their friends had already been set the melancholy task of packing up the effects of poor Dreyer and Ince, and I now got down to writing to their parents. At least I was able to say that they could not have known anything about it. Dreyer—the most recent recruit from the well-known Naval family—was a fair haired, fresh-faced, cheery boy who took life lightly but was loyal and reliable when it mattered; Ince, a more reserved type, was tall and dark. Very intelligent, he had a quiet way with him that was always most effective. Both were popular and sadly missed. The former was a 'Dart' but Ince a 'Pub' who had only joined the Navy seven months before.

As soon as seaworthy, we weighed anchor and sailed south to Rosyth, entering a dock which would be pumped dry by the next morning. I had the middle watch (00:00-04:00) that night and was just thinking that nothing ever happens to relieve the aching boredom of that watch when there was the sound of frantic feet up the steel ladder that ended inside the quarterdeck lobby. Out rushed Lieutenant (E) Wildish to say that there was an unexploded 15-inch shell in the bottom of the ship, immediately beneath us. I sprinted aft to wake the Captain, then the Commander and everyone else who should know, feeling very relieved that the galaxy of talent that tumbled down the hatchways, buttoning coats over pyjamas as it went, was between me and the awkward decisions that would have to be made.

All possible damage control precautions were taken while Guns and Torps (the Torpedo officer, Lieutenant Commander R.F. Harland, who had the distinction of looking exactly like the King! I think he had a responsibility for bomb disposal) tossed up as to who would deal with the unwelcome guest. The former won (or lost!) and when a hole had been cut in the ship's hull, he and the Gunner's party lowered the shell through with a 14-inch grab attached to a chain purchase. A picture was eventually taken of them and the Captain in the bottom of the dock, the latter with his foot on the shell like a trophy of the chase.

73

Certainly belonging to the salvo that had drenched us in the after director, this projectile had probably caused the slight jolt I had noticed at the time. Wildish, as Damage Control Officer, knew we had been hit as the special gauge for the purpose indicated inexplicable flooding of the watertight compartment at this point. He reported to the bridge but could take no further action. As soon as the lengthy process of pumping water out of the dock allowed, he went down with another officer or senior rating to look. There was a large, clear-cut hole just above the bilge keel. They climbed through it—into what was normally an empty compartment—shining torches around to discover another hole in the next bulkhead inboard. This was the outer wall of an oil fuel tank. Clambering through this second hole, with difficulty as everything was slimy with oil and sea water, they found yet a third hole in the inner wall. Through this again into a third compartment they found an indentation—but no penetration in the next and third bulkhead. There were three to four feet of oily water in the bottom of this last compartment, normally empty, and procuring a boat hook Wildish poked around until contacting an object, the shape of which he could not explain from his knowledge of the hull. At the very moment that the truth struck them both they were in the presence of a monster intruder in the form of an unexploded 15-inch shell, the large auxiliary diesel engine (for providing electric power in harbour) started up just the other side of the dented bulkhead, with its usual frightful clatter and vibration. Appalled and very frightened, they shot up the compartment's vertical ladder and down into the diesel room to shut it off.

Next day Dick Wildish went off to get married, a much pleasanter occupation, as, for the record, did Dick Beckwith.

Curiously enough, many people had tried to develop a shell that penetrated under water but so far as I know only the *Bismarck*, with this freak effort, succeeded. Having lost its long pointed nose-cap (there was no sign of this) it had come in horizontally through the anti-torpedo 'liquid sandwich' of air, oil fuel and air, to hit the 2½-inch armoured bulkhead and fall to the bottom (the ship's double bottom did not start till the other side). What astonishing luck that it failed to go off! A 2,000-lb shell, detonating in very close proximity to both oil fuel and diesel oil, could at best have started a major fire and blown out the side of the ship at that point. 'Y' turret magazine was only yards away and at worst there could have been an explosion in all too faithful emulation of the *Hood*.

★   ★   ★

Well wot a to-do. I shall sleep through any thriller film in future. We are waiting for Alexander to speak after the 21:00 news as we hope he's going to say something about *P of W*. We are all a bit bitter as the papers have got hold of the wrong end of the stick. I'm sorry about Dad's telescope and lots of things. Have got some hefty souvenirs. It is rather good to have been in a first class big ship action and a very good view of it too! Two Midshipmen were killed, as you probably saw, which was very sad. I can't tell you anything about it of course . . . I imagine you're wondering what happened, especially old Haw-Haw saying we were left in a sinking condition! We take off our hats to the *Bismarck* as a jolly fine ship and a very brave crew too. She did marvellously well and was apparently unsinkable by gunfire in a short time. The penny press and all their vulgar exaltation (apart from natural jubilation) and not knowing anything about it, rather annoy one.

A good deal was released about the *Bismarck* operation, presumably to counteract German propaganda concerning our losses; 'Lord Haw-Haw'—last met when he 'sank' the *Ark Royal* in the North Sea—was doing his best with the *Prince of Wales*. Her hits on the *Bismarck* had not been confirmed and I expect our bitterness was due to the press inadvertently echoing his remarks. They were not, of course, told everything and painted a pretty fanciful picture of the whole affair. It was widely stated that the *Hood* was destroyed by a lucky hit penetrating to a magazine. This was not the case. However fine a ship in her day (20 years of flag-showing round the world had built her up into a legend), she was latterly an old battlecruiser; 'old' meant that her design—particularly her armour protection—was out of date and 'battle-cruiser' meant that she was fast and lightly armoured to begin with; not intended to fight a battleship at all.

The 'hefty souvenirs' were some bits of 15-inch and 8-inch shell about the size of cricket balls, one of the latter—from my cabin flat—being nicely decorated with perforations for taking the copper driving band.

Several VIPs came to look over the ship, among them the socialist A.V. Alexander who had relieved Mr Churchill as First Lord of the Admiralty. Guns was introduced to him in the Wardroom and the following conversation took place: 'Did you hit her, boy?' 'Well, sir, we straddled several times but . . .' 'Did you hit her or didn't you?' 'Sir, with armour piercing shell they go off inside and although I'm pretty certain . . .' (back turned, conversation over). An awkward silence was broken by Mr Alexander's private secretary: 'Terribly sorry, but we're due at the Co-op in Edinburgh and are running late already . . .'

We stayed in dockyard hands for a month, got in some more leave, many a pleasant visit to Edinburgh (Aitken Dott were surprised to get my birthday picture back for cleaning in such a terrible state and Gieves did excellent business) and then returned to Scapa. Just before leaving Rosyth the Captain went to hospital for a hernia operation. He was relieved for a short time by Captain C.H. Harcourt who took us back to the Flow (passing HMS *Repulse* on the way, the first time we had fallen in with this near relation to the *Hood*). Envious visitors from other ships—many of whom had seen neither action nor leave since the war began—came to hear about our doings and look around. 'Line-Shoot' number one was a scimitar-like piece of steel that curved down from the Wardroom deckhead. A legacy from the shell that had killed the radar operator above, it had been left as an honourable scar and painted white. A bulge in the deckhead of my cabin flat also went unremedied. Other areas of damage had been restored, though in point of unpleasant fact the compass platform never quite lost tell-tale reminders of that day.

Robin Buller and my cousin Darby George were still Midshipmen in *KG V* and I heard from them of the *Bismarck*'s end. They had some Polish snotties on board and in the closing stages these were discovered in the Midshipmen's chest flat, sharpening knives and bayonets, as they thought that boarding was imminent with the chance to pay off old scores.

There was, of course, nothing untoward about our temporary CO, in fact he shortly became an Admiral, but naturally he was not held in such affection as Captain Leach. The depth of this affection was well illustrated on the latter's return. It was the middle of the forenoon when the Captain's boat was seen approaching. With a flash of inspiration the Commander—presumably after a word with the substitute skipper—went to the Bo's'n's Mate's microphone in the adjacent lobby and said, 'Captain Leach is returning to the ship. Those of you who would like to welcome him back may lay aft'. The forward end of the quarterdeck and the whole of the after superstructure overlooking it suddenly began to sprout sailors, unseen by the Captain who by now was under the lee of the stern. As he appeared at the top of the gangway the Commander took off his cap and shouted 'Three cheers for Captain Leach!' who was taken completely by surprise. The cheers rang out from a solid mass of men and heaven knows what the other ships thought was going on. It was all very irregular but most satisfactory. The Captain stood astonished for a second, then waved his hand and went down to his cabin with his stand-in. He passed close to me and I saw that tears were glistening on his cheeks.

Gunnery and other exercises were resumed, including a 14-inch 'throw-off' shoot at the cruiser *London* (the guns being suitably offset from the director). The edge of our training had been somewhat blunted by the fleshpots and, though it was not as hectic as before, life became

76

one again with the well-known Scapa routine. A difference was the summer weather. On some days the Flow was pure glass, mirroring the cottonwool clouds that hung motionless in a blue vault or drifted slowly over the green and brown hills to mottle them in passing, just like they did to the Downs at home.

We were under way but stationary on just such a day, probably awaiting the start of an exercise with another ship or target-towing aircraft, and I was Officer of the Watch. The Captain was beside me looking intently through his glasses at some distant object—almost into the sun—when I saw his lips curl into a slow smile. Without shifting his gaze he said 'Look, Brooke—an immoral mosquito!' I put up my glasses and burst out laughing. In the distance were two Walrus flying boats at anchor, looking in the haze like grey mosquitoes. One was beyond the other and, because of our high vantage point, appeared to be well and truly on top of it, bobbing gently the while.

Captain Leach was a keen ornithologist and when in the open sea would suddenly point to a scudding shape and ask 'What's that?' At first one had little idea but soon learnt the difference between a petrel and a puffin, and of course it helped to pass the more uninteresting hours.

There was plenty of intriguing practice with our own Walrus aircraft, Sturdy little biplanes with a pusher engine between the wings, they were known irreverently as 'shagbats'. One would be run out of its hangar on to the catapult with wings folded back, turned to face the sea on one side or the other, made ready and fired by a fat brass cartridge that went into a breech like a gun. The discharge was frightening to watch, the heavy little aircraft reaching about 90 mph in the width of the ship, but I eventually screwed up enough courage to ask Lloyd, our Gunroom aviator, to arrange me a passenger flight. When this was forthcoming almost the entire complement of the Gunroom was present, grinning expectantly at the discomfiture of the Sub. Those who could see my face on departure cannot have been disappointed. The sensation was excruciating, a stomach- and brain-numbing pain that increased unbearably until I blacked out. On coming to—probably but seconds later—we were climbing gently to starboard under full throttle and everything was delightful. The Flow shrank to a big lake as we gained height, there was the odd ship cutting its grey surface like a skater's blade, the *Prince of Wales* like a huge toy—for the first time I appreciated what a vast expanse of deck she had—and all around the islands of Hoy, Carva, Flotta, Burray . . . with Scapa bay to the north where lay the *Royal Oak*.

*   *   *

At the end of July strange things began to occur, many felt and some seen. Senior officers went about giving the impression that they knew something. By August 1 there were too many physical manifestations to be denied. Some officers had to vacate their cabins and double up—a sure sign of VIPs in the offing—and a Captain Pim and a 'two-and-a-half' arrived from the Admiralty. They set up a War Room in a large office and I was deputed to assist them, painting in parts of a huge chart of the Atlantic. On this they stuck flagged pins showing the positions of convoys, escorts, ships in company or detached units and U-boats, the latter represented by little black coffins. Extra communications ratings arrived on board and a stream of signals began to flow in to the War Room, from which the positions were continuously updated. There was also a map of the Russian front, which had recently erupted.

HMS *Prince of Wales* was fitted as a flagship, the Captain normally living in the Admiral's palatial quarters, but he now vacated these for his sea cabin on the bridge. Everyone was agog. Obviously we were due to receive someone of importance, but whom? Rumours abounded. Some wag in the Wardroom organised a sweepstake of personalities and their destinations which included: 'taking Hess back to Germany', 'taking the Grand Duchess of Luxemburg to Canada' and 'taking Mrs Cochrane's young ladies to Dakar!' 'Taking Mr Churchill to see Roosevelt' was drawn but not thought much of.

August 4 arrived and all our questions were answered. As the only RN Officer in the Officer of the Watch's 'union' (otherwise comprising Lieutenants and Sub-lieutenants RNVR), it was ordained that I should officiate on all important occasions, having the necessary experience to cope with the ceremonial and other niceties that I now thanked my *Nelson* days for supplying. This was often irksome but in the next three weeks paid dividends indeed. So I was OOW on the quarterdeck when HMS *Oribi*, one of our newest destroyers, shaped up to come alongside. No doubt there were several in the know by this time but I was not. Who was that stocky figure on the bridge in a British Warm and Service cap? The Prime Minister. Winston Churchill!

As the *Oribi* glided in towards us the general salute was sounded, the Commander brought the ship's company to attention and the bugle blared. Mr Churchill returned the salute. By now we could see the cigar. The *Oribi* eased alongside, there was a brief thrash from her propellers, heaving lines already across brought her wires to bollards on the *Prince of Wales* and in moments a brow was being run up to our quarterdeck. Mr Churchill came up it to the shrilling of the side party's calls and came forward to shake hands with Captain Leach.

There was a momentary relaxation of tension and then the First Sea Lord was on the brow followed by a General whom one recognised as Sir John Dill, Chief of the Imperial General Staff; then an Air Chief Marshal, small and dapper, who proved to be Sir Wilfred Freeman,

Vice Chief of Air Staff; another small, dapper figure in plain clothes (Sir Alexander Cadogan of the Foreign Office) and the bulky and recognisable scientist, Lord Cherwell. They were followed by a round dozen lesser luminaries, including the well-known authors, H.V. Morton and Howard Spring, who we learnt were to chronicle the coming events.

Special Sea Dutymen was sounded off as the last newcomer disappeared below and in half an hour the ship was under way. Just as had occurred ten weeks before, three destroyers picked us up outside the Flow, course was set for the Atlantic and the Captain broadcast to the ship's company. He said that we had on board the Prime Minister and the Chiefs of Staff and that we were going to Placentia Bay, Newfoundland, where they would meet the President of the United States, Franklin D. Roosevelt and his staff. We would be four and a half days at sea . . . that is, excepting any diversions on the way. As the little groups who had gathered round loudspeakers so as not to miss a word drifted away, there cannot have been a man who did not realise that here was a prize of truly historical proportions for Hitler to grasp.

The weather got up after 24 hours and at 20 knots the destroyers were leaping about in such agonies of effort that our 10-inch winked a consoling message before we forged ahead, to let them drop out of the picture. There was a brief pause at Iceland, where, the weather having moderated a little, three others from a recent convoy joined (*Ripley*, an ex-American 'four-stacker', *Restigouche* and *Assiniboine*, both Canadian). After the reported position of a U-boat had been skirted, little occurred beyond the daily round of dawn action stations, bridge watchkeeping, dusk action stations and night watchkeeping while the ship drove on across the Atlantic at three parts speed, creaking and groaning as her plates protested, cabin articles dancing and the entire environment shaking in a way we hardly noticed but which was anathema to the unfortunate non-naval guests.

Mr Churchill found sleep so difficult that he was transferred to the Admiral's sea cabin on the bridge. A long way from the thundering propeller shafts, and at the ship's point of balance, he slept well. Characteristically, he made the decision on the spur of a tortured moment and went forward (the expression hardly does justice to his progress, bent double under swaying hammocks, along a corkscrew path between watertight doors and hatches—most of the latter reduced to manholes—and then up a dozen steel ladders with very inadequate chain handholds) in the company of a Lieutenant with a torch. The latter was full of praise the next day, as apparently Mr Churchill said nothing throughout. Perhaps at 66 he was conserving his breath!

He had brought a good supply of films with him and these were shown every night in the Wardroom. There was no room for Gunroom officers but we heard that between reels he would sometimes turn from where he sat with the other VIPs and give a little homily on the story. One, *Lady Hamilton*, all about Nelson, he was seeing for the fourth time. On these occasions 'the Prime' as he had been dubbed, wore the mess dress of the Royal Yacht Squadron, a mess jacket with brass buttons but no stripes. He worked with his advisers most of the day but one got occasional glimpses of him in the famous 'siren suit' of blue denim, with which the cherubic face and portly figure combined to resemble a huge baby in rompers, zipped up the front. He took to sleeping most of the night—obviously the pressure of work was less than usual—to the great relief of his entourage who normally had to be on call at all hours and get their routine work done as well.

I was sent for on the third day and told to take General Dill over the after director; the forward one was, of course, ready for action. Somewhat awed at first, I found him very easy and charming—as all accounts agree—a handsome, rather aesthetic looking man. When I had got him through the cramped entrance and settled in the Control Officer's seat, I was describing the sequence of events when he missed a point. Rather over-engrossed, I said testily 'No, of course not, you obviously haven't understood', and then suddenly remembered I was talking to the Army's 'First Sea Lord' and became confused. He thought it a good joke and from then on we never looked back; in fact I found myself very reluctant to deliver him back to his papers.

Over halfway across the Atlantic the weather subsided pleasantly, though this made the U-boats' task easier. All the time our position and the Atlantic situation was pinpointed in the War Room. This was no stamping ground for Sub-Lieutenants and one had to await publication of H.V. Morton's *Atlantic Meeting* to get a real peep inside. The position of the *Prince of Wales* on the map was, of course, of outstanding interest. I often went in to find out where we were and also to look for the nearest U-boat; and some seemed to me quite near enough! Delighted on one such occasion to see the death of a U-boat, I said to Captain Pim: 'Has that U-boat been sunk?' A well known voice took me to task. Winston Churchill had quietly entered the Map Room. 'Only British submarines are sunk', he said with a smile. 'German U-boats are *destroyed*!'

On the day before our arrival there was a rehearsal on the quarterdeck of the President's reception on board, with Sir Alexander Cadogan representing Mr Roosevelt and the Prime Minister, an interested spectator, breaking in from time to time with a suggestion. August 9 proved calm and grey. Three American destroyers appeared and eventually led in towards a misty streak on the horizon that materialised into low-lying hills, not—at that distance—unlike those we had left. But Placentia Bay proved to be much larger than Scapa Flow and the hills heavily wooded. Of habitation, however, there was little sign. But it was not at the land that we looked as, rounding a promontory, the American force was revealed at anchor.

In the centre was the cruiser *Augusta* which was known to have the President on board, flanked by another, *Tuscaloosa*, the battleship *Arkansas* and a flotilla of destroyers. With strange single-float seaplanes cavorting overhead, the *Prince of Wales*, which must have looked oddly weather-beaten to the curious American eyes, with her inevitable streaks of rust from hawsepipe and bow flare, was led close past the *Augusta*. Our ship's company were fallen in and as Officer of the Watch (aft)—on entering harbour this post was in addition to the OOW on the bridge—I could see little until the *Augusta* was nearly abreast of us. Mr Churchill and staff were close by on the quarterdeck, and with him at the salute the band played *The Star Spangled Banner*. The National Anthem came back to us over the water and one saw an awning spread on *Augusta*'s fore turret, under which was a small group. Prominent was a tall man in a fawn suit, hat in hand and leaning slightly on an army officer at his side; obviously Mr Roosevelt, who one knew had been a polio victim.

The tremor of the cable running out on the fo'c's'le heralded the 'G'—one long note on the bugle—at which gangways went down, booms swung out, cranes raised their heads over boats to be lowered, and the Jack was hoisted at the bows. All the business of arrival ensued and the Captain duly appeared after his first proper bath since Scapa. Morton, an unobtrusive but keen observer of the scene, went up to Captain Leach, whom he had not then met. They talked and he later wrote 'I said something about the responsibility of taking Winston Churchill across the Atlantic in wartime, and received in reply an eloquent glance of tired blue eyes and a weary but contented smile'. Admirals had staffs to advise and share some of the load during the war, but Captains of ships were alone with their responsibilities. Captain Leach's must have been one of the heaviest in naval history.

The Prime Minister, with the Chiefs of Staff, went over to the *Augusta* at 11:00. We could see him greeted by Mr Roosevelt, to whom he handed a letter from the King, and then all went below for the first of several conferences. During the afternoon, launches came over from the American ships with a carton for every man in the *Prince of Wales*. Each contained an orange, two apples, 200 cigarettes, half a pound of cheese and a card inscribed 'The President of the United States of America sends his compliments and best wishes'; a very kindly human touch amidst all the pomp and ceremony. But it was Saturday and an orgy of hospitality began to bubble through the surface courtesies, officers and men from both Navies circulating freely in each other's ships. They showered us with cigarettes and as far as the officers were concerned we reciprocated in the only way we could, 13:00-23:00 non-stop. The US Navy is 'dry' and so this was a success.

From then on a pleasant peacetime atmosphere warmed the whole visit, but what really brought things nostalgically home to us was that all ships remained brightly lit at night, a luxury we had not known for nearly two years. No one was allowed ashore, except a handful on official business, but it did not seem to matter.

The American Midshipmen were some three or four years older than mine but our being at war, and recently in action at that, evened the conversational scales. It was somewhat inflating to visit them—I went on board the *Arkansas*—and be plied with questions, though my tact was exercised to the limit when asked directly how I thought the very old battleship would fare. The questioner was a southerner with an attractive *Gone with the Wind* drawl and later we were walking about the upper deck of the *Prince of Wales*. The sun shone, the band was playing catchy tunes and life felt good. Dozens of foretopmen were washing the bridge from wooden stages, lowering themselves down its face as they progressed. The band struck up a current transatlantic favourite, *Paloma, my pretty little poppee* . . . at which they began whistling the tune. My new-found friend turned to me and said 'Say, your boys sing *our* songs?' It is hard to say which of us was the more incredulous. Whenever I hear *Paloma*—it seems to have been revived lately—I see the two of us looking up at the great grey facade, with all the men whistling.

That first Saturday evening, his boat's wake turning the limpid reflections of the other ships' lights into a thousand sparkling points, Mr Churchill went over to dine with Mr Roosevelt. One of the things they discussed was the morrow's 'Church' in the *Prince of Wales*, which turned out—another deft touch among the weightier considerations—to be a most successfully integrated affair. It was conducted by our own and an American padre with both British and American hymns and sailors from all the ships present (at Mr Churchill's express request there was no 'marching about', the visitors being met informally at the gangway and led aft to the quarterdeck).

At the last moment the destroyer *McDougal* cast off from the *Augusta* and came alongside and when all was ready Mr Roosevelt, in a dark blue suit and with an ivory-handled stick, came slowly across the brow, leaning heavily on the arm of the same officer (who proved to be a son in the Air Corps). Officer of the Watch again, I scrutinised him as closely as I dared; a fine, lined, tanned face with an alert air despite his disability, and distinct aura of authority. Then came Admiral King, Admiral Stark, General Marshall, General Arnold; also Mr Sumner Wells, Mr Averell Harriman and Mr Harry Hopkins, all to sit in the stern facing the big guns of 'Y' turret. The service began and about a thousand sailors, singing like they used to sing in those days, must have made a brave sound as their voices rolled out over the water to the other ships and the dark green hills beyond. One felt it was an ill omen for our enemies. When the last hymn had died away I saw to my horror men of both nationalities advancing on the Prime Minister and President with cameras. Officers on the spot began to wave them away but the two targets beckoned them on and so there was a photographic free-for-all lasting some minutes.

Mr Roosevelt was then taken on a tour of the upper deck to see places of interest especially to do with the *Bismarck* action. McMullen told him how narrowly the US Coastguard cutter *Modoc* had come to disaster and the President (who was preparing US psychologically for war) replied that it was just as well nothing like that had happened as he would have had a very difficult time 'explaining it to the great American public'. Mr Churchill then entertained Mr Roosevelt and his Chiefs of Staff to lunch, which took place in the Wardroom. This, of course, was the WR messman's big moment and he had asked me if I could do something special in the way of menus; so I produced a set with British and American flags crossed at the top and pen and ink drawings of the ships in Placentia Bay at the bottom.

After lunch there was an incident that gave me a considerable kick. It was arranged that all the officers of the *Prince of Wales* should be introduced to the President, seated in the Wardroom anteroom. They would file past and shake hands, the mess president concerned introducing each by name. The Wardroom officers went in first. When they had finished I led in the Gunroom officers, was introduced by the Captain and then stood beside the President to do the rest of the introductions. The last Midshipman was departing when I sensed drama. There was no sign of the Warrant Officers! The Captain moved forward and, looking most embarrassed, bent to say something; but I suppose Mr Roosevelt had taken in the hiatus because he asked me a question about the Midshipmens' training. I answered it and he asked another. Seeing us getting on satisfactorily, the Captain retired discreetly and I then had ten minutes' fascinating conversation with the President. He had been Naval Secretary and knew everything there was to know about the US Navy. I think he was genuinely interested in how we trained our officers and men and I had to go through it all, with many questions. He then gave me a graphic rundown on the US methods, laughing heartily at his own description of certain reservists as '90-day wonders'. When I eventually saw the rotund Mr Luxton— president of the Warrant Officers' mess—hovering very breathless in the doorway (someone had forgotten to tell him) I tactfully closed our conversation with genuine regret. It is a measure of Mr Roosevelt's magnetism that I had quite forgotten those around us, including the

Prime Minister!

After his guest had returned to the *Augusta*, Mr Churchill went ashore in a whaler, towed by a motorboat, with four others. He was in his siren-suit and on return was seen to be happily clutching a bunch of pink wild flowers. It was just as well (perhaps carefully arranged) that he dined with Mr Roosevelt that evening, because the Wardroom held a guest night attended by about 20 American guests. The usual rough games were played and the rear part of the ship resounded to the goings on. Lieutenant Ian Forbes played his bagpipes and in the middle of the racket an American officer said to Anthony Terry (who, as recounted, had already been sunk three times) 'I guess you boys take this war very lightly'. Little did he imagine that poor Terry would be sunk three more times before March was out.

A day later salutes were again exchanged as we steamed past the *Augusta*, the central actors in the week's drama waved to each other and soon we were clear of the harbour behind a screen of US destroyers. As Placentia Bay, with its brief glimpses of a kinder world, reverted to the grey streak we had first seen and then disappeared, defence stations were sounded off, soon followed by night action stations, and the realities of wartime life crowded in again.

Halfway across we overtook a convoy of 72 ships, to steam slap through the middle and fly the signal 'Bon voyage. Churchill.' He enjoyed it so much that he asked for an encore, so we doubled back and came through again, with all the ships hooting. There was a brief call at Iceland and then course was set for Scapa, the voyage in general continuing uneventful. Not in the Gunroom, however. The first evening out we entertained the three Chiefs of Staff to drinks. Very friendly and interesting, they did not know it, but were really acting as a sort of aperitif. I was aiming higher, having put out feelers about Mr Churchill visiting the Gunroom. The next day there came a message to say that he would be delighted and would bring Sir Alexander Cadogan, Lord Cherwell, H.V. Morton and Howard Spring.

The Gunroom was given a special scrub and when the appointed hour arrived we awaited the great man with some trepidation. I met him in the passage and led him into an expectant but unusually abashed semi-circle. With a drink in his hand he darted amused glances round him—after the initial pleasantries conversation was not exactly humming—and then said 'I know what you boys want; you'd like to ask me questions!' There was a chorus of 'Yes sir!' 'Very well—pull up a chair.' We pushed an armchair into the middle of the ante-room and clustered round. Questions came thick and fast. Was America going to come into the war? Were the Germans likely to overrun Russia? What did he think about this, what did Mr Roosevelt say about that . . .?

Hess, Hitler's deputy, had landed in Scotland by single-seater aircraft just before we left; nothing but the bare fact had been given out and the whole country was agog to know more. 'What is the truth about Hess?' I asked. He replied that Hess thought we were ripe for peace negotiations and that he would be able to return to Hitler with the UK on a plate. 'Where is he now, Sir?' Mr Churchill named some prison. 'What is he doing?' 'Writing voluminous memoranda to me.' 'Do you read them?' 'No!' rasped Mr Churchill, 'there's better use for paper like that!' At the ensuing guffaws he grinned impishly round at his delighted hearers. There is no doubt that an impudent schoolboy streak, particularly appealing to the young, was one of his most endearing traits. I said once: 'When are we going to start bombing civilians?' and he whirled round on me and stuck his lips out so that the cigar looked like a 16-inch gun and said 'What d'you think we've been doing for months?' At this I said lamely that I thought we still at least kept up the pretence of military objectives, at which Churchill said 'Civilians *are* military objectives!' and grinned all round. I asked him whether the Japanese were expected to come in against us. 'No, I don't think so' he said, and then added 'if they do, they'll find they've bitten off more than they can chew.' The inquisition went on and Sir Alexander Cadogan said that he had never heard the Prime Minister asked such awkward questions, or answer so directly. We found him (Sir Alexander) and, indeed, all of them, most affable, doubtless hand-picked by the Prime Minister for this Gunroom ordeal. The next day he went through it all again in the Wardroom (word must have got out!) but we felt we had drawn first blood.

The morning of August 18 saw HMS *Prince of Wales* off Scapa Flow and at action stations. There was no cause for alarm, however, just a full-scale demonstration of the ship's firepower for 'the Prime's' benefit as 14-inch salvoes, 5.25-inch salvoes and hundreds of rounds of close-range ammunition were loosed in impressively noisy abandon. The free world nearly lost its champion, though, because a UP bomb (an unreliable device that descended by parachute and was soon discontinued) became entangled in the rigging just above Mr Churchill's head and took some getting down.

The ship anchored in the Flow and a destroyer came alongside to take the Prime Minister off. He made a farewell speech to the ship's company—all gathered forward—about the historic occasion in which we had played a part; at the finish he brought out a cigar at which a great roar went up. When the destroyer accelerated away the Captain called for three cheers and for the second time in days, the sound rolled out and back from nearby hills, a fitting curtain to a memorable time.

A charming postscript was the receipt of a copy of Churchill's book *World Crisis*, with 'From Winston Churchill—Question time in the Gunroom!' on the flyleaf.

4

Prince of Wales and Repulse

We found to our embarrassment that, if previously envied for her lucky embroilment with the *Bismarck*, the *Prince of Wales* was now the '*Daily Mirror* Ship' (all the papers having been full of the Placentia meeting and the resulting Atlantic Charter) and one took care to provide intriguing tit-bits only when asked.

The usual sorties for practice shoots and other exercises were renewed and on return from one of these, late in the evening, the Captain tried a new approach to our buoy. It was a failure; the bow 'payed off' in a sudden breeze and as there was insufficient room to manoeuvre on the spot we had to go out and come in again from the normal direction. This lost an hour or more, washing out a much anticipated run ashore to the fleet canteen after a gruelling spell. To the surprise of many Captain Leach apologised to the ship's company over the loudspeaker, explaining that he had tried to save time but muffed it. This seemed to me unnecessary, even a mistake, but it went down very well indeed with the troops, especially the 'HOs' ('Hostilities Only'; ie, non-regulars). Doubtless he understood what I cannot have at the time—that these new, half-trained and civilian-minded seamen who now formed the majority of the ship's company should be treated with greater consideration than their hardened messmates who were used to taking the rough with the smooth.

The '*Daily Mirror* Ship' was not left kicking her heels for long. On September 15 she embarked Vice-Admiral A.T.B. Curteis and sailed for the Mediterranean to come under the orders of Admiral Somerville (now flying his flag in the *Nelson*). Confirmation soon came that the object was to force an important, mainly troop-carrying, convoy through to Malta in what was called Operation Halberd. Though just such an assignment had been successfully carried out in July, the Mediterranean was no longer a British preserve and both surface and heavy air attacks could be expected. Particularly around besieged Malta British ships were furthest from their base but the reverse applied to our enemies. It was therefore with a considerable sense of anticipation, that we found ourselves in blazing sunshine, surrounded by blue sky and blue sea, steering east, not far from the convoy and its close escort.

All was quiet for two days, most of which were spent at Repel Aircraft Stations, searching the sky endlessly with only the occasional diversion when *Ark Royal* turned into wind to fly off or land on reconnaissance aircraft or fighter patrols. Then suddenly (it was the morning of the 27th) she warned of enemy aircraft in the vicinity, speed was increased, and as one watched and waited, the tension grew. All at once it was 'Alarm Port!' and there they were, dropping down—not my side—to come scudding in over the sea. The port close-range weapons started up, the reassuring *pomperty-pom, pomperty-pom* of the 'Chicago pianos' mingling with the Oerlikons' more staccato chatter. All ships were acting independently—turning towards—to avoid torpedoes. On the starboard side it was difficult to keep one's attention on the clear sky with all this going on behind. There was a buzz of excitement and, succumbing to temptation, I darted across the small Air Defence Position in time to see a big splash subsiding. We had shot one down. The line had hardly been re-formed before there was another attack on the port side, the big ships turning again to avoid the bubbling tracks. Again the *Prince of Wales* shot one down.

Those of us on the disengaged side were beginning to feel out of things. The port pom-poms began again, followed immediately by the cease-fire gong, its steady, raucous message going unheaded. Consternation. An aircraft coming in behind the Italian torpedo planes and fired at by both *Rodney* and ourselves had not been recognised as a Fulmar fighter and it too was shot down. At last it was 'Alarm Starboard!' with several aircraft coming in fast. They seemed to be the same type as met in the *Douglas*, the red, white and green stripes showing clearly as they dropped their torpedoes and wheeled away. We hit one twice in the tail but it stayed up, floundering like a wounded pheasant. It was hard to feel quite the hatred one did for the Germans and I found myself half wishing the fellow luck in getting home.

There were further attacks on my side, all successfully avoided, during one of which a Fulmar was on the tail of a Savoia Marchetti and firing steadily, shot it down right abreast of the *Prince of Wales* (unimpeded by us, thoroughly chastened by now). Shortly after this the destroyer *Duncan*—a sister ship of the *Douglas*—reported that she had picked up two British airmen, presumably our birds, which was good news. *Legion* also reported that she had picked up two Italian airmen. All this time *Ark Royal* had been acting independently of the rest of us, constantly turning into wind to operate fighters, and had worked her way out some distance on our starboard beam. She suddenly opened up and we saw she was having a private battle with enemy planes that were probably taking advantage of a landing-on period. The firing died down and with relief we saw she was unharmed, her fighters—and also her reconnaissance Swordfish—being keys to the whole situation. We did not appreciate it at the time, but the former had had much success some distance from the fleet, the Italians that attacked it being those who had managed to get through.

It all seemed a piece of cake. But cake can crumble and although it was not as bad as that, there were some long faces soon. It was early afternoon when an attack by three torpedo bombers developed on my side. One made for the *Nelson* ahead of us and its torpedo could be clearly seen to drop. A minute later, engrossed, I heard someone say the *Nelson* had been hit and when I could look my old ship was certainly slowing, had a slight list to starboard and was down by the bow. It transpired that luck was certainly not with her as, having turned to comb its track, she was hit right on the stem by a 'fish'; a few feet either side and her bow wave would have deflected it. However, she enjoyed a measure of revenge—shared with the destroyers on the starboard wing of the screen—as between them they accounted for the last of the three aircraft. A quarter of an hour later there was a concentrated attack on the port side which had the close-range weapons banging away again and the ship heeling to sudden helm for the umpteenth time, but nothing for either side to claim.

We were not properly back in station before an RAF aircraft reported two Italian battleships, four cruisers and 16 destroyers, 80 miles ahead of the convoy, steering so as to close it. Within moments Admiral Somerville had ordered Vice Admiral Curteis in *Prince of Wales* to take *Ark Royal* and *Rodney* with two cruisers and half a dozen destroyers under his orders and move out to give battle. *Ark Royal* was to launch a torpedo attack (her Swordfish were already coming up the lifts) while the damaged *Nelson* would follow as best she could.

We went to action stations which sent the AA supernumeraries like myself back to their proper quarters and, settling down beside Beckwith and Sheridan* in the after director, it certainly looked as if we were heading for some excitement, probably much more prolonged than on the last occasion. Again, one found oneself fidgeting with spotting knobs, adjusting headphones and making trite conversation. The difference was the bright sunshine (most of us were lobster red by this time) instead of the cold, inhospitable Atlantic. It did not seem quite right to be hell-bent in such pleasant conditions. Perhaps the Italian Admiral thought so too, because soon all was anti-climax. The enemy turned for home, our torpedo bombers failed to find them and at 17:15 we were recalled.

---

*Lieutenant G.T.B. Sheridan, RM, had relieved Tom Baker-Creswell, who was to take part in the Anzio landings and subsequent fighting ashore, so putting the Royal Marines' *Per mare per terram* very much into practice (as indeed the others were to do in time).

The convoy got through to Malta with the loss of only one ship (all her troops were taken off), the result of a moonlight action. Several Italian submarines attacked us on the way back to Gib, necessitating emergency turns, retaliatory depth charges and the sinking of one of them by *Legion* and *Gurkha*. Admiral Somerville came on board on arrival but to some an equally welcome visit (though Guns found it embarrassing) was that of the unfortunate Air Defence Officer of the *Nelson* who had been sent over to find out 'how we did it', ie, shot down aircraft. The ship's first encounter with hostile aircraft had certainly gone well. The whole operation had, in fact, exceeded all hopes and the double success provided yet another fillip to the confidence and already high spirits of the *Prince of Wales*. She sailed later that evening to arrive at Scapa on October 6.

Only 16 days later it was evident that something special was afoot, yet again. Ammunition lighters came alongside, we filled up to the brim, stores of all sorts followed and on completion the ship sailed, with *Electra* and *Express*, anchoring in the Clyde on October 23. Next day Vice Admiral Sir Tom Phillips, up till then Vice Chief of Naval Staff at the Admiralty, and a full staff embarked. Though nothing was said it was perfectly clear that HMS *Prince of Wales* was off on a long voyage. No leave was given but, of course, some had duty ashore at the Naval offices at Greenock and I prevailed on Dick Beckwith, whose wife was near, to give her my large Peter Scott print for collection some time later. (I expected to leave the ship on getting my second stripe in December and did not relish the idea of carting this about.) We sailed on the 25th—with the same destroyers; it turned out they were to be our permanent escort—and the Captain soon gave out that Freetown, on the west coast of Africa, would be the first port of call.

A week's steaming saw us back in whites, the dog watch deck-hockey players stripped to the waist and sunbathers taking their constitutionals up and down the fo'c's'le. Awaited with some anticipation, Freetown did not disappoint. Jack Egerton, Ed's father, who was Naval Officer in Charge, sent a car to take me and a load of Midshipmen to a beautiful palm-fringed beach and after dark the bazaar, selling every sort of weird memento, lit by oil lamps and throbbing to native music, seemed to our unsophisticated eyes to be the heart of Africa itself! I bought my girl of the moment a little figure in leopard skin and returned to the boat well content.

Though Captain Leach probably knew the rudiments, it is probable that few on board outside the Admiral and his Chief of Staff, Rear Admiral Palliser, were aware that in the corridors of Whitehall a sort of high level poker game—basically between the Prime Minister and First Sea Lord—was in its final stages. Mr Churchill had wanted for some weeks to send a 'propaganda' fleet, with at least one modern battleship, to rattle a cutlass at the Japanese, who were becoming more and more bellicose; Admiral Pound, who was quite unable to send a force of the necessary strength, did not want to invite a heavy reverse.

By mid-October the more-or-less-agreed plan was to concentrate the *Prince of Wales*, the *Repulse* (ordered to Colombo from Durban, whence she had escorted a convoy) and the new carrier *Indomitable*. But the latter, working up at Jamaica, most unfortunately went aground on November 3. *Illustrious* and *Furious* were being repaired in the States and on November 14 our overall carrier strength was still further reduced when *Ark Royal*, so often sunk in the German imagination, finally succumbed to a U-boat in the Med. So no carrier was available. If anything had been learnt in the naval war so far it was that a force needed air protection—preferably its own—when operating within range of shore-based aircraft. The Japanese were now in Indo-China, and the RAF in Malaya was weak. One can guess that the argument whether to press on with just the battleship and the battlecruiser must have been unbearably acute. Mr Churchill had his way but it appears that, as a sop to Admiral Pound, the final decision about sending the *Prince of Wales* on to Singapore was not to be taken officially until she arrived in Cape Town, though it has been said that Admiral Phillips—who of course had been at the centre of all the deliberations—was in no doubt about our final destination from the outset.

The Admiral, who was very small, gave me the impression, in the comparatively short time he was on board, of a somewhat reserved intensity. Perhaps he was just preoccupied, as well he might be, the operation on which we were embarked being nothing but a gamble. Fortunately, the rank and file knew nothing of this; the sudden excursion was all a bit of a lark in the best tradition of the last ten months. True, the question mark that hung ominously over Japan indicated Singapore as our probable destination, but the fact that we had never been given the chance to work up really properly—every exercise period had been cut short by some special development—did not, I think, concern we junior officers much. The *Prince of Wales* was undoubtedly as efficient as possible under the circumstances; morale, after several successful performances, was high; and above all she was a happy ship.

After a hilarious crossing-the-line ceremony, during which most of the officers, from the Commander down, were daubed in chocolate (that had gone bad in the canteen), whitewashed and ducked, the *Prince of Wales* duly arrived at Cape Town with its enormous flat-topped backdrop that is Table Mountain. We were given a wonderful reception. Officers were entertained privately, functions arranged for the men and an orgy of shopping indulged in. A surprise visitor was my cousin John Tothill; now a Commander, he was refitting his destroyer *Janus* following an

90

action with some Vichy French ships off Syria. They used dye in their shells which sent up different coloured splashes, useful for spotting, and the *Janus* received several hits, one on the bridge. The Engineer Officer, who told me this, went up to report the engines out of action, and on reaching the top of the bridge ladder was aghast at the sight, everyone casualties except the Captain who was standing at the binnacle, lurid red and green all over. The red was other peoples' blood and the green (which took weeks to get out of his beard) the dye. Apparently he was completely unruffled and chatted to the EO (who was not), as if it was all an exercise. Years later he, Cousin John, told me that his mother had given him a St Christopher on a chain and he had just hung it on the Captain's chair when the shell struck.

A day or two out of Cape Town we became suddenly aware of a close air escort on our starboard quarter. A number of huge albatrosses came within yards to glide uncannily along beside the quarterdeck, with no visible signs of life except the blink of a yellow eye as they returned our interested stares. Ever since the Ancient Mariner the albatross has been a bird of ill-omen, but I do not think anyone worried. The ten-day passage to Colombo, broken by brief stops for fuel at Mauritius and Addu Attol, was pleasantly uneventful. I did a large sketch, for eventual water-colouring, from well aft, taking a lot of trouble with the difficult perspective of 'Y' turret, the after superstructure tipped with 'my' 14-inch director, the 5.25-inch batteries and so on. It went rather well; a shame it never got beyond the pencil stage.

HMS *Repulse* was already at Trincomalee, the naval harbour on the east coast of Ceylon, when we arrived at Colombo on November 28. A graceful if elderly half sister to the *Hood*, she had six 15-inch guns (only one turret aft instead of the latter's two) and had been very little modernised since the early 1920s. As a battlecruiser she was much more lightly armoured than the *Prince of Wales* but had the same top speed of about 29 knots. Her Captain, Bill Tennant of Dunkirk, was senior to Captain Leach and when Admiral Phillips, who had just been promoted to full Admiral, flew straight on to Singapore to confer with the authorities there (including Admiral Sir Geoffrey Layton, C-in-C China, whom he was to relieve), the *Repulse*, after rendezvousing south of Ceylon, led us on the final leg of our five-week voyage. In an oppressive, damp heat, quite different from the drier atmosphere of India, the squadron had Singapore in sight to port—a distant smudge to the east—about noon on Tuesday, December 2 1941.

With only the sketchiest knowledge of the area I studied the charts with interest. Indo-China (now Vietnam, Cambodia and Laos) recently delivered, to all intents and purposes, by the French to the Japanese, ran down opposite the north part of the Malay Peninsula—from which it was separated by the Gulf of Siam—to end in a huge, blunt point.

This was only about 160 miles across the sea from Kota Bharu, a place just inside the Malayan border with Siam. Singapore Island, I saw, was about the size and shape of the Isle of Wight, with Singapore City in the middle of the south coast. The naval base, opposite it on the north coast, was approached via the Strait of Johore which separated the island from the mainland by amounts varying between a half and two or more miles.

Having passed Singapore, which sprawls along a considerable frontage, the two ships steered in for the easterly mouth of this Strait and were soon steaming up the gently winding channel. The naval dockyard opened up eventually after a turn to port and the *Prince of Wales* secured alongside. As various VIPs flowed up the brow, the *Repulse* came to a buoy nearby and Force Z, as the two ships and their destroyers were now known, had arrived.

Introduction to the tropics had dealt the Gunroom beer supply a crippling blow and one of my first duties was to order 120 dozen. We had not seen a lot of *Repulse* before, and there was naturally much inter-ship visiting. My opposite number was a fair-haired, lively little Sub called Pool who told me that he had got into the Captain's bad books by constantly volunteering for Motor Torpedo Boats (hardly a ploy likely to commend itself to the CO of a capital ship!) There had also been a spot of bother at Durban over some of the Midshipmen bathing with girls in the nude, though it was at a private bath and Pool himself was not involved.

The newspapers and radio were full of the arrival of the squadron, described as 'HMS *Prince of Wales* and other heavy units'. Presumably to mention the 25-year-old *Repulse* would be a bit of a come-down. The '*Daily Mirror* Ship' was in the limelight again and we felt very bad about it. I have read that there was some rivalry and bad feeling ashore between the two ships, which is nonsense. Apart from this publicity there was no cause and in fact no time for such a thing to develop, beyond the odd individual case that often arises.

The unfortunate engine room department got down to boiler cleaning, having been denied the expected opportunity at Cape Town. The Commander (E) is on record as having to give the Captain a 'friendly ultimatum' on the subject.

The next day three or four of us took a taxi the 20-odd miles to Singapore. As we drove, fascinated, through kampongs (villages) scattering chickens and children, usually Malay but sometimes Chinese or very dark skinned Tamils, we gasped at the colours. To start with the road wound about, often among strange trees that threw deep shadows; nearer the city some of the gardens were breathtaking and all the time a bright blue sky provided a literally dazzling back-cloth. In a back-handed way even the damp heat, which I found very oppressive with my shirt sticking close back and front, came up to scratch. This was a beautiful place where everything seemed to be bursting with ripeness. But as we found ourselves on the outskirts of Singapore, among rambling stone and wood buildings, often built over the pavements so that arched and pillared walkways shielded the jostling pedestrians from the sun, a dreadful unspoken query, so far overshadowed by the unfolding scene, became real. Where on earth were the fortifications? We had travelled the full depth of the island and not seen one military mite. So much had been heard about 'Fortress Singapore'—put out with extra intensity of late—that we expected Maginot-like emplacements, barbed wire, cleared fields of fire and so on. There was absolutely nothing and the shock was great.

As we downed stingahs (whiskies and soda) at the elegant Raffles hotel and then wandered among the fine buildings in the heart of Singapore, I at any rate could not shake off a feeling of unease. But the Americans were at this moment engaged in diplomatic discussions with the Japanese and surely something sensible would be worked out. It was not to be. On December 5 a large Jap troop convoy, with powerful escort, was sighted off the south-west point of Indo-China, steering for the Gulf of Siam and the *Repulse*, which had sailed for Port Darwin to show the flag in Australia, was recalled.

The 7th was a Sunday. The Admiral returned from a conference with the Americans at Manila, but—at least from a Gunroom viewpoint— nothing else happened. The *Prince of Wales* had been moved into dry dock for a quick scrape of her bottom. (This was, of course, to remove speed-reducing weed but was to prove helpful to many of her people in a way none could have dreamed of.) The immediate effect, sitting as we were in a reflecting cauldron of baking concrete, was of terrific, damp, enervating heat*. The engine room department was already having serious problems concerning the heat, but fortunately this was no concern of mine. One yearned for the self-made breeze of a ship under way. It was not long in coming.

Sleep was brutally rent in the early hours of the 8th by the urgent bugle call 'Alarm to Arms' and the dry 'Hands to repel aircraft stations—Hands to repel aircraft stations', not entirely successful in excluding a tremor of excitement, set cabins and messdecks disgorging humanity like ants from an upturned stone. Overshadowing both the effort to banish sleep and the physical struggle into an overall suit, was the grim realisation that this was war with the Japanese all right. I

---

*In all the millions of words written about the fall of Singapore I am sure too little weight has been put on the debilitating effect on newcomers of its damp heat, which many need months to get used to. In my opinion it is not surprising that our PMO (Principal Medical Officer, Surgeon Commander F.B. Quinn) was to report: 'Though the morale of the ship's company was good I am of the opinion that the men were fatigued and listless and their fighting efficiency was below par'.

fought my way up to the ADP to find the night surprisingly cold. The moonlight picked out those in white uniforms like ghosts, tin hats pushed back and eyes on the sky. The drone of planes was overhead. Very high, they were on their way to bomb Singapore and I think it was on their return that we opened up with the 5.25s, such guns firing from a ship in dry dock being probably unique. A Bofors somewhere let go optimistically, the graceful parabola of its tracer shells falling far short of the little silver crosses that were plain in the searchlight beams. Continuing unimpeded to their Indo-China airfield, they must have passed near the Japanese transports that had been landing troops successfully at Kota Bharu in the north for two or three hours. (Offered stiff resistance at first from raw Indian soldiers, the enemy had prevailed and were to press on to take the all-important local airfield before the day was out.)

Breakfast was a sombre meal. News had just come in of a devastating carrier-borne attack on Pearl Harbor, the main US Pacific base, which seemed to have caught the Americans completely by surprise. Hong Kong too was under heavy attack and the Philippines, Guam, Midway and Wake. Nearer home the Japanese were also landing at several points in Siam, notably Singora, just north of the border. When more details were known about Pearl Harbor it was clear that the US Pacific Fleet had suffered heavily. The balance of naval power in our hemisphere had plummeted towards the Japs overnight, the implications of which were incalculable. In command of the sea, they could spread unchecked, and then what of Australia, or India? Not only was this shattering, but the ruthless efficiency with which it had been effected struck chill. The declaration of war on Japan went almost unnoticed.

Steam had, of course, been ordered for full speed but some boilers were still open for cleaning and, in fact, the last pair were not connected until after the ship sailed.

Back alongside the wall there was much coming and going. The most poignant meeting must have been that between Admiral Phillips, the Commanding Officers of the *Prince of Wales* and *Repulse*, and the destroyer Captains of the force. The Admiral said he considered that, given fighter support and the element of surprise, there was a reasonable chance of at least preventing reinforcement of the enemy and cutting the communications of those already ashore. In any case we could not remain inactive while the enemy continued to land. He asked for comment and apparently Bill Tennant replied for the meeting that there was no alternative.

Again these sombre sentiments were not aired to the rank and file and when we sailed it was with a tingle of anticipation rather than anything else. Force Z slipped and proceeded at 17:35, retracing its steps to the open sea. The big ships then turned on to a north-easterly course and the destroyers took up their positions ahead. There were now four of them, our faithful 'Es'—*Electra* and *Express*—being augmented by the veterans *Vampire* and *Tenedos* from the local flotilla. The Chief of Staff had been left ashore at the combined HQ, and about 100 miles had been put between Singapore and the Force when a signal of the utmost importance was received from him. It said 'Fighter protection on Wednesday 10th will not, repeat not, be possible'.

The absence of air cover when out of range of Singapore fighters— about 500 miles—took away the main prop of Admiral Phillips' assertion that the operation was feasible. Nevertheless, because it was impossible for the Navy to remain inactive, he had no option but to press on and on the morning of the 9th put out an unvarnished description of the state of affairs:

Force Z from C in C. The enemy has made several landings on the north coast of Malaya and has made local progress. Our army is not large and is hard pressed in places. Our air force has had to destroy and abandon one or more aerodromes. Meanwhile fast transports lie off the coast. This is our opportunity before the enemy can establish himself. We have made a wide circuit to avoid air reconnaissance and hope to surprise the enemy shortly after sunrise tomorrow, Wednesday. We may have the luck to try our metal against the old Japanese battlecruiser *Kongo* or against some Japanese cruisers and destroyers which are reported in the Gulf of Siam. We are sure to get some useful practice with the HA armament. Whatever we meet I want to finish quickly and so get well clear to the eastward before the Japanese can mass too formidable a scale of an attack against us. So shoot to sink!

With our present desire for concealment the weather on the morning of the 9th was ideal—low cloud, intermittent rain and generally poor visibility. Having left the Anambas to port at breakfast time course was set northwards preparatory to a run into Singora and by 17:00 we were 170 miles from the southern tip of Indo-China (and near the latitude of Kota Bharu, where the other main landing had taken place). Half an hour later the visibility suddenly improved and to our consternation there was a plane on the horizon, soon joined by another and then another. They hung about maddeningly, obviously reporting our every detail to the Japanese fleet that was certainly covering Singora. The advantage of surprise had gone the way of our air cover.

By this time *Tenedos* had come to the limit of her fuel endurance and as dark closed in was detached to return to Singapore. At 19:00 the bridge signal lanterns flashed for an alteration of course (to a little north of west) and an increase of speed to 26 knots. The dash to Singora had begun. Shortly afterwards *Electra* sighted a flare in the sky some miles ahead, but nothing further transpired. The dash to Singora was shortlived. By 20:15 Force Z was swinging round to south-east, the exact reciprocal of the morning's heading, with speed reduced to conserve fuel. The operation had been cancelled—causing general disappointment—and we were returning whence we had come. Whether the Admiral started the western move as a feint I do not know, but not long after turning back he received a reminder from Admiral Palliser that must have confirmed his decision—'Enemy bombers on S. Indo-China aerodromes are in force and undisturbed. They could attack you five hours after sighting and much depends on whether you have been seen today'. He added that there might be carrier planes in the area (in fact our discoverers were from cruisers).

At midnight another signal was received from Palliser 'Enemy reported landing Kuantan, lat. 3° 5°N'. Kuantan was in a south-westerly direction about 180 miles off. For various reasons it was a likely place for the Japanese to land; Admiral Phillips ordered course to be altered for Kuantan and speed increased. So another dash was on, continuing for the rest of the night.

Action stations were sounded off early the next morning and we settled down to see what daylight would bring. I had with me in the after director a small canvas action bag with essentials in it, rubber life-jacket (which I should have been wearing but found too hot), first aid items and so on. Daylight brought nothing; for the second time in 24 hours there was an anti-climax. Our Walrus was catapulted to search but still saw nothing and was told to return to Singapore. By 08:00 Force Z was right off Kuantan and the *Express* was sent in to have a close look too. 'All is as quite as a wet Sunday afternoon' she reported. It was a calm, grey morning with the sun behind the clouds, but not low, rain clouds as on most of the previous day. Visibility was good and later the sun was out more often than not. We trained the director on to the distant land and I had a good look through the powerful binoculars. It was greatly tree-covered, a long line of variegated greeny-grey.

A southerly course was resumed that would have kept roughly parallel to the coast, but soon after *Repulse* had catapulted her Walrus for anti-submarine patrol, we turned back north-east to investigate some barges seen earlier but by-passed. At 09:50 *Tenedos*, who had almost reached the latitude of Singapore (but was still well to the east to avoid possible minefields) reported that she was being bombed. This was a most unpleasant turn of events as she was considered to be at the very limit of the enemy's range. The barges were left to themselves, a south-westerly course resumed and speed increased to twenty-five knots. Shortly after, it was just before 11:00, an aircraft was picked up on the radar at maximum range. It stayed there, presumably watching us and then there were more echoes, closing rapidly at considerable height, fine on the starboard bow.

By this time we were at Repel Aircraft Stations, which found me on the Air Defence Position (ADP) as usual. The *Repulse* was on our starboard quarter at four cables (800 yards), her rakish bow carving majestically through the water and a long white road streaming out astern. One destroyer was ahead and another on each bow. The day was warming up to a sticky heat and the *Prince of Wales* was vibrating to the few knots less than her maximum. A temperature of 136° had just been recorded in the boiler rooms, with several stokers collapsing, and one felt uneasily comfortable on the ADP, basking in the man made breeze of some 30 m.p.h. However, any contentment was short lived as the lookouts began to yell and one saw them plainly, eight or nine twin-engined plump looking bombers high up ahead.

On went anti-flash gear and tin hat, to start sweat oozing and running into every fleshy crevice. Our forward 5.25s crashed out, quickly followed by the *Repulse*'s 4-inch. Seconds later the 5.25s again as the first shells began to wink among their quarry and spatter them with black puffs of T.N.T. The enemy came on steadily, beginning what appeared to be a run on the *Repulse*. I watched their relentless advance with grudging admiration; some shell bursts were close enough but the formation remained tight. We altered course to starboard and then back to port. They were overhead when the *Repulse* all but disappeared in a forest of fountains that rose up around her. As the water subsided, brown smoke billowed out from somewhere amidships. With a hollow feeling one realised she had been hit. But she kept on, apparently little the worse. The bombers, now making off, had kept high throughout—about 10,000 feet—and were certainly most competent.

For some time Force Z sped on unmolested. *Repulse* got her fire under control and signalled that she was operationally unimpaired. I had taken off my anti-flash gear for a breather when the most ill-timed call of nature of my life made me descend two decks to the bridge heads. I was no sooner seated than every gun in the ship except the 14-inch seemed to open up. The heavy jarring of the 5.25s, the steady bang-bang of the new Bofors* and the rhythmic coughing of the multiple pom-poms mocked me as, frantic with annoyance, I sped my departure. I was nearly out when there was a tremendous reverberating explosion that shook my little steel cabinet and had me staggering. It continued as an ominous, muffled rumble that seemed to come from a long way off. My hand was on the door knob when another, peculiar noise percolated through the rest. The gunfire had died down. The noise was rushing water, the sea pouring into our ship, the sound being transmitted up the lavatory waste pipes with chilling clarity. Back up top I was in time to see three or four black dots disappearing towards the horizon.

*Fitted at Cape Town.

Nine Mitsubishi 'Navy 96' twin-engined torpedo bombers had dived out of cloud to port, turned towards us and attacked in line abreast. It was some consolation that I would have been on the disengaged side. One aircraft had been shot down, crashing close alongside the ship, but all had released their torpedoes and some had machine-gunned the bridge as they passed near, killing two men on the wings. It seemed that one torpedo had hit the *Prince of Wales* right aft. We were now describing a turn to port, slowing considerably, and had taken on a noticeable list, also to port. The alteration continued, which we in the ADP watched with disquiet, worst fears confirmed when eventually the 'not under command' balls—two big black canvas spheres—went up at the yardarm to denote that HMS *Prince of Wales* could not steer.

The damage must be bad, but just how bad one could not tell until reports began to come in from various stations to the Gunnery Officer nearby. The electrics of half the ship—her rear half—had gone, one of the worst results being that the after 5.25-inch batteries (four twin turrets in all) were virtually useless. They could be worked by hand but for AA purposes this was but a gesture. There was also no communication with the affected area, a situation full of menace. Presumably part of the ship's electrical ring-main and one or more generators were damaged but there was a well tried system of switching to alternative routes or sources of supply, not to mention portable leads that could cross-connect to undamaged sections and doubtless the damage control parties would soon have power restored. But the minutes ticked by and there was no improvement. The ship continued to circle to port, the ominous black balls remained aloft and we began to wonder. As far as we knew there had only been one torpedo hit and, however powerful, its effect was shockingly greater than it should have been. Though nothing was voiced it would be idle to pretend one was not shaken, at least temporarily. Moreover, it was only a question of time before we were attacked again and it was about 150 miles to Singapore. Where the hell were our fighters? We did not know and all we could do in the ADP was to sweep the hostile sky with our glasses yet again.

Soon—it was just before mid-day—a formation of high-level bombers was seen approaching from the south—I do not remember if they were picked up by radar—which shaped up for a run over the *Repulse* a mile or so away from us. We fired a few salvoes at long range and she met them with a steady stream of 4-inch fire before disappearing for the second time in a maelstrom of splashes. Hardly had we observed with relief that she was unharmed, when another formation—of torpedo planes this time—came in low on the other side of her in an almost perfectly co-ordinated attack. She put up a 4-inch barrage as they dived towards the sea and when they levelled out and came in at the defiant old ship, her close range weapons opened up with a continuous chatter and she sparkled with fury from a dozen points.

The attack died away and again she was unscathed. With licence from the Admiral to act independently from the outset, she had opened out during the first action and evasive manoeuvres had taken her still further away. She now closed again and in answer to a query made 'Thanks to providence have so far dodged 19 torpedoes'. Meanwhile the *Prince of Wales* still circled—it was learnt that the rudder was jammed—and the list increased. 'S1' and 'S2' turrets, the only 5.25s on the starboard side with electrical power, could not now depress enough to engage torpedo bombers.

Minutes later (the time was about 12:20) it was 'Alarm starboard!' again and I got ready with my indicating pointer as another nine planes came in low, beyond the *Repulse*. They broke up into small groups and went for her. She turned away from us towards the leading sub-flight of three, guns banging away. After they had dropped their torpedoes, banked steeply and made off, it looked as if Bill Tennant had done it yet again. But another aircraft, very well handled and possibly unnoticed, had worked its way to our side of her and, having started a run for the *Prince of Wales*, suddenly turned sharply and headed back for the *Repulse*. It was followed by two more and in seconds there were three torpedoes racing towards her. It was almost inevitable that one would hit, committed as she was to the wrong direction, and in another moment a tall grey plume shot up from her side, plumb amidships.

But this was only seen out of the corner of the eye because the next half dozen came straight on for our starboard side, three being almost in line abreast. I should say the ship was doing less than ten knots. All were engaged by pom-poms, Bofors and Oerlikons, my mounting taking the middle aircraft, and the sound was deafening. I expected to see all three of them disintegrate but on they came, seeming to bear charmed lives.* The left-hand one—opposite the ship's bows—let go first, then the right-hand one and some time after, the centre, three silver cigars slicing into the water in precise sequence. The foremost aircraft came straight on at the ship and for a moment appeared to be bent on flying into her. At the last moment the pilot pulled up over the fo'c's'le and the large machine with its two radial engines, red sun marking on the side and the crew plainly visible, passed within yards of the four-barrelled pom-pom on 'B' turret, under Ian Forbes the bagpipe player. (One could not tell at the time because of the din, but the gun had a stoppage caused by faulty ammunition.) The other two aircraft banked and roared away astern to leave us in the company of three

---

*One has read since that nearly all the enemy aircraft concerned were hard hit; they looked, and must have been, very robust.

speeding torpedoes.

The first track to be seen was the left-hand one, a narrow, pale green streak of rising bubbles that came on, straight as a die, for the bows of the *Prince of Wales*. We watched fascinated. Never have I felt so helpless. There was a resounding thud, our surroundings trembled as if shaken by an unseen hand and a great column of water, much like the shorts from the *Bismarck*, rose up alongside 'A' turret to a height above us on the ADP.

Next came the right-hand torpedo. As sure as fate it sped to the quarterdeck where an exact repetition took place. There goes my cabin I thought. And then the third. It seemed to be coming straight for the bridge, almost underneath me. I remember thinking 'Am I going sky high?' On and on came the line of bubbles, right up to the ship's side just forward. Knowing that the torpedo itself was well in advance of its track, I thought—for a split second—that it had passed underneath. But then came a great crash. Everything around seemed to jump and bounce as I gripped the steel parapet in front of me; and then what can only be described as a world of filthy water—I suppose smoke and water mixed—shot up in front to blot out all vision. It spread out and then cascaded down on top of us with crushing force. I shut my eyes and clung to the parapet for dear life. The noise was like all the rainstorms ever invented. When it had subsided there was silence except for the sound of water—it was ankle deep—running away through the drainage scuppers. For the moment there was an indefinable feeling of despondency in the air. Guns obviously sensed it too and with true inspiration shouted to another comically bedraggled officer 'My God, you don't look half as good as Dorothy Lamour' (we had just had the film *Hurricane* in which Dorothy Lamour spent most of her time in a drenched sarong). A spontaneous laugh went up and the moment passed.

According to the records we were hit by a fourth torpedo in this attack. I have no recollection of it at all but presume that in concentrating among a lot of noise one can miss such things. (The compass platform narrative, kept by the Captain's secretary, only noted three on the starboard side.) Scrutiny of the *Repulse* showed her to have a slight list to port but no great reduction in speed. If only one could say the same of the *Prince of Wales*! Heaven knows the Japanese had been lucky to get a torpedo home in a vital spot so early on, but someone was loading the dice too heavily against us. It was bad enough to be without air cover but to be fighting, from the first few minutes, with our hands tied behind our backs . . . 'Alarm starboard!' On tin hat again for another attack, but they were not concerned with us this time. No doubt the enemy had seen we were crippled and could wait while they concentrated on the indomitable *Repulse*.

Above *Mr Churchill on the quarter-deck of HMS* Prince of Wales *on the way to Placentia. The after 14-in gun director (with three rectangular ports) is on the superstructure behind the pom-pom.*

Left *USS* Augusta *with President Roosevelt aboard, coming alongside. Author is foreground figure facing camera.*

Left *President Roosevelt and Mr Churchill; behind them are Admirals King and Stark, USN.*

Right *Mr Churchill and AB Kelly watch the unloading of presents from President Roosevelt.*

Below *HMS* Prince of Wales *arriving in Singapore, December 2 1941. On the right, in white, is Captain T.K.W. Atkinson, Captain of the Dockyard.*

103

Survivors of the Prince of Wales *abandon ship to the destroyer* Express *as she passes up the starboard side, some time before the author left from the after end of the fo'c's'le.*

We were then subjected to a ringside view of the end of that gallant ship. There can be no more dreadful sight than that of a large vessel, full of one's own kith and kin, being hounded to the bottom. The seemingly inexhaustible supply of aircraft with which this was accomplished indicated to the impotent watchers what could be in store for us too.

This time her tormentors came in individually from all directions. It was agonising to watch the gallant battlecruiser, squirming and twisting her way through what we knew was a web of crossing torpedo tracks, guns banging and crackling defiance. One plane flew between the two ships from aft on a parallel course to the *Repulse*. She hit it just before it came in line with us and a fire started at the tail. The flames ate their way towards the cockpit and the machine began to porpoise as the tail lost directional control. Although it was clear the men inside had only seconds to live I watched with undiluted pleasure. The plane slowed, its whole fuselage a torch, and then the blazing mass dived into the sea. A cloud of smoke went up and we all cheered. Turning back to the *Repulse* I was just in time to see another plume shoot up from her port quarter. Her port screws and rudder must be damaged and this, one knew, was the beginning of the end. Even as the thought registered there were three more hits in quick succession, two on this side of her and one on the other. As the last aircraft pulled up and away the *Repulse* had a severe list and her speed was right down.

She was now about four miles away. The sea was calm and grey, as was the sky. At the end she was steaming slowly at right angles to our line of sight, from right to left. She was still making headway when her bow began to go under like an enormous submarine and terrible to see. As the waves came aft along her fo'c's'le—tilted towards us—and then engulfed the great 15-inch turrets, still fore and aft, she listed further and remained so for a time. Then she rolled right over, upperworks, mast, funnels and all splashing on to the surface of the sea. She lay on her side for a few seconds—perhaps longer—stopped at last. Then her keel came uppermost and she began to sink by the stern. The last thing I saw was the sharp bow, pointing skywards, disappearing slowly in a ring of troubled water.

Two of the destroyers were speeding to succour the black dots that speckled the area. I found myself watching with a dry mouth. Had Bill Tennant gone down with her? And Pool? Were they fighting for their lives at this very moment? But there was no future in such thoughts and hard as it was I concentrated my mind on our own predicament. Not to much comfort. The ship, in which we had great faith, was designed to stand many more than half a dozen torpedoes. But facts were facts. We were unmanoeuvrable and there were no powerful ships that could come to our aid. Up till now I had contrived a mental blanket that kept out thoughts of disaster but the evidence of one's own eyes is hard to discount. The *Repulse* might have been old but at least she had begun her death struggle in a fair condition. Only a few of our 5.25s were still in action. Though the list had been temporarily reduced—either by counter-flooding or the results of the last three torpedoes—it had begun to worsen again and the close-range weapons would soon be difficult to handle (the electrics of some had failed and they were using the unfamiliar direct sights). Above all, where the *hell* was the RAF? Even a few fighters would make all the difference . . .

'Periscope! Green eight-0, there's a submarine there Sir!' A Petty Officer, the senior PTI, just below me, was pointing at the water a few hundred yards away. I told him to pipe down (it had disappeared) and refused to take any notice. The pom-pom director's crew was being distracted, there was not much we could do about it and there was no point in adding fuel to our troubles.*

It was now about 12:40. The list was steadily increasing and reports began to come in from some close-range mountings that they could not depress enough to counteract this. Others followed. For some minutes we remained at our virtually useless stations and then a Petty Officer of Quarters of one of the pom-poms came up to the Gunnery officer and saluted. 'Permission to fall out my gun's crew Sir please?' Guns thought for a moment and then said 'Yes', subsequently dismissing the remainder who could not fire, including mine. I was taken aback but no doubt Guns appreciated the gravity of the situation better than I.

With nothing on hand, and being a supernumerary of the Air Defence organisation anyway, I left the ADP and began to make my way down without any particular intention. I was passing a plotting office when there was the drone of bombers. Going outside I saw someone looking up and made out a formation that was just about over us, high up to port. One or two of the forward 5.25s fired and I went back into the plotting office. Two ratings were on all fours under a small table. I snapped at them to behave like men and come out. They emerged sheepishly and were making a show of resuming their duties, when the ever increasing whistle of descending bombs, and large ones at that, froze the three of us. A second later there was a heavy detonation nearby, and the ship trembled with a now familiar convulsion. I could not very well give the two men the usual 'Get on with your work' because I knew and they knew that there was no longer any work to get on with, so I scowled appropriately and left. There was a lot of smoke about on the catapult deck but no exact indication of where it had come

---

*I put this in the personal report that most of us were required to write later (it came to be mentioned in the confidential book on the action) and then forgot it until reading many years afterwards in a Japanese account, that a submarine, which had expended its torpedoes, was in fact a close witness of the scene.

from. (In fact a large bomb had penetrated on the port side to burst in the recreation space beneath.)

The Flag Lieutenant (B.R. Armitage) was standing on the starboard wing of the Admiral's bridge, looking aft at the quarterdeck where some wounded were gathered. He was a very pleasant, large RNVR (an amateur boxer, I believe) whom I had got to know quite well in the very few weeks he had been on board. 'Thank God it's a calm day for a bathe' I said. 'Oh it's all right for you to joke about it', he replied 'I can't swim'. I said not to worry, just catch hold of something floating, there was sure to be lots of it about. Neither of us had our rubber life-belts with us. We talked for a bit and then I heard (though there was no official order) someone shout 'Abandon ship!' So this was it. A glance aft confirmed that the end was not far off. A destroyer had come alongside the quarterdeck, the port side of which appeared to be almost awash.

I then remembered that my inflatable life jacket was in my action bag in the 14-inch director, right aft, and decided to go and get it. I went down on to the catapult deck and, crossing among buckled plates, climbed up a steel ladder that led to the boat-deck, two pom-poms each side of the second funnel and eventually my goal. Though it was awkward going in some places, I was still not unduly worried and was 'making haste slowly'.

Suddenly I saw that the sea was lapping at the support of the lowest pom-pom mounting. The sea near the base of the funnel! It struck me in a flash that not only was the ship heeled over but also very low in the water and the end probably a matter of minutes. The life-belt forgotten, I retraced my steps as quickly as possible. Ships' bows always seemed to sink last and I had long since determined that the fo'c's'le was the place to aim for.

From the top of the steel ladder I saw that the destroyer had moved up the starboard side so that her waist was abreast the catapult and hands along her side were casting heaving-lines up to the *Prince of Wales*. Our men were gathering at the guardrails opposite her and also on the higher level of the 5.25-inch turrets. Recrossing the catapult deck—with some difficulty due to the list—I climbed back up past the 5.25 battery and found several patient queues formed at the upper deck guardrail just forward, where the heaving lines from the destroyer—now relatively stationary—had been secured. Several men were dangling from each, jerking themselves along, hand-over-hand like puppets. I decided to join the nearest queue, rather than go forward. It seemed to take an age—though probably only a couple of minutes—to get near the front and this offered ample opportunity to look round.

There were hundreds of men gathered along the side in both directions. Some were already jumping off forward. A dozen lines down

107

to the destroyer were thick with wriggling figures. There was no untoward noise of any sort, all concerned were simply going about the business of saving themselves with proper determination. The sea between the two ships and for some distance around was now black with oil fuel and the pungent smell of it assailed the nostrils. By now one could sense the heel of the deck increasing under one's feet, underlined by the fact that the gap between the ships was growing infinitesimally. A macabre race ensued. I reckoned the chances were even and made ready for a dash towards the bows in reversion to my original plan.

Someone on the other side shouted 'Stand by!' It was the destroyer Captain, a sandy-bearded Lieutenant Commander (F.J. Cartwright), a picture of coolness as he lent on his forearms at the corner of the bridge, watching the side of the *Prince of Wales*. On the deck beneath, a seaman stood at each line, knife poised over the taut rope, eyes on his Captain. At last there was no one in front of me. I gave my precursor a few feet and went too, the half-inch diameter rope biting into my hands with considerable intensity. It was surprisingly tiring work, now with the nightmare element that, as the battleship heeled increasingly away, the men at the other end of the rope had to pay it out, nullifying most of one's efforts. When the last few yards became a steep uphill haul—the weight of bodies kept the rope well down—I felt for a moment too exhausted to go on but a glance at the oily water in which men were already struggling provided the spur of desperation. A last effort put my wrists within the grasp of eager hands and in one exhilarating heave I was over the destroyer's rail. Crawling out of the way to regain my breath, I saw the man after me come safely over and then 'Slip!' roared the destroyer Captain.

The row of knives flashed and, as I struggled to my feet, all the ropes swung down, heavy with men, to crash sickeningly against the battleship's side. 'Starboard ten, full astern together', came from the bridge above and, as the engine room telegraph clanged, the grey wall opposite began to roll inexorably away. There was a heavy bump and we began to heel violently outwards. Grabbing at something I realised that the *Prince of Wales'* bilge keel had caught under the destroyer. Her skipper had left it too late! But the next instant she swung back, the powerful propellers began to bite, and gathering sternway we surged clear. The destroyer stood off a cable or so and in silence except for the hum of her engine room fans, we watched aghast.

The great battleship continued to roll slowly away; as her upperworks dwindled and then vanished, the grey paint on her hull changed to brown as the dividing black line of her boot-topping rose out of the water, and the men at the guardrails began to climb over and slide down this treacherous slope. Those still hanging on to the severed ropes found themselves lying on a near-horizontal surface. Some scrambled to their feet and joined the long lines of men moving at ever increasing speed, as if running on a giant treadmill.

The bilge keel that had hit the destroyer in its upward climb from the depths, reared out of the water, a massive six-foot steel wall that now bore down threateningly on the advancing throng. They climbed desperately over it and continued on. The ship was now nearly bottom up with the main keel rolling, if more gently, towards them. She then slowed to a standstill, a 700-foot waterlogged cylinder of brown, the forefoot higher than the stern.

How long she stayed like that I do not know, a minute or two I think, as if doing her best to give the last of her men some sort of chance. They were slipping and sliding into the water, now uniformly black with oil fuel and littered with débris. Two or three of the ship's boats were floating away on the other side.

Then we saw that the huge hull was disappearing. The bows rose higher and higher. A perimeter of broken water marked, as if with throttling fingers, the exact extent of the ship that remained. This closed in steadily towards the bow as the main body of the hull settled deeper. Again there was a pause when the sharp bow alone was visible— poised like a stark memorial to the brave men she was taking down with her—and then in a last turmoil of foam it slid from view.

The surrounding water, for some time a great confusion of eddies and swirls, was a mass of black specks as the heads of swimming men showed in exact and dreadful emulation of *Repulse*'s end. Some made for the boats which soon became little islands of packed humanity. Others struck out for us and another destroyer that had closed in. By now our side was almost covered with scrambling nets and ropes of all sizes. Tired men were soon clinging to them and being hauled up. Some were wounded or too exhausted to do anything but just catch a hold, and fell back when their full weight was lifted clear. Sailors from the destroyer went down to the bottom of the nets to help the swimmers and several jumped into the sea to bring in the worst cases. Nearly all were covered in oil fuel, very painful to the eyes, and those who had swallowed any were coughing and retching.

We worked like beavers hauling on the ropes. If the sea had been at all rough the numbers saved would have been very much smaller. Soon there were more men on deck than appeared to be left in the water and we took turns at the hauling. Some of *Prince of Wales'* Engine Room staff were dreadfully scalded, presumably from escaping steam; in particular I remember the little Senior Engineer (Lieutenant Commander (E) R.O. Lockley), on whom the brunt of the responsibility for his department had evolved, with the flesh hanging from his chest in dreadful white bights.

There were soon several hundred survivors on board, crowded all over the ship and, where I was on the fo'c's'le, shoulder to shoulder. For the first time it dawned on me that the Japanese were missing a big chance. Stopped, the rescuing destroyers presented easy targets but so far nothing had happened. Relief at being safe was immediately replaced by what seemed certain knowledge that the worst was still to come. Suddenly the communication number of 'A' gun shouted 'Alarm port! Follow director!', the interceptor switch on the gun was slammed shut with the familiar double click and I said to myself 'Here we go'. At the same instant I ducked to avoid the barrel of the gun as it passed slowly and purposefully over my head. Someone said there were two or three of those cursed 'Navy 96s' quite close. I put my fingers in my ears, shut my eyes and remained bent double, as did everyone else. The discharge of a 4.7 was the most unpleasant of any gun in the Navy, those of us just in front of its shield were packed too tight to move away and as I waited it struck me that this was a damn silly way to pass out. But nothing happened.

Unplugging my ears I heard the drone of aircraft and following the direction of the muzzle saw a fat Jap bomber about a mile away. I quickly resumed the previous attitude. Though frightened of the effect I thought 'why the devil don't we open fire; they'll get *us* next'. But still nothing happened, and there ensued a curious pantomime that has never been properly explained. Several Japanese aircraft flew round and round, eventually coming very close and inspecting the effects of their handiwork (or more likely those of their colleagues) while the guns of the destroyers kept 'on' and the fingers of the director layers remained poised. Fortunately, and it says a lot for steady nerves and good drill, no one opened fire. If they had there is no doubt of the eventual outcome.* Eventually they all flew away—chased by fighters that had suddenly arrived from Malaya—and we breathed again. Tubby, radial-engined ex-American Brewster Buffaloes, the new arrivals criss-crossed over our heads and it was just as well they could not hear what we were saying about them.

HMS *Prince of Wales* had sunk at 13:20. At the end of an hour our destroyer was absolutely jam-packed and an air attack still on the cards. The other two were not so crowded and accordingly the Captain was told to set course for Singapore. The sombre scene faded gradually astern; the black sea, the occasional island of humanity where a carley float or oil-grimed boat waited patiently for succour, and the two small ships.

Room was found below for anyone in a bad way and this eased the congestion a little. Feeling suddenly very tired I picked my way to the

---

*It is now known that there were two more squadrons of Japanese aircraft in reserve. A total of 96 aircraft were used that day, most of which took part in the attacks.

quarterdeck and lay down. I found myself beside the body of an officer who had a handkerchief over the face. He seemed familiar and I raised the handkerchief to see who it was. The calm features of the Flag Lieutenant who I had been speaking to such a short time before were revealed. He appeared to have been drowned. Though I had witnessed many unnerving sights that day without effect this somewhat overcame me. For the first time I felt unworthily lucky. No doubt he had waited on the Admiral till the last and had had little chance; I had not even got my feet wet.*

So far there was no news of our senior officers. The wounded were everywhere below and as the sun went down one of the ship's officers lent me an overcoat to keep out the cold. Some time on this melancholy trip back it struck me that I did not know to which of the 'E's we were so deeply indebted. It was the *Express*. Good old *Express*. Looking around her pulsating deck, heaped with dozing forms, among which the lifebuoy sentry and 'Y' gun's crew, hunched against the breeze, were the only signs of life, I saw her again—was it only three years ago?— when Bowles and I from the *Esk* had so often been on board. Instinctively my eye strayed to the handrails, chromium-plated by her First Lieutenant with the treble barrelled name. Of course they were painted over, as all brightwork had been at the outbreak of war. She had certainly got away with murder today; it looked as if we were not going to be molested now.

It was after midnight when she nosed alongside at the Naval Base. What a contrast to our bold exit two days before! *Electra* and *Vampire* disembarked their bedraggled passengers some time later and it was not long before the survivors of the *Prince of Wales* were shocked to a man to discover that neither the Captain nor the Commander were of their number.

Captain Leach had remained on the bridge and his body had been found floating by Lieutenant W.M. Graham, who supported it until forced by his own exhaustion to let go. The Commander had stayed in the tiller flat, after dismissing those working with him, wrestling until the end with the jammed rudder.

Both were of the finest stamp of Naval officer, efficient disciplinarians who knew how to unbend, not to say the most likeable that one could serve under. One felt a very personal loss, especially regarding Captain Leach. His son was a Midshipman in the cruiser *Mauritius* refitting at Singapore and our hearts went out to him.† Tom Phillips was not a

*When I told a member of Armitage's family of our conversation on the Admiral's bridge, I was surprised to be told that he was a very good swimmer. 'Presumably he was pulling your leg' this person said, 'it was a habit of his'.
†To become Admiral Sir Henry Leach and First Sea Lord.

survivor either, which was a major tragedy, though it can be appreciated that this unfortunate Admiral, whose star was virtually in the descendant as soon as he left England, had not had time to impress his personality on us in the same way.

I went straight over to the cruiser *Exeter*, which had arrived since our departure and was now the spearhead of the Royal Navy in the Far East! Pat Brougham of my term—we had had adjacent chests at Dartmouth for nearly four years—was on board and lent me a pair of grey flannel trousers and a shirt, plus somewhere to doss down.

Next morning our sagging spirits received a terrific boost from the sight of our Royal Marines parading; they were fully armed and in brand new uniforms, drawn overnight. The two ships' companies were mustered for a roll call so that accurate lists could be constructed of the missing. It took time and we sat around in groups swapping experiences. Two such stick in my mind. The Warrant Telegraphist in charge of the *Prince of Wales'* main wireless office told me that as soon as the action started he naturally expected to be ordered to send a signal for air cover. As hit after hit shook the ship and she began to list, the absence of such instruction became too much for him and he went up to the Admiral's bridge. Enquiring diffidently of one of his seniors, he was told that efforts to persuade the Admiral to ask for air cover had failed. He accordingly 'took his life in his hands' as he put it—advice to Admirals not being one of a Warrant Telegraphist's responsibilities— and, approaching Admiral Phillips, asked if he should not make the signal. The Admiral just shook his head. From this incident it might appear (but this is entirely personal conjecture) that the Admiral was mentally dazed by the disaster that was unfolding about him.

In fact, at a fairly late stage, Captain Tennant, finding that the flagship had made no signal of any sort, himself reported the bombing and his position. The Buffalo fighters were airborne within minutes. On arrival an hour later, their senior pilot was so impressed with what he saw that in his report to Admiral Layton he said 'During that hour I had seen many men in dire danger waving, cheering and joking as if they were holiday-makers at Brighton . . . It shook me, for here was something above human nature. I take off my hat to them, for in them I saw the spirit which wins wars'. I am afraid that there were also men who shook their fists at the fighters, in the belief that they had let us down. As far as I know this unfortunate impression was never put right; certainly not for those survivors—about three quarters of the total— who were shortly dispersed to Indian or home-based ships.

The other recollection concerned the Captain's Secretary, Paymaster Lieutenant W.T. Blunt, whose face was such a mass of bruises that he was almost unrecognisable. His action station was beside the Captain and his duty to keep a record of occurrences (which he saved) and any other details that the latter might require. He said that at the end the following were on the compass platform (bridge): the Admiral, the Captain, the Officer of the Watch (Lieutenant Commander Lawson), Chief Yeoman Howell and Blunt himself, destined to be the only survivor of the five. When the list finally began to accelerate they all left; the Admiral and Lawson paused at the Admiral's bridge—one deck down—and climbed out on the superstructure to sit on the rim of an Oerlikon sponson; Blunt, wishing to retain freedom of movement, stood (on the side of the Admiral's bridge) by the sponson; the Captain and Howell elected to descend the next ladder and this was the last Blunt saw of them. There is no doubt that the Captain jeopardised his chances of survival through remaining with the Admiral.

When the superstructure was nearly horizontal Blunt jumped, hoping to reach clear water, but was immediately overwhelmed and swept back by a rush of water, either into the compass platform or Admiral's bridge. With the whole plunging deeper and deeper he was knocked about like a ball in a can. When near the end of his tether he sighted a gleam of light and, swimming towards it, managed to last out until the surface was reached. The Side Party's copper punt was not far off and when he reached it and looked back the ship was gone. (It had been Blunt's habit to practise holding his breath under water in his bath and, despite the jeers of his messmates, had worked up to more than two minutes. He probably owed his life to this eccentricity.)

We were still congregated for the roll call when I saw Bill Tennant and an officer threading their way among the groups, looking for someone. When he came to me he said 'Thank God' and walked out. In the midst of all the other responsibilities of the moment he sent a cable to my parents to say that I was safe.

We heard of the last attack on the *Repulse* from someone who I think must have been his navigating officer, Lieutenant Commander Gill. Mutual understanding between them—Tennant had himself been a navigation specialist—had clearly reached the highest peak. He, Gill, stood by the voice pipe (to the chief quartermaster 60 feet below) while the Captain strolled from side to side of the bridge saying nothing but indicating with circular movements of his hand the direction in which the wheel was to be put. In this way the great battlecruiser was flung about the ocean with a dexterity that avoided, as reported, 19 torpedoes.* Eventually *Repulse* was hit by five in all (and one bomb).

When it was clear she was going the Captain ordered 'Abandon

---

*He was to write 'I found dodging the torpedoes quite interesting and entertaining until in the end they started to come in from all directions and they were too much for me'.

I saw Bill Tennant several times after the war but we never discussed that December 10. It was not a day we wished to remember. Youthful to the end, he became an Admiral, KCB, and Lord Lieutenant of Worcestershire before dying in 1963.

Ship'—doing so in good time saved many—and himself went down to 'B' gun deck. From there he told the assembled men that they had fought the ship well and wished them luck. He later told my father that the ship rolled over on top of him and he found himself—just like Blunt—being sucked deeper and deeper, the water changing from green to dark green to black. He was making ready to end it all with a long gulp when he suddenly realised that his surroundings were getting lighter again. Just managing to hold his breath until reaching the surface, he was hauled onto a carley float, considerably dazed as his head had hit something on the way up.

Wandering about during the roll call was a grim experience as one discovered who was missing. Time and again some slight chance had saved one and done for another. The failure of the broadcast system must have taken a very heavy toll. The padre (the Rev W.G. Parker, a New Zealander) was tending wounded men and refused to leave them when the hatch above him had to be closed. Of the Gunroom, Sub-Lieutenant J.B. Womersley, RNVR, Midshipmen D.R.W. Tribe, RN and P.A.B. Hunt, RNVR, were lost, which was tragic, and everyone was saddened to find that Lieutenant Commander Ferguson (probably handicapped by only having one lung) had not survived. I found myself hit almost as much as anything by the news that my servant, bandsman Brooks, was dead. To this day 'J'attendrai' and 'Begin the Beguine'—records with which he would wake me—recall his shy smile.

It was discovered that the *Prince of Wales* had lost 20 officers and 307 men, the *Repulse* 27 officers and 486 men. The fact that the latter had gone quickly was not surprising in view of her older 'tween decks design; but the vulnerability of her modern consort was a shock to us all and in time to the whole Navy. The original damage and flooding on the port side were greatly in excess of that to be expected from one normal torpedo hit and detailed study shortly concluded that the explosion—though a good way forward of the propellers—had inexplicably forced one of the fast turning shafts out of true. Rotating concentrically, it had torn breaches in bulkheads which in turn had caused flooding of electrical generator rooms and rupturing of fire mains, oil pipes and so on, leading to failure of half the ship's electrics. Of course, the lack of communications aft had made the damage control parties' tasks immeasurably more difficult. All in all it seemed the enemy had been supremely lucky in that particular hit, even as one of our own shells had been in the case of the *Bismarck*. (The mystery of one hit doing so much damage was not resolved until divers inspected the hull in 1966. They found that there had in fact been *two* torpedo hits on the port side; the second, right aft and curiously unnoticed—it was probably simultaneous—had torn off the 'A' bracket that supported the port outer shaft, as well as blowing a hole in the stern, with the results described.)

The fact that the torpedo bombers seemed to bear charmed lives was partly because most of our pom-poms suffered stoppages at critical moments due to shells becoming separated from their brass cases, a fault of manufacture. All the ammunition at the guns had been changed only days before but the same occured with the fresh supply. The high level bombers were fortunate too. Japanese records provide a postscript to the effect that in the final run over the sinking ship no less than five aircraft were hard hit (by only two turrets). Dick Beckwith and a Gunner's Mate did sterling work bringing another turret into action by hand, but it was only of value to morale.

I saw nothing to be ashamed of in the whole action, with the minor exception of my friends under the table; but then one would have been surprised otherwise. Contrary to a vague but hurtful insinuation by a civilian writing over a generation later, the ship's company was well disciplined and its morale high; in addition succour was on the spot and well handled, the weather was kind and so was the victorious enemy. The forbearance exhibited by the Japanese airmen in not impeding rescue work was discussed by all. Most settled for the theory that the recently untried Japanese Navy, the élite of their forces, wished to create a humanitarian tradition. But subsequent atrocities such as the wanton shelling of unarmed craft that had been stopped and the machine-gunning of men in the water raise doubts, and perhaps the strange mutual forbearance was just a curious accident played out by the men on the spot.

The pros and cons of the whole operation were debated back and forth but all were agreed that the Admiral could not possibly have kept us inactive while the enemy landed. Force Z's disastrous sortie was in the proud tradition of Admiral Cunningham's 'It takes the Navy three years to build a ship. It would take 300 to rebuild a tradition'—and no one should take that from Tom Phillips.

There remains the question of not asking for air cover that fateful morning. It is thought that he originally considered that this would be arranged automatically by the Chief of Staff and that the breaking of wireless silence was therefore unwarranted. The official view (in as much as the *History of the War at Sea* is official) appears to be that this was expecting too much of Admiral Palliser, especially since he had not been advised of the diversion to Kuantan. Of course there was no merit in wireless silence once the enemy knew where we were.

There had, in fact, been a very near miss on our last night. At the time that the *Electra* had sighted a flare (dropped in error by a Japanese aircraft over their cruiser *Chokai*), the enemy fleet, approaching from the north, had turned away. This was only minutes before contact would have been made. With our radar and bigger guns things would probably have gone our way in a night action, but had it been inconclusive other meetings with the numerically superior Japanese fleet would have been only a question of time.

It was on the public at home, where the outlook was already grim, that the blow appears to have fallen hardest. Many people have said that the loss of the *Prince of Wales* and *Repulse* was the worst news of the whole war, and Mr Churchill's personal anguish as he answered the early morning call from a hoarse Admiral Pound is easily appreciated. At the time I could not help remembering his pronouncement to me on the Japanese: '. . . if they do they'll find they've bitten off more than they can chew!'

5

Fall of Singapore

My Midshipmen were sent, lock, stock and barrel, to the cruiser *Exeter*, except one lucky fellow, David Cremer. He had jumped into the water as the ship went down and broken his ankle on some floating object. Hauled into a boat, he had lain on the bottom and been trampled on, ending up in hospital for some time. So he missed the ship and also three and a half years in captivity. HMS *Exeter* sailed from Singapore to be sunk three months later off Java, her survivors being taken prisoner by the Japanese. I was to meet two of the others, Peter Anson and David Roome*, doing refresher courses after the war and to hear some wonderful stories of courage in adversity.

For a day or two I was left to my own devices except for the settling in of the two ships' companies. Some, including myself, went to the Fleet Shore Accommodation (FSA), a fine new barracks of airy, white blocks, widely dispersed on a grassy hill overlooking the dockyard. Others were accommodated in a hutted camp, presided over by Dick Beckwith who appeared one day in the mess with a grim photograph handed to him for censorship. It showed the *Prince of Wales* bottom upwards, a minute or two before she went; hundreds of men were clearly visible standing upright or sliding into the water. He confiscated it as being bad for morale.

What news we could obtain of the fighting in the north was not reassuring. But it was far away—about 400 miles— the enemy still had the advantage of an attacker's initiative, and everything would surely be all right. On the morning of the 14th I was wondering idly what was to become of us, when Sub-Lieutenant Kempson, RNVR and I were told to get ready for a trip up north. Kempson was a very large, competent, good-natured fellow with curly reddish hair and a strong face that reminded one immediately of his father, the headmaster of Dartmouth.

No-one seemed to know much about our mission except that two RNVR Subs and about 20 ratings had gone up the day before to run ferries between Penang, which apparently was an island, and the mainland. I was to take charge of the party, bringing with me a third

*Now Rear-Admiral Sir Peter and Captain, Royal Navy, respectively.

crew. Kempson's duty was unspecified. A brief glance at a map revealed that Penang was off the west coast and about level with the fighting. After drawing revolvers, mine a huge .45 that soon wore a sore place on my boney hip, we joined a coaster and darkness found her hugging the coastline northwards.

Approach to Penang coincided with that of a reconnaissance aircraft, recognised as Japanese, but it paid us no attention. Fires could be seen burning in the town as the ship anchored and on the way by car to the municipal buildings it was clear that there had been a recent heavy air raid. Houses were smouldering and bodies still lay where they had fallen. We were taken to the Senior Naval Officer, Penang, Commander Charles Alexander, who was on a verandah at the back with some officials. Grey and sparse with an overall sand-coloured tan that denoted a good spell in the tropics, he exuded a calm, authoritative aura that made a strong impression. He told me that three large, steam-driven ferries were the main communication with Butterworth on the mainland; their native crews had deserted as soon as the Japanese had started bombing; Naval crews were already operating two. There had been a partial collapse of essential services and general alarm on the part of Asiatics. It would be best if henceforth the ferries were to run only by night, the crews resting in their commandeered bungalow by day. Information from the front line was sketchy but he would keep me informed; we were believed to have adequate food for the present. He turned to Kempson and I made off.

The sun was in full blast as, having disembarked at the wooden landing stage at Butterworth, I walked inland to find myself in an obviously well-to-do European residential quarter. Large 'bungalows', in reality solid two-storey houses, mostly white with tiled roofs, stood well back in their own grounds. Gardens were beautifully cared for but something was wrong. For a moment I could not put my finger on it and then realised that the whole place was deserted. There was no movement and no sound except the incessant scraping of crickets.

Further on there was the sound of voices and, seeing figures in a garden, I turned in at the drive. There were several steps up to the front door where one of the Sub-Lieutenants now appeared, a fair-haired open-faced fellow called Sheldon from the *Repulse*. He had hardly said 'Well, *am* I glad to see *you*!' in ominous tones when the other Sub rushed out in a state of some hysteria. I rounded on him when we were indoors, after which a Petty Officer took me aside to warn that this officer had got the ratings jittery. A pleasant start!

The situation was not one to soothe the nervous. They had moved into the bungalow to find a meal ready on the dining room table and many other signs of headlong flight. Inactivity in the steaming heat, still new to us, was irksome, and we were lying about in sweaty discomfort when, halfway through the morning, a sudden buzz of conversation came from the hall. The men were clustered round a soldier in tropical battle rig but without arms or helmet. Proving to be a Corporal in a County regiment, he said he was one of the few survivors, if not the only one, of his unit. They had been cut off and annihilated in an action a few miles to the north. I questioned him further and received a lurid account of the fighting which had ended with his officer rushing forward and firing his revolver until shot down. He went on to say that the . . . bastards would be on us at any moment and that if we had any sense we wouldn't stay another . . . second. He himself would be on his way to Singapore as soon as he had had some . . . food. This most unwelcome visitor was a sleek, glib type, rather pleased with the sympathy he had so surprisingly stumbled on. Presumably a deserter, he stayed all day. I should have sent him packing but it is easy to be wise after the event. He may not have been near the fighting; on the other hand one did have the uncomfortable feeling that the garden might suddenly sprout other things than flowers.

We embarked as the sun went down and it was a relief to be doing something. The ferries, though cumbersome two-decker affairs which took in vehicles on the lower deck, presented no technical difficulties. Throughout that night we ploughed back and forth with an endless stream of Europeans and Asiatics, all afraid of being cut off by the enemy, who one learnt was coming closer and closer.

Early next morning Sheldon's ferry had a breakdown and it was broad daylight before we got it alongside, an anxious business with one eye on the dazzling sky. The two crews, returning to the bungalow together, arrived to the unwelcome news that (for reasons that escape me) we were down to two ferries doing the job of three. Later Commander Alexander telephoned to say that Penang was to be evacuated that night. The army had had another reverse (I think at Gurun) and was retiring a longish way in order to reach ground more favourable for defence; Penang thus lay exposed and whether the Japanese turned up sooner or later was entirely up to them. We were to continue ferrying—mostly army units—until the job was completed, heading south for Singapore when ordered.

The day passed uneventfully except that a Petty Officer, who was very fat and probably came from the *Repulse* as I did not know him, was found face downwards in a flower bed, sobbing, his nerve having given way. Night found us hard at work. The heavens opened to produce the sort of tropical downpour that was another new experience. The shaded lights of vehicles, reflected in the streams on deck, lit or silhouetted the throng of bewildered humanity, to lend the long night a wild, Wagnerian quality. Very much in keeping, some sepoys sat on their haunches and, swaying in unison from side to side, came out with a dreadful, moaning dirge. 'What the hell are they doing?' I asked a shadow at my side. 'Dunno sir'—it was Petty Officer Aldred—'but I wish they'd keep it for a funeral.'

It was again full daylight—the enemy 'air' having missed a first-class opportunity—before a Lieutenant Commander Hegarty embarked and we were told only one more load, keep them on board and sail for Singapore. Later a small white steamer, full of people, closed to hailing distance and a black-moustached Colonel shouted that we were to make for Port Swettenham instead, a place about halfway to Singapore. Presumably the greater distance at our slow speed was considered too dangerous. There was nothing to indicate the immense influence this Colonel was to have on my destiny.

We said goodbye to the effective old ferry at Port Swettenham and returned to Singapore by rail. I had to kick my heels at the FSA for a time while one after another the spare junior officers disappeared on exciting assignments up country. They manned motor boats and made themselves generally useful in the creeks and mangrove swamps on the left flank of the army. When their boats were put out of action they made themselves useful ashore. Now and again one would appear at the FSA, bearded and dirty, to collect stores and have a bath, the centre of envy on the part of the rest of us. Though having the whale of a time, one and all had the same story backed by tired eyes and a sad resignation; it was impossible to move by day without attracting bombs or bullets from the air. There did not seem to be any British fighters. Nearly all movement was done by night. The enemy had tanks in considerable numbers and we had none. Some of the harder-pressed units who had to fight all day and every day were at the end of their tether. In addition, the Japanese—who seemed to have abundant reserves—were proving frighteningly adept at jungle warfare and in places that we had apparently deemed impassable. Here the speaker would hitch up his holster, give us 'base wallahs' a pitying appraisal and disappear again. Dickie Pool was one of these, at last realising his ambition to command a small, fast craft. Kempson turned up once or twice but I never got round to asking him exactly what he had been doing. Sadly, he was later reported missing and did not survive.

A boost to morale was provided by my promotion to Lieutenant, celebrated by the receipt of a lot of white uniform, ordered on our arrival and forgotten. This was followed by another bonus. The Captain of the Dockyard feared an attack by parachutists. Since it was the heart of the Naval Base and thus the biggest single plum in Malaya, this was quite on the cards and I was delighted to be told to form a special anti-parachute force, some 150-strong, with top priority in men, equipment, transport and anything else required. To be known as the Naval Guard, we would come directly under the Captain of the

Dockyard and on reporting to him I received yet another pleasant surprise; it was Captain T.K.W. Atkinson, who had been my popular Commander in the *Nelson*.

A Warrant Officer was appointed second in command, there was a Chief Gunner's Mate plus several other senior rates and, having armed everyone to the teeth and drawn a huge American saloon for myself and lorries for the remainder, I got down to field training and small-arms practice. Sentries, who were visited at all hours, were placed on the many strategic points of the area, discipline was very strict and morale high. About the worst punishment my men could have was to be thrown out of the Guard and returned to the main pool. However, no parachutists obliged, the only time I had my pistol out in anger was to fire (slightly high) at some looters in a deserted machine shop, and our only casualty was an AB who lost a finger (very neatly, he was only away for ten days) when the lorry roof support he was holding swayed against a tree.

To improve the less than shining hour, news came that Borneo had fallen. Anthony Terry and I had managed to get to Singapore for a fling on Christmas Eve, but it was not a success. There were big parties in the various hotels, where everyone tried to produce the right sort of spirit, but it would not take off. Hong Kong fell on Christmas Day after a brave defence, followed shortly by news of terrible atrocities there. Meanwhile the Japanese advance in Malaya continued relentlessly. From about January 7, and due to successive British airfields falling into enemy hands, serious bombing of the Naval Base took place most forenoons, on and off from 09:30 to 12:00. Either the dockyard, the FSA or the oil fuel depot at nearby Senoko received attention. Fortunately, shelters at the FSA were well constructed and adequate for the bombs that rained down. Night raids—sometimes three times a night—soon became commonplace. They were usually directed against the city or Keppel Harbour to the east of it, but not always, and as the bombers came first over the Naval Base, sleep was a desultory affair (especially for one who was paying several calls on sentries in addition). Low-level incendiary or machine-gun attacks were made by lone aircraft on occasions, usually against Senoko, which miraculously escaped until three tanks were hit about January 18. The off-duty Guard were rushed there to lend a hand to the hard-pressed dockyard fire brigade, but we could not do a lot. The gasometer-like tanks were blazing, making approach difficult and sending up dense black smoke that blotted out the sky so that one moved about in an eerie red gloom. The fire brigade, Malays under British officers, were magnificent. The dockyard itself was not too badly damaged, bombs falling mostly on roads or open ground, though at least one big machine shop received a direct hit. By this time hardly any native labourers would work in the dockyard and it became oddly silent.

One incident provided a terrible disappointment. During a night raid I was approaching a small river bridge where I had a sentry with a Lewis gun. The searchlights and AA guns were weaving and grumbling around Singapore to the south, when there came the noise of an approaching aircraft, flying very low. It was following the river towards the bridge and I stopped the car to watch with a feeling of pleasurable anticipation. To my horror the twin-engined bomber flew straight over the bridge unmolested and continued northwards. Roaring up I leapt out of the car and asked the young sentry why the hell he had not fired. 'They were flashing a recognition signal at me, Sir, I didn't know whether they were ours or theirs.' Somehow I controlled myself and explained patiently what I thought the simplest Tamil girl knew; that there weren't any of 'ours'.

This was just about true. Certainly, by the end of January all our few bombers had left for Sumatra. None of us ever saw any, though this does not mean they did not do sterling work elsewhere. The fighter picture was a little, though not much better. The Brewster Buffaloes that had come out too late to help the *Prince of Wales* and *Repulse* had proved no match whatever for the Japanese Zero fighters, the excellent performance of which had taken the RAF completely by surprise. However, 50 Hurricanes duly arrived, some flown off the carrier *Indomitable* (repaired after the grounding that had cost Force Z so dear) and some in crates. They could have made a considerable impact *en masse* but of necessity were thrown in piecemeal.

The Naval Guard were used increasingly for *ad hoc* duties that arose and when the new Motor Ship *Sussex* arrived at Stores Basin to unload crates of Hurricanes, guns and other important items, I found myself there with a large contingent. The native labour would not work after dark for fear of the bombing and we took over from 17:00 to 05:00 for several nights. The aircraft usually came over in 'V' formations of 27, though sometimes of nine, the bombs landing over a considerable area to raise acres of ascending smoke and debris. As a matter of fact this was preferable to the sneak raids of single aircraft. One gauged the course of the 'V', and if it was not coming directly over, worked on.

A rasping, nasal Japanese voice on Penang radio took to announcing where the bombers were going to next—the city, the Naval Base, Keppel Harbour, and so on—underlining the impotence of the defence. Formations were usually escorted by Zeros—superior to the Hurricanes, which had mostly inexperienced pilots. The latter went up again and again most gallantly, but their numbers diminished every day. I met one Squadron Leader who had shot down a goodish number and was a byword, but he was killed eventually.

The First Officer of the *Sussex*, one Ian Posgate, and I became very friendly. Just before she sailed he said 'you know this place isn't going to last, why not send your kit home with me?' Although little had gone right for us I think this was the first time I had heard the possibility of defeat actually mentioned openly. Anyhow, I handed over a trunk full of all the gear I could spare. (Following tactful enquiries after my health, it turned up at home and a good time later.)

Raids on the base continued and we all became somewhat tired. Lack of sleep is a morale reducer as modern secret police well know. As far as the general run of the ratings was concerned, it appeared that they were serving no useful purpose ashore, a difficult notion to refute; and with the constant bombing, comparative idleness and increasingly bad news as the army continued to retreat, morale was not too good. Personally I was lucky in having a special antidote. I would report daily to Captain Atkinson and his cheery 'Hello Brooke, what's up today?', followed by a breezy description of some happening and what he wanted me to do, delivered as if he was 'telling off the hands' at Portsmouth, was a tonic.

By mid-January the enemy had taken Port Swettenham and Kuala Lumpur, the virtual capital of mainland Malaya. In little more than a month he had gone from Siam to Johore. However, there was one bit of news that cheered us all. A Major Rose of the Argyll and Sutherland Highlanders had been given a special force which was taken up the west coast by Lieutenant Commander Victor Clark* (ex-*Repulse*) in large motor launches. Landing well behind enemy lines, they ambushed and destroyed a column and were embarked again with minimal loss. Shortly afterwards, Clark (eventually to receive a DSC and Bar), took the gunboats *Dragonfly* and *Scorpion* to rescue a brigade cut off near Batu Pahat. Four nights running, boats were got up a shallow creek, Clark and his officers often swimming as the Japanese were within ear-shot, to ferry the 2,000 exhausted soldiers down to the waiting ships. (I overheard one of *Dragonfly*'s ship's company describing these dashing exploits to another sailor who remarked that his CO must be very brave. 'Too bloody brave for my liking!' was the heartfelt reply.)

I was in charge of a section of the FSA for ARP (Air Raid Precautions) purposes and unless away with the Guard, had to remain in a ground floor office during an attack. This was no fun, and in retrospect, rather stupid. A heavy steel plate was imported to put across the entrance, behind which a Petty Officer and I cowered ignominiously. One bomb landed 15 yards away, fortunately in soft ground, though the steel plate did its stuff all right. Only four buildings eventually escaped damage, the two most serious losses being the galley and the officers' club (used as an overflow Wardroom), both of which

*When Singapore fell, Clark got away in a launch, but was sunk by a destroyer in the Banka Strait and taken prisoner after swimming for a whole day with a badly broken arm.

were completely wrecked. But on the whole the FSA buildings stood up to it well, probably due to their free ventilation design. Cooking now had to be done on a field kitchen in the open, fortunately arranged before the war by Commander Livingstone, the Maintenance Commander.

With no battlefleet and the few elderly light cruisers and destroyers based on Singapore becoming ever more vulnerable, Admiral Layton sent them all to Colombo in mid-January and repaired there himself. This left Rear Admiral, Malaya, as the senior naval officer. He was Rear Admiral E.J. Spooner, my one-time Captain in the training cruiser *Vindictive*. On hearing that the constant bombing was having a bad effect on the ratings at the FSA he ordered that the 'Jim Crow' system (instituted by Churchill whereby factory workers did not take shelter until actually told to by a watcher on the roof) should be implemented and came up to impress it on us himself. This excellent intention was dramatically dashed. It was 'clear lower deck' one morning on the parade ground, with every man-jack clustered round a small wooden dais on which stood the Admiral and the Captain (Captain L.H. Bell, who had been on Admiral Phillips' staff). He had just begun to speak when the drone of bombers heralded the inevitable 'V'. He took no notice though all eyes were fastened intently heavenward. It was clear they were coming straight over us—a target too good to be true—and it soon became hard to hear the Admiral above the shouts of Petty Officers preventing men on the outskirts of the throng from making off.

The Captain eventually took a hand and Admiral Spooner gave way, ordering the disperse. A headlong rush for the shelters was only just completed when the familiar whistling began, to end as hundreds of bombs crashed all round. The Admiral, who had taken cover in the nearby Regulating Office, was hit on the head by a brass clock that was shaken off the wall. He made his way back to his car amidst all the dust and rubble and, though one felt sorry for its champion, that was the last we heard of Jim Crow.

The officers working up country continued to appear briefly with increasingly pessimistic tales. Everyone was exhausted, though it was hoped that now the line was back in Johore we really would hold them. It did not happen.

Drafts of naval personnel had been leaving, mostly for Ceylon, as suitable ships put in and by the end of January there must have been less than a dozen officers and 300 men remaining at the FSA, though there were staff officers and others accommodated there. The Admiral was clearly in a dilemma. There was nothing worthwhile for us to do; we were in fact 'useless mouths', but wholesale evacuation of the Navy would undoubtedly be bad for general morale.

It must have been January 29 that some of us received an urgent message to report to the War Room in the dockyard, there to be told by Captain Atkinson and the Staff Officer (Operations), Commander St Aubyn, that the Army was going to withdraw across the causeway into Singapore Island that night. We were to provide boats for a Dunkirk operation if the causeway became impassable. We received the impression, soon confirmed, that it would be more a question of *when* the causeway became impassable. Commander Hoffman, Captain of the gunboat *Grasshopper* which had escaped from Hong Kong, was in overall charge, Ian Forbes was to be beachmaster for a couple of hundred yards of sea-wall to the west of the causeway, I the same on the eastern side.

There was no time to lose and we dashed off to make the necessary preparations, detailing crews and collecting boats, ropes, scrambling nets and Jacob's ladders and securing them along the sea walls. Preparations were about complete when word came in the evening that the operation was postponed 24 hours. Finishing touches were put the next day after which there was nothing to do but wait. I had a look round Johore Bahru, the main feature of which was the Sultan's palace with its tall castellated tower. The causeway, a solid boulder-based embankment rising some 20 feet above the water and wide enough to carry a road and railway line, led straight to a crossroads among pleasant white stone houses where the main road to Malaya came in from the left. One imagined that its tranquil length would be hotly contested; it was already covered by machine-guns and an armoured car stood ready to give battle at the edge of some trees. I went over and talked to her red-haired, tam-o'-shantered Captain. He was in good spirits and together we investigated an empty shop (civilians had been evacuated) full of radiograms and expensive English tennis racquets. We swung them in the confined space, childishly discovering the ones with the best grip, the realities of the world outside somehow far away.

Lieutenant Hayes of the *Repulse* was liaison officer on the staff of the Corps Commander, Lieutenant General Sir Louis Heath, and towards evening he sent a message to say that I was invited to dine with the General and his staff. This surprising and welcome happening was an education. The Corps HQ was in a group of huts on a nearby hill and we sat down at a long table decked out with glass and gleaming cutlery and attended by mess waiters, just as if it was Aldershot (or rather, Simla; General Heath was Indian Army*.) Talk was bright, varied and on anything but the war, which was not mentioned once. Cricket seemed to be the main topic. Eventually the General, a fine looking, powerful one-armed man reminiscent of Haig, pushed back his chair and said 'Well gentlemen, it is time to draw stumps'. The shirtsleeved

*The victor of a brilliant campaign in East Africa culminating in the capture of Keren.

khaki diners reached for their map cases, rose as one and dispersed into the darkness. The carefree atmosphere went with them and down by the water a cold breeze blew.

A party of engineers, including a Naval officer, were putting finishing touches to a dozen depth charges they had buried in the causeway. The plan was for the Army, numbering some 30,000, to retreat across it under cover of darkness. Even for a sailor there was no difficulty in grasping the delicacy of this undertaking. One and all predicted it would be sticky. Two possibilities made it plainly doubtful. These were failure to disengage from the Japanese, when they would have sitting targets as the last troops crossed the causeway, and their bombing of the latter should the ambitious extent of the retreat be discovered; the chance to trap our men in Johore would be too good to miss. In which case the beachmasters would naturally be the last to leave.

The sun went down with its usual suddenness and the first of an endless stream of motor transport, guns, Bren carriers and ambulances began to trundle across. The moon came out making their shaded stern lights hardly necessary. Of course, there was no question of sleep and hours later the scene had not changed. About 02:00 there was still no sound of battle, though if the job was not completed by daylight the fat would surely be in the fire. I could have gone up to the bungalow whence the bridgehead units were being commanded to hear the official news of progress but preferred to let events overtake me.

At last the motorised cavalcade thinned. It ceased; and then came the infantry. Dawn found me beside the road, fascinated. The steady tramp of feet seemed to embody time; crunch, crunch, crunch, crunch. Small men, big men, tall men, lean men, brown men, red-faced men, and all sweating, dirty men, not a few bleeding. There was not one without a happy glint in his eye as he came in sight of the shining water. Over the other side they saw haven, at any rate a relief, rest for a spell. Most of them had fought galling delaying actions all down the peninsula, outnumbered, out-equipped, it must be admitted in some cases out-generalled, and always without air support in face of vicious attacks. Singapore, the bastion of the east, was waiting to take them in. What a broken reed she was to prove!

It grew lighter as I watched, and those of us waiting cast many an anxious glance at the sky. They came on and on and on, like an eternal brown crocodile, platoons on alternate sides back to the crossroads and then along to the left, where the armoured car still stood, battened down and ready.

Soon it was daylight, and still they came on. Would they never end? Norfolks, Leicesters, East Surreys, Australians, Gurkhas, Sikhs, Punjaubis . . . I raised a smile from many a grimy face. The sight of a Naval officer ashore, and an unnaturally clean one at that, tickled them

126

a lot. Several gave me the 'thumbs-up' sign. Later I was joined by a few sailors from the boats who were also finding the wait a bit irksome and was proud to hear one Tommy say 'The Nighvy's here at any rate!' The bearing of all was so good, that we just had to watch; we felt we were seeing something.

And then the dreaded moment came. It was broad daylight, about 07:30. The drone of bombers drowned even the marching feet, and there to the north-west was a formation of 27, flying as a great 'V', straight for the causeway. We scattered for cover. I made myself very small beside a Bren-gunner in a slit trench and, screwing up our eyes, we watched. They came overhead; we listened, trying to detect the well known screech, ready to flatten. Not a sound. Hardly able to believe it, we watched them fly on, and out of sight, towards Singapore.

Australians and Gordons of the outer bridgehead were coming in now and I got the order to stand by to leave. So it had come off. Even if disaster overtook us now, the main army was over, however late on schedule.

And then I heard the pipes. Pealing, whirling, screaming derision at all enemies of Scotland; a wild, thrilling sound that, coming at a moment of dramatic relief to nervous tension, made one want to cry and sing at the same time; rising and falling, mad, exultant. Two pipers were fallen in by the side of the road. This was a strange setting for those highland airs—the square white houses, the lush green vegetation, the bright blue sky and behind, the jungle. They skirled and rang in the sultry air, lighting the faces around and bringing an added jauntiness to their step. It came to me that many of their number were still in that jungle, stiff in the attitudes in which they had fallen, or dying slowly of thirst and wounds; unmarked, save by parakeets or a chance Jap infantryman lucky to enhance his equipment. I thought to myself that one day the enemy would pay; one day these impudent Japanese would be made to grovel. I made an inward resolution I would be there to see it.

Australians, marching to the pipes, were nearly through, and the men of the inner bridgehead (a semi-circle of strongpoints and carefully sited machine-guns, last to retire) awaited the word. They were Argyll and Sutherland Highlanders, a shadow of the battalion which had gone into action five weeks before. The honour of covering the retreat was their due.

The Bren beside me folded with a snap as its owner ran off grinning to form up. The Commanding Officer, (Lieutenant Colonel Stewart, who had recently received the DSO) came down the steep grass bank from Headquarters' bungalow. The curtain was going to fall in style. Hayes, who was with him, waved to me, crossing his arms above his head in the seaman's sign which means 'Secure; all finished'.

I stayed for a last look before going down to the boat and away. They came swinging past behind the bagpipes, mostly small men, I noticed. Hard, dour, and as tough as leather, they marched with a long supple stride and there was an arrogant confidence about them.

The pipers were playing 'Bonnie Dundee' as I ran down to the boat. We went off at full speed towards the Naval Base. Halfway across, the air was shattered by a huge reverberating explosion and a pyramid of black smoke and masonry rose ponderously into the air, seeming to fan out and hang like a giant toadstool before thundering back to earth. The causeway had gone up, like a drawbridge behind the Army. I shaded my eyes with my hand and strained my ears.

Just visible at its Singapore end were the last miniature figures strutting away, and over the lazy water, above which the air was already a shimmer with the torpid Malayan day, came the strains, thin, proud, defiant, of 'Bonnets over the Border'.

The FSA, separated from the water by a few football pitches—and about four miles from the causeway—was now in the front line and evacuation in full swing. Our two Marine detachments were despatched to join the Argylls and as the ships had been West Country ones the combination became the 'Plymouth Argylls'. Told to report to the RAF transit camp at Seleta, near the west coast about five miles away, I found Terry and the rest of the men in attap huts on a rubber plantation. Forbes was appointed to the *Grasshopper* and I did not see him again.

Instructions had apparently been received to leave everything at the Naval Base untouched for the Army to take over. The first part of this was carried out but not the latter. Word came through that nothing much was happening there (clearly the enemy were resting and preparing for a final assault on the island) and I returned over the next few days to collect useful items, movement becoming more restricted each time. It was strange to have to slink about the irrigation ditches and run crouching past gaps among buildings, where so recently everything had been normal. I joined a Gurkha unit that was keeping watch from the top of the canteen. Their British officer pointed out the Japanese positions opposite and through his glasses I could see figures moving about. His men wanted to hear about the destroyer *Gurkha*, about which I was fortunately well informed and he translated word for word to the little grinning desperadoes with their vicious kukris.

The odd puff from a Japanese gun or mortar rising from the jungle opposite was visible from time to time, followed by the rush of shells arching overhead to land in the dockyard. Though an Indian AA gun nearby had taken a direct hit from a bomb, killing all the crew, nothing seemed to be happening beyond this whine and crump in the dockyard, probably intended to annoy any troops in possession rather than demolish buildings. The FSA was not being molested, except for occasional sniping if one showed oneself. Overall was the uneasy feeling of calm before the storm.

We continued to be employed on *ad hoc* emergency jobs as they arose, usually unloading stores or fighting fires in Keppel harbour. It must have been there that I watched the men from the unfortunate 18th Division disembark, with the realisation that they were destined for disaster. One could see by their pink skins that the poor devils needed months of acclimatisation and special training before they should be faced with a fanatical enemy, flushed with success. Most were to be fighting for their lives within ten days and marching into captivity in 20.

Another forenoon in the docks I was caught in the middle of a 'pattern', only just getting under a lorry in time. The din was almost unbearable but between the tremors and flashes I could hear different and reassuring detonations, accompanied by the unmistakable tinkle of cartridge cases falling on to a steel deck. With the sort of urge a homing pigeon must know and rather shaken I crawled out in a lull and made towards the sound. It was the Australian cruiser *Hobart* secured on the other side of some go-downs. As I went up the gangway another formation came over, her 4-inch guns opened up again and it was like moving into another world, mentally as well as physically.

Stalwart guns' crews, mostly in the hoods and gloves of anti-flash gear, worked methodically at their guns, passing the gleaming ammunition from its stowage to the shell handing numbers; the twin breeches recoiled with the discharge almost as soon as the brawny arms rammed home, fists clenched against the brass-based ammunition. Smoking shell cases bounced out on to the deck to lie in awkward piles until cleared away and the whole scene, in contrast to the jittery world only yards away ashore, was enacted with the unconcern of Melbourne ladies passing cups. When the last wave of aircraft had gone the men pushed the white hoods off their faces and mopped perspiring brows. With great reluctance I took myself ashore.

The Naval Guard had been disbanded shortly after evacuation of the base but nobody seemed to want my car back and, of course, it was very useful. Another one became the cause of a severe fright. Abandoned cars were two a penny, often with doors open and ignition keys in place, their owners having just driven up to the dockside and embarked. They were also to be found elsewhere and I was not at all surprised to come upon a brand new green MG 'TC' sports, chromium gleaming, parked with keys in place among some trees at Seleta. After two days I decided it would be more convenient, and much more fun, than my big Ford saloon and made the exchange. The little car burbled happily along on return from somewhere one evening and my thoughts were anywhere but on personal trouble. Anthony Terry came out to meet me as I switched off the engine. 'Now you've done it!' he said. 'That car belongs to a Surgeon Commander Stephenson. You have been reported to the Admiral as having taken it and he wants to have you shot.' I put my head back and roared with laughter but he cut it short. 'I am deadly serious. I've been arguing for you most of the afternoon and he is not decided yet. As you know, the penalty for looting is death. They shot a sepoy yesterday for stealing a motorcycle and the Admiral says there should be no favouritism just because you are white and an officer. He's not at all averse to making an example. I tell you its touch and go.' He turned back to his hut leaving me aghast. Rear Admiral Spooner, undoubtedly under severe strain, had been making some other strange decisions, and Terry was not exaggerating as I soon learnt from several sources. The owner of the car was actually very nice about it and good enough to be somewhat upset at the turn of events. As can be imagined the following day or two went rather slowly. However, I heard no more about it.

The next alarm, which must have been about February 7, was in its less dishonourable way, just as narrow a squeak. A summons came from Commander P. Reid (who I think was liaison officer with 3rd Corps) for an officer to take charge of the water part of a raid on the Japanese positions across the strait from Seleta, and I found myself conferring in an attap hut with half a dozen Army officers. Men of the Norfolk Regiment were to be towed across in 14 pontoons to land among mangroves and attack the enemy from behind. It was to take place that night. This was real action at last and I was gripped with excitement until someone detailed the towing craft. These were one diesel and one 'hard chine' petrol motor boat. The latter, of which I had plenty of experience as a Midshipman, was of the sort designed to plane out of the water at high speed. Two minute rudders were adequate for this but, combined with the flat bottom, were useless for manoeuvering at slow speed; also the boat would sound like a sports car and its clutches, not designed for towing, would soon burn out. Even if we got to the other side, we would certainly not get back, with or without enemy assistance. The obvious solution was to procure another boat but there was not time. I glanced at the faces around, catching in only one a glimmer of understanding. A young Gunner Captain with a small blonde moustache, who had provided maps, returned my look with a grimace.

The Colonel asked whether I was in agreement with the plan, at which all turned to me. Terrified they would think me afraid, I said yes and the meeting broke up. Outside I buttonholed the Gunner Captain, who turned out to be a small boat enthusiast; 'Pretty nonsensical' he replied.

Back at the camp I described the meeting to Terry who said nothing at all. The next thing was to select crews for the boats; they too were pleased at the prospect of positive action but I could not help feeling sorry for them. I had decided that the whole thing was suicide and had managed to reconcile myself to the thought. And then realisation dawned. We were to create a diversion while something more important took place elsewhere! Three or four officers and a number of men were quite expendable under the circumstances. The same sort of thing probably went on all the time. I was thankful that I had not voiced my misgivings, probably to be told with icy politeness to carry on just the same.

The boats were prepared and finally—for the second time in a fortnight—there was nothing to do but wait. As the light failed I prayed that I would acquit myself well and lay down for an attempted nap. Some time later we were roused by a distant but continuous cannonade, shortly after which a message was received that the Japanese were landing and that the raid was cancelled.

A sense of anti-climax was shortlived; morning brought the staccato crack of shells bursting in the rubber trees all round. We ran for the somewhat shallow trenches fortunately prepared, pressing ourselves into the rich red mud and cursing as each salvo whistled and crashed. Nobody was hit though the odd hot fragment would smack into the ground alongside one. There was a 25 pdr battery close-by and this was presumably the real target. The shelling went on all day. The enemy had presumably got guns across the strait (damage to the causeway proved not as great as hoped) and there was no future in this spot as a static base. Accordingly we were withdrawn into Singapore that night and quartered in the Oranje Hotel near the sea front, about a mile east of the centre of the city. It had already been stripped of unnecessary fittings and made a good enough centre for our spasmodic activities.

The enemy made immediate progress (due I believe to communication failures on our side to do with the guns and searchlights that should have made his crossing of the water an expensive business) and was irrevocably consolidated on the island by the following morning. Fighting was heavy and continuous from then on, marked by a steady rumble to the north that drew closer and closer. Bombing and strafing of the city, the docks and various troop concentrations became more or less round the clock, unopposed by fighters. What was left of the RAF retired to Sumatra about this time and I personally never saw any of our fighters again.

My recollection of the last few days is a jumble of disconnected incidents, mostly trivial, which are impossible to unravel into the right sequence. I remember the flat of an RAF family, there seemed to be two generations there, where I was invited for a quick meal. My host was married to a very beautiful Eurasian girl of about 18 and one could not help wondering what her future would be when the Japs arrived. There was no doubt, by this time, that the end was not in question. They had seen us off all the way down the Peninsula and only a miracle could turn the tables now. Civilians leaving, mostly women and children, had grown to a rush, every ship sailing full up. One saw heartrending scenes at docksides as families said goodbye, husbands and grown-up sons turning back to a grim future. Of course the enemy were bombing ships as they put to sea and the securing of a place in one was no passport to safety. I had some business, forgotten now, with the survivors of the liner *Empress of Asia*, set on fire and sunk as she neared Singapore.

The Japanese continued a steady if slow advance, mainly down the Bukit Timah road to the west, occasionally breaking through and being thrown back. Rumours abounded but no-one seemed really to know the state of affairs. Rubble in the streets opposite the occasional yawning gap often made one's progress slow, mushrooms of smoke rose gently in the hot air to mark the latest bombing which in some places combined into a brown pall, and always one moved with an eye cocked on the sky. Fortunately most roads and streets had wide open drains which afforded excellent temporary shelter. A Zero fighter was shot down near the Oranje Hotel and I passed it, its red-blobbed tail high in the air like an encouraging monument, on the way to and from assignments.

An unpleasant development was the appearance in the streets of Australian soldiers in their bush hats and leather equipment. They came to us asking for food, hung around at street corners and a number eventually congregated alongside HMS *Laburnum*, the Naval Head-quarters ship, which was approaching through a sort of small park. Instructions came from the Admiral that we were to evict these undesirables and I arrived with a dozen bluejackets to be rather alarmed at the sight of several hundred soldiers camped on the grass. Plumping, perforce, for the velvet glove, I told my men to fix bayonets but stay in the lorry, and advancing with as much nonchalance as I could muster, picked out an officer in the middle of the throng and gave him his marching orders as pleasantly as possible. There was a long moment while he conferred with his immediate entourage and then to my relief they got to their feet and ambled off. Going round the other groups was not difficult and soon they were all on their way. This may have been the party that eventually stormed a merchant ship, shot an officer who went to stop them and forced the master to take them to Java.

These Australians let their country down disgracefully, though fortunately for them there were few witnesses who escaped to report the fact. We had no idea of their origins and I was later to feel somewhat ashamed of my anti-Australian sentiments when it became known that they were recent arrivals from recruiting camps with virtually no training. Of course the original Australians of the AIF in Malaya fought well to a man, as did their brothers in the Middle East.

Three or four more days and nights followed each other; living for the moment, one lost count. For the first time I experienced a strange feeling of unreality, not even engendered by the sinking of the *Prince of Wales*; surely things couldn't be as bad as this? It must be all a dream.

By February 10 the rumble had turned into a series of clearcut explosions intermingled with machine-gun fire. They were in the outskirts of the city. By day billows of brown smoke covered the western horizon where oil tanks had been deliberately set on fire and at night the sky over Singapore was permanently lit by conflagrations. Rumour had it that the enemy had taken the main water reservoirs and if this was true the end must surely be near. There was still a number of quasi-naval ships in the harbour, some armed, some not, and we knew that if the Admiral was going to embark us for a getaway it would have to be soon. I suggested to Terry I should get a list of all the ships and their exact whereabouts so as to be ready, and obtained this from the Naval HQ in the Municipal Building. Captain Atkinson was there, unruffled as ever, Commander Alexander of Penang and other officers.

At last, on February 12, the expected orders came. I sometimes feel that if I never have any more luck for the rest of my life it will only be fate re-adjusting the balance. We fell in on the ground floor of the Oranje Hotel for Terry to go down the ranks with a paper in one hand, which he consulted for the names of ships, while 'cutting off' the ratings in batches with the other. Thus were the remaining officers and men of Force Z consigned to death, captivity, or in a handful of cases, freedom, according to the fate of the vessel assigned. There were six I think: the *Kung Wo, Ping Wo, Shuan Quan, Tien Quan, Mata Hari* and possibly another. I was to see three of them sink; none got through. Terry and I and a hundred men were to go in the *Kung Wo*, as far as I knew an old China coast steamer pressed into Naval service.

No-one was to embark until the evening and that afternoon we were all employed commandeering tonkans and sampans—that were moored up the river mouth that cuts into Singapore—and securing them along sea-walls. Presumably they were to assist evacuation and some were doubtless used later by enterprising troops. Anyway, it was good employment for the hands, even if not enjoyable having to eject a protesting Chinese family from its home-from-home, 'cheese-eyes' (babies), pots, pans, dhobey, dried fish and all. In the middle of this I was shouting directions from a bridge to some sailors below when suddenly surrounded by my friends the Australian soldiers, all saying 'Where's he going?' 'Can we have one?' 'How do we get down there?'

High level bombing of the harbour and dive bombing, I think of Fort Canning, the Army HQ, was incessant the whole afternoon and one worked, as usual, with many an interruption. It was necessary for me to tow some craft to the far end of Keppel Harbour and on return I found the others had gone to join their ships. Presuming that the *Kung Wo* would need food for its suddenly inflated passenger list, and to collect my few belongings, I went back to the Oranje Hotel, loaded up the car in competition with several other parties, collected my one kitbag and said goodbye to a malacca cane and other treasured but unreasonable articles. A sound habit of recent days of eating whenever the chance presented itself took me into the so-called Wardroom and I was enjoying the pleasures of anticipation, as the froth subsided on a glass of beer, when there was an almighty bang outside, well above the background noise. I was looking out of the window when there was another that shook the building, and a cloud of yellow dust drifted along the street from the left. This was followed by another somewhere behind. People were streaming down the road. The beer was only half gone when a major detonation rocked the whole house, to be followed by the crash of glass and sound of falling masonry. A shell had hit the roof and bits of the big domed skylight were everywhere as, descending the stairs, I congratulated myself on having left the car facing in the right direction.

The ground floor disgorged blaspheming figures, adjusting tin hats and cramming tins of food into pockets. Sub-Lieutenant Wood, who was getting into a lorry he had just taken from some Chinese looters, threw me a crate of beer as I crossed the pavement and in a second I was doing 70 mph past the crashed fighter. The bangs multiplied and I really thought the Japs were close behind. In actual fact I believe it was mortar fire. My destination was *Laburnum* where the *Kung Wo* was berthed.

Laburnum presented a scene of activity and no little confusion. MGBs, launches, Fairmiles (large patrol boats) etc, were three or four deep, embarking passengers, gear and provisions. I found the *Kung Wo* had gone, no-one knew where. She must have sailed earlier than expected and my spirits rose. Instead of being tied to an ancient death-trap I could now take my pick with a clear conscience of the small, fast, mostly well-armed craft that would stand ten times the chance of slipping through the net the Japanese had undoubtedly spread for us. As I looked around, a small vessel nosed alongside and Dick Beckwith called out cheerfully from her bridge. I had not seen him for weeks and we exchanged a few words. Eventually I picked out a sizeable armoured motor launch bristling with tommy guns and recognised Sub-Lieutenant Dunbar on the bridge. 'Got room for a passenger?' 'Yes of course, come along!' I unloaded my kitbag and the crate of beer—grate-fully received—and got it on board. 'I'm supposed to be in the *Kung Wo*' I said, 'but thank God she's sailed.' '*Kung Wo*?' said someone, 'she's

134

gone down to the coaling wharf; she burns one hell of a lot of coal and with steam up for the last ten days has run very low.' My heart sank. 'Are you sure?' 'Oh yes', said my informant casually.

For a moment I was torn in agonising indecision, then I humped my gear ashore again and, saying goodbye to Dunbar, made for the coaling wharf. As it happens, to the best of my knowledge, poor Dunbar and his launch were never heard of again*.

AA guns a few hundred yards away disappeared temporarily in a brown curtain of bomb bursts as I left for Keppel Harbour, giving a lift to two soldiers on the way. The blue sky was permanently speckled with bursts where aircraft dived in ones and twos or droned relentlessly over. In the lulls the background cannonade seemed nearer than ever. I hoped, not for the first time, we had not left it too late and put my foot down. When we came to the docks 'You'd better slow down here, Sir, this is "the area"' said one of my passengers, adjusting his tin hat. I did so, remembering my last view of 'the area' from beneath the lorry. The enemy were paying even closer attention to the docks than usual; they appeared deserted except for the bobbing heads of Asiatics looting smouldering warehouses, or of soldiers sent to stop them, both of whom peered at one from drains at the side of the road when a mutual sense of discretion sent them to ground. The road was pitted with bomb craters and the atmosphere of deadness was completed by motor vehicles of all kinds that were dotted about, many undamaged. Dropping the soldiers, I took a wrong turning and getting out to look round, saw a large lorry, full to the top with tinned provisions.

The ship was located at last, having just completed coaling and ready to go. Terry's bearded face welcomed me from the rail with 'Where the hell have you been? We gave you up for lost. You've nearly missed the ship!' I refrained from saying how right he was, took my hands back to the lorry and was busily employed when a voice said 'Looting eh?' It was a Captain in the Indian Artillery whom I happened to have met somewhere before. '*The Navy going?*' he repeated incredulously and then, visibly shaken, helped me to unload. He was pathetically optimistic—someone had told him that the Loyals had pushed the Japs back six miles in the Pasir Panjang district—and I felt very bad as we worked alongside each other, I with some chance, he with none. Eventually I gave him the keys of my car and said goodbye, leaving him looking up at the *Kung Wo* from the desolate dockside.

An ancient Yangtse river steamer of about 5,000 tons, very tall and straight with a single thin funnel amidships, she was not unlike a Mississippi steamer at first glance with curious balcony-like

*Dick Beckworth's gallant end was not to be known until after the war. See page 275.

135

protuberances built out over the water. Closer inspection revealed her to be completely unarmed and in superficially poor condition, many near misses having peppered her above the waterline. She had been converted to minelaying (though there were no mines on board) and was nominally Naval, her Captain and the half-dozen officers being reservists.

Having put my kitbag in an upper deck cabin liberally ventilated with splinter holes, I repaired to the saloon to find Terry, Surgeon Commander Stephenson of the MG and a rather unlikely assortment of civilians including an attractive Chinese girl in blue trousers. She belonged to a party—under the auspices of a Captain Steel who seemed a cheery character—representing the remnants of what is now called the media, accredited to Singapore command. After a few minutes' enjoyment of the luxury of being served with a drink I found myself prone between the mine rails on the waterline aft, listening to the whine and *BRUMF* of bombs nearby and feeling the tremor of those that burst in the water. When the 'All Clear' sounded, merely a blast on somebody's whistle, as the local sirens had given up the unequal struggle, I found I had brought a glass of sherry all the way down from the upper deck. We slipped immediately to anchor in the harbour.

Everyone was in good spirits and supper went with a swing even if it was eaten with no lights and little cutlery. The Chinese girl, who did not lack attention, was called Doris Lim, and had apparently been left in the lurch by her MGM cameraman boss. There was Yates McDaniel, an American of Associated Press, Athole Stewart, an Australian I think of the Public Relations Office, an Australian Flight Lieutenant called Downer and a man called Wellby from the censorship department. So far the *Kung Wo* had borne a charmed life and we fervently hoped this would continue, especially as it was now only a few hours off Friday the 13th. She had been bombed at Hong Kong before being brought down to Singapore, bombed again at the Naval Base—taking a direct hit just forward of the funnel that had wrecked most of the cabins near the saloon—and narrowly missed several times earlier in the day while coaling. However, she could still do a fairly respectable 14 knots.

Awaiting the signal to sail—every hour of darkness that went by without it seemed like a nail in our communal coffin—we congregated on the upper deck. The long searchlight beams groped desperately for their tormentors, weaving silver patterns above the mottled pink and black of the glowing, smoking shore. The sea, which should have been her mainstay, threw back the last agony of Singapore in a glittering kaleidoscope. We stood in a row at the rail and watched, our faces lit by the glow, the air foul with the smell of burning. Sometimes a flare-up—demolition—would reveal every expression. There was little talk; I

Aboard Sederhana Djohanis: *Cox, Holwell and Fraser.*

Above *Putting in at the last island for coconuts and water and to land the native crew.*

Below *The sternsheets: Waller, Broome, Gorham, Davis and Lind.*

Above *One of the author's watercolour paintings depicting* Sederhana Djohanis *menaced by a waterspout.*

Below *View from bowsprit: Rowley-Conwy on left, author on right.*

Above *The MV* Anglo-Canadian *stops for us; Campbell has put on uniform for the first time in 37 days.*

Below Sederhana Djohanis *drops astern–not very shipshape!*

suppose we realised we were watching one of the biggest things of the war. Further disasters, hitherto only speculation, were now certain. The Dutch East Indies would be the next to go, and then what of Australia? Or India? 'Singapore cannot fall' . . . 'Singapore *will* not fall' . . . It was all terrible. But at least for a serviceman it was but one more example of 'what we had joined up for'; the plight of civilians was infinitely worse. How would the victorious Japanese behave? One turned from the thought with shudder. At about 21:00 Lieutenant Commander Pickard—who I think was Assistant Harbourmaster— came out in a launch and shouted for information on the numbers on board and number and state of the lifeboats. The answers were 120 naval personnel in all, some 20 non-naval passengers and three boats, all damaged by splinters, at which he went away. Later another launch loomed up containing many women and children; on hearing the state of our boats it too made for another ship.

By 23:00 several vessels had gone past us and out, and there were none left that we could see. The Captain signalled by lamp to *Laburnum* for instructions; after some delay a reply came from a motor launch, saying he was alone and waiting to embark Rear Admiral (Malaya). After passing some further information about minefields he suggested that we sailed. I wondered if it was Dunbar*. The anchor was weighed just before midnight, without further orders, but we had apparently been forgotten and the few remaining hours of darkness were now beyond price. Getting clear of the harbour was a tricky business with the many small craft about but at last the *Kung Wo* was in the open sea and on her way (straight through a minefield, though I did not learn this until later).

From a distance Singapore was strangely like London in peacetime with the same overhanging ruddy glow. On our other quarter the island oil depot of Blackang Mati was a sheet of flame. This was a night if ever there was one. Comparatively well off as we were, I felt a strong foreboding not allayed by conversation with the Surgeon Commander as we sat in deckchairs before turning in. He said that running the gauntlet to Batavia, our destination in Java, would of course be no joke with the Japs having complete command of the air and sea. If we survived the first bit we would have to pass between Batavia and the enemy-controlled Banka Island. This gap—the Banka Strait—had become known as Dive Bomb Alley and was almost impassable.

*39 years later I discovered it was Pool! He and his Fairmile had taken part in the Rose Force operation and then excelled in a night action in the Johore Strait, sinking Japanese invasion craft (for which he was to receive the DSC). He did evacuate Admiral Spooner and Air Marshal Pulford but met a Jap destroyer near the Banka Strait and had to beach on an uninhabited island. When Pool was captured many weeks later, the Admiral, Air Marshal and most of the party had died of disease or starvation.

Although touched on often enough recently, my thoughts on evacuation had never progressed beyond getting on board a ship. Colombo via the Malacca Strait had been the obvious route until lately denied and I had never studied the southern alternative. In fact I was crassly ignorant of the whole area. Stifling uneasiness, I felt I could go into this next day and, after laying out the rubber lifebelt issued, turned in and slept soundly.

A cold bath was very pleasant at 07:30. It was fortunately over and I was nearly dressed when the ship began to vibrate and I heard the sound of running feet, above, change to an urgent clatter as they came down successive ladders. Two seconds saw me flat on the deck in the passage outside. There was a roar overhead and then the unpleasant period of suspense . . . *Crump, Crump, Crump*. The ship shuddered, lurched and then righted again. I thought we had been hit, but all seemed well and someone said 'Coo—narrow shave!' At once there was a rush down to the mine flat, which served as a very effective shelter, being three decks down and with steel channels in the deck into which one could wedge oneself. I grabbed my tin hat and followed suit. The place looked like a giant sardine tin, thick with bodies. Some were burrowing among the baggage piled in a corner, though one man stood by a port watching two aircraft. Completely unarmed as the *Kung Wo* was, it was likely that we would just have to take it, the aircraft going back for more bombs if necessary.

'Coming round again' said the man at the port and lay down between the rails. Above the laboured breathing one could make out the engines (they were fighter-bombers with small calibre bombs) coming nearer. They increased to a roar. I squirmed a bit closer to the motherly steel rail. *Swoosh . . . CRASH! . . .* The ship shook violently, and a series of minor thuds ensued. I leapt up and went to look at the damage. We were hit amidships, the bomb bursting on the second deck and blowing out the side of the ship and superstructure there, as well as making a gaping hole in the deck. Dust rose all round and up through the breaches. Fortunately very spectacular from the air, but no serious harm done, and no casualties.

'Take cover!' sent us all dashing back to the mine flat again and a repeat performance. This time they came low and made sure of it. Two heavy shots rang out in quick succession, which turned out to be an enthusiast with an elephant gun, blazing away from the bridge. There was a vivid orange flash, an earsplitting explosion and a wave of scorching air. The deck leapt and bounced under me, showers of metal fragments seemed to clang everywhere and then came the hiss of escaping steam. They had put one, possibly two, almost into the same hole as the first, so that it burst somewhere over the engine room and just forward of the mine flat. Stokers came tumbling up the ladder from

142

below, staggering through the smoke and dust and followed by white clouds of steam. The noise of it escaping became almost unbearable. I went through the steel door and down a few rungs of the engine room ladder but was forced back. The Chief Engineer appeared outside. He was very fat and rather past it, asking 'What's happened . . . What's happened?'. I went up to the bridge to ascertain the situation. The ship had stopped and had a considerable list to port. Either the first near misses which were just off the stern, or one of the hits, had started her plates and it was presumably a question of time. There was a chain of islands about six miles to the east of us, small, steep and thickly wooded; surf could be seen breaking on the sands of the nearest.

After flying round us for a good inspection the aircraft made off. All at once the steam stopped, the ensuing quiet seeming strange after the last hectic minutes; the Second Engineer had got down and found the valve, a fine piece of work. The engine damage proved irreparable and we at once set about organising our departure.

The three boats were lowered in rather unnecessary haste, the first setting off before full up and with no extra provisions. Terry took charge from that moment, which was just as well and not unreasonable—though a passenger, he was the senior officer present. He forbade any baggage beyond a single bundle per man, but the ship's company had already got at the canteen store and were loading up large cartons of cigarettes until stopped and dispatched for tinned food. Water had appeared in the bilges of the other two boats and as they made for the shore one could see those men not rowing baling furiously.

Those of us left on baord set to, making rafts and securing them to the side. Barricoes were filled with water—the supply or lack of the latter ashore would determine our fate—and every possible receptacle pressed into service. The scene of confusion was considerable, the ship being mostly wood and very thin, poor steel. Girders and stanchions were twisted into grotesque contortions, bulkheads were riddled with holes, and large sections of the deck were missing. One walked on a carpet of splintered wood, glass and other fragments, in and out among fallen beams and festoons of wire rigging. I half expected her to sink before the boats returned.

Suddenly there was a cry of 'fire in the bunker', a most unhealthy locality, and a chain of buckets was organised. It spread to a pile of wood which had been the middle deck planks and was only accessible from the hole above. This looked serious, but was eventually extinguished. There was no breeze and the heat was terrific. When there was nothing more to do we sat down and discussed the possibilities, which did not help much. The outlook was not good. Even should we make it ashore in the unseaworthy boats there was the small matter of getting away again with the enemy everywhere; they might

143

even be on the island. We were 80 miles from Singapore, 400 from Batavia and some 30 from Sumatra, still, as far as we knew, in Dutch hands. But we were at least fortunate in having land as near as it was and only one casualty. A Chinese foreman had been discovered stiffly upright in a corner of the coal bunker, stone dead with a bit of shrapnel through the temple.

I went to my cabin and chose what I would take away. It seems incredible that I could have overlooked the value of some things, though I believe other people looking back have found the same. I would have given the earth for an overall or blanket a few hours later, on the first of many encounters with mosquitoes. The war correspondent, McDaniel, provided considerable relief, as he would pop up at the most annoying moments, Leica to eye and notebook ready. This was going to be the biggest scoop of his career!

The little white boats grew smaller and smaller. We saw the first skirt one island and make for the next. Suddenly the drone of an aeroplane made our hearts sink. Here they were, back to finish us off. It was a single-float seaplane this time. He circled round and round very near. The observer could be seen watching through binoculars, and we walked cautiously round the deck, keeping something in the way in case he should turn bellicose. Apparently satisfied, he flew off to look at the boats. With experience of the *Prince of Wales* I hoped it might be Japanese policy not to machine-gun boats. We continued to watch anxiously and then to our relief he departed.

A bottle of hock was discovered and split between the war correspondent, the girl, the RAF and myself, which did not go far, especially as the RAF broke the neck off much too far down, but we drank to the future and hurled the glasses against the saloon mantle-piece—now at an angle of 15 degrees—in the right style.

After some hours two of the boats could be seen returning, and eventually took us all off, except for the First Lieutenant and half a dozen volunteer seamen, who had to remain. We pulled away from the *Kung Wo*, baling hard all the time. The tide was out when we made the island. The sun was beginning to set and our figures cast long shadows across the sand as we waded round the boat, trying to pull her in across uncomfortably sharp coral. Someone came splashing out with the welcome news that an Australian soldier had found a stream of good water. This was an enormous relief. Things seemed even better when the appointed victualling staff announced that there was three or four days' supply of tinned food. The beach was backed by jungle, where tropical trees, shrubs and creepers grew in dense profusion, but as far as could be seen there were no coconuts or other eatables on the island.

After a meal of corned beef and biscuits, we curled up on the sand for the night, with the setting sun a sheet of gold behind the black shape of the ship. Though tired enough, sleep was much interrupted. The recent luxury of mosquito netting had made me forget these tormentors, and I was woken several times by eerie touches here and there which proved to be little hermit crabs. Two or three times we were forced to move further up by the tide, so that morning, heralded by a particularly insistent type of cricket that always starts at the same time, found some of us amongst dead trunks of rotting vegetation.

It was the strangest awakening I have had, and there were to be many with which to compare it. Birds twittered, the sea lapped a few yards off, and the yellow sand of the very pleasant little bay was littered with stretching figures, all wondering where the hell they were. Worries started immediately.

Two small, grey, sloop-like vessels were anchored by the next island. The *Kung Wo* was still out to sea, although she had drifted a little, but our best lifeboat, which had gone out at dusk to take off the remainder of the crew, was nowhere to be seen.

Suddenly a grey launch put out from one of the other ships and went alongside the *Kung Wo*. Things looked very black. It could hardly be other than Japanese and had probably been sent to clean us up. Our boat was either captured or had escaped in the dark. We expected to be taken prisoner within minutes. There were too few arms (about a dozen rifles and revolvers) to effect resistance, even if that were advisable, for if we beat them off we should be left to starve on what was expected to be an uninhabited island. Succour from our own people was surely out of the question. Better to eat Japanese rice than none at all! Those who had any began the destruction of documents. I got rid of a letter or two addressed to HMS *Prince of Wales* as I had heard of Japanese ability to extract information and there might be things about her they wanted to know. We began discussing their treatment of prisoners, little being known beyond their appalling behaviour at Hong Kong.

The launch was seen to take off the men from the *Kung Wo* and then make straight for us. That seemed to clinch it. We stood on the beach and waited. All at once our lifeboat rounded a headland close inshore and grounded on the beach. The Second Officer and its crew climbed painfully out, exhausted. They had never got to the ship at all, having been swept away in the dark by a current they had been rowing all night. The launch from the *Kung Wo* came in as near as she dared, while we scrutinised her minutely. A white-uniformed figure stepped on to the fo'c's'le and gesticulated; he appeared to be European! Our hearts leaped. 'Send a boat out' came to us across the water. It was Monro, the First Lieutenant, who had been left behind the day before.

The news was unbelievably good. The two other ships were the *Kuala* and *Tien Kuan*, fleeing from Singapore and trying to hide from aircraft by day. The launch belonged to a planter evacuating from his estate in Sumatra, who had happened to look in on the *Kuala* on the way. An officer in the latter had persuaded him to go out and have a look at the derelict *Kung Wo*, in case there was anybody on board. The planter came ashore (I regret I never learnt his name but I think he was Dutch and he had a beard) and a conference was held. Even as this was going on, to a background of hammering as the beached boats were being plugged and patched with tingles, a steam tonkan—sort of bluff commercial maid-of-all-work—rounded the other point and came in. Her origin is forgotten (if ever known) but she too had come to help. It was decided that as many as possible were to go in the planter's launch and the tonkan that night to Sumatra, whence Terry would arrange further nocturnal rescue trips by the same or other requisitioned craft. It all seemed too easy. We merely had to wait for the dark. Sumatra was only 30 miles away and, even if in enemy hands, was a vast and friendly country. Eventual onward transport to its west coast, and British ships to India, seemed well in sight. How the situation had changed in the batting of an eye!

I thought it would be a good plan to contact the *Kuala* and the *Tien Quan* to exchange information about plans, so that if all three parties were not lucky in getting through, the survivors might be able to do something about it. This agreed, I borrowed the launch (which was quite large with a Malay crew of four) and set off for what, on the chart the Captain (Lieutenant Commander Thompson) had salvaged, was called Pohm-Pohm island. The two ships had moved to anchor very close inshore, rather unwisely near each other I thought, in a very small, horseshoe bay. Both were auxiliary naval vessels of about 600 tons, taken over from shipping companies. The crews were engaged in ferrying branches of trees from the island to camouflage the ships, an optimistic task (since wisps of smoke from both funnels wound up in the tropical air) but doubtless good for keeping the men employed.

I boarded each in turn. One had about 350 of all three services on board, and about 50 civilians, mostly service wives and families. The other had 450 women, mostly hospital nurses, a few children and a contingent of the RAF. I wrote out our situation for the two Captains and what we intended to do. They showed me their courses for Batavia on the chart and one kindly gave me a Very pistol, parallel rulers and Pilot Book of the district. I saw Lieutenant Rafferty on board *Kuala*, and a few other people I knew, including PO Tailor who had been one of my Guard Petty Officers. He was standing at the top of the ladder as I came on board. 'Good God, Sir! What are you doing and how on earth did you get here?' He was brandishing a huge spanner and told me he was self-appointed quartermaster of the stores, needing the spanner to keep certain people off them. Bodies were strewn about the decks and passageways and it struck me there was very little apparent organisation. I thought how ghastly it would be if these ships were bombed, with all the congestion. The RNVR navigator, whom I had come across before, was very nervous about the danger of aircraft. I tried to reassure him that if they were coming, they would probably have done so already, as we were attacked at 07:45 the previous day and it was now 10:00.

Little did I realise the emptiness of my words.

Having given and received all communications that could be of mutual help, I started on the return journey. The launch was new and ran very sweetly. She was about three-quarters of the way back when there was the sudden explosion of bombs and, following the shaking finger of the Malay cox'n, I saw spouts of water round the *Kung Wo*, out to sea. I increased to full speed, got in the lee of a chain of very small islets that jutted off the end of our own island and slowed down to make the rest of the passage with as little disturbance as possible.

A formation of nine big bombers circled round the *Kung Wo*, which they had missed, before running in again. She was hit squarely and disappeared in a cloud of smoke. When it cleared she was almost on her beam ends, and sank in a moment. Munro's luck was indeed in. Not so the unfortunate people on board the other two ships. I felt a terrible dread, almost seeing the confusion that must be taking place. Some of their boats were probably inshore . . . it was not a long way, but they only had seconds to go. The island had no beach, indeed the scrub jungle came down at an angle of about 45 degrees and dropped sheer to the water, amongst brown rocks. The bombers flew round in a large circle and made their run at about 5,000 feet, straight for Pohm-Pohm. Their path took them right over me, and the Malay crew grew frantic, donning life jackets and cowering in corners, while the cox'n shouted for the engine to be reversed and put the wheel hard over for the shore. With few words of Malay I made noises of infuriation and, pushing him off the wheel, tried to get at the throttles; this he could not understand and kept resisting (it was not possible to steer and work the engine at the same time). Keeping the boat straight and warding off his efforts was not easy and I expected to hear, momentarily, the grinding of coral.

Then came the sound of bombs again and I saw a direct hit on one ship and the sea around a mass of near misses. The launch's crew got to their feet and I had fears of their overpowering me. The bombers came round again, much lower and right over our heads. Although I did not expect them to trouble about a launch, it was possible one might spare me a bomb and so I went hard astarboard at the right moment.

Nothing happened until they were over the luckless Pohm-Pohm island. Again the black spouts rose all round the ships, though neither seemed to be hit this time. *Kuala* was smoking. I wondered if I would do best to go back and help as much as I could; but it would take about

147

half an hour and after that time it would be much better to go with the doctor who was quite close. I was also very doubtful of the Malay crew, especially when they arrived on the scene of action.

There was still a short distance to be covered and I steered in for the cover of some overhanging trees. It was an unfortunate move as there were four plops in quick succession. The crew were overboard. I was making the boat fast to some fishing stakes when one of the Malays, an old man, began to splutter and cry out. He obviously could not swim and was going to drown. I cursed the old fool and then, with the idea that as well as saving him I might gain the confidence of the others, dived in and effected a spectacular rescue. He sat on the beach and vomited while I called to the others who had disappeared in to the jungle. One by one they came back like frightened children and cowered together when yet another bombing attack took place. I then made a big show of jumping in and swimming back. Fortunately they followed suit, clustering round the old man who was hauled on board. The engine was still running and we were away in a second. A lasting annoyance was that my watch fell out of a top pocket in the course of the aquatics.

When I got back Terry, the doctor, and a Sick Berth Attendant boarded the launch and with our few medical supplies set out for Pohm-Pohm again. They were over there a long time and it was dusk when we heard them returning. Terry shouted for us to come out; we were to embark as arranged.

The launch had many badly wounded women on board and some who had died on the way over. They had been bombed nine times. Several people had been killed both in the ships and in the water, and there were some 40 wounded on land with few medical supplies and very little food. One ship was sinking but the other was afloat though holed. Only a tiny stream had been found on Pohm-Pohm, which was a small island, basically a thickly wooded mound projecting out of the sea. The survivors were lying among trees with hardly any water. A strong current had swept some away, and next to no gear had been brought ashore. Here was a terrible state of affairs.

6

On the run

Although repaired as far as possible, our lifeboats were in poor shape. Help from Sumatra was essential and it was decided that the launch and tonkan would set out that night, each towing one boat. Everyone was mustered at the water's edge and a long crocodile began to wade out, slipping and blaspheming as coral cut mercilessly into flesh. It soon became clear that there would not be room for all of us, so Munro and I said we would stay behind and I called for volunteers.

Eventually about 30 men were taken into the tonkan and the same number in the boats. The rest of us, wet and rather crestfallen, splashed back to the beach. As we listened to the engines dying away an AB beside me said 'Well, anyway, we've got rid of the panic party* Sir!' To the good could be counted 60 fewer mouths to feed which increased our rations to eight days and after a muster it was apparent that the call for volunteers had indeed rid us of the panic party and grumblers. Except for Monro, the 60 remaining were all *Prince of Wales* and *Repulse* ratings, plus an Anglo-Indian engineer called Thompson who spoke Malay like a native (a rifle shooting enthusiast, it was his elephant gun that had greeted the aircraft) and three British officers of the Singapore Fire Brigade. The senior, Mackintosh, was fluent in Chinese and Malay and the others spoke the latter well too, so we were unlikely to have language problems. The senior rating was Chief Engine Room Artificer Roper and I made him Master at Arms. There was a seaman Petty Officer (Pickard) and a PO Cook (Hobbs) but not enough Leading Seamen so I rated up the two best ABs (Witherley and Brown) to acting Leading Seamen on the spot. I fear they never got paid as such! All were in fairly good heart once the initial disappointment had been absorbed.

Monro was a most likeable, stocky, close-cropped Scot in his mid-thirties—though years in the tropics made him look older—who perhaps should have taken charge but the men naturally looked to me. Anyway, he was a tower of strength and we took major decisions together. After Roper had organised the men into parts of the watch and detailed lookouts there was nothing more to do, and we turned in, higher up the beach this time.

*'Panic party' is a naval expression of derision rather than more serious abuse.

It was a flat calm and, though lulled by the lapping of the water and gentle whispering of leaves in the jungle behind, sleep did not come to me for a long time. Ordeal by mosquitoes was not the only cause. It was true we had water, and food for a bit (the first thing to do would be to explore inland for more) but our chances did not look good. The poor devils on Pohm-Pohm would have to be taken off before us, while every day would see the energetic Jap spreading south. I prayed, very hard, with the fervent hope that past laxity when times were good would not count too much against me and realising how my old, familiar nursery prayer was now starkly apt ('. . . Thou has warmed me, clothed me, fed me; please listen to my evening prayer'). I had never gone short of food or clothing in my life and it was salutary to think of all the times I had repeated these words without much feeling. Curiously enough, it must be said that, though there were to be moments in the next two months when hope seemed to be gone, I never lost the underlying certainty that all would be well in the end. I do not know whether this was Naval training, religious faith, or what. Though doubtless helped by the necessity to appear outwardly confident, it was not natural optimism as I have a volatile Irish temperament sometimes given to depression. Ultimately this feeling took the form of seeing myself, in my mind's eye, walking into the drawing room at home and saying '*Am* I lucky to be here?'

Daylight brought two surprises, one seemingly good, the other seemingly bad. *Tien Kuan* was gone, perhaps having got away with all the survivors to leave us top of the list for nightly rescue. And one of the lifeboats was high and dry. It proved to be holed and battered, an expedition along the sand returning with the news that the second boat was in the same state some way away. Our hearts sank. It looked at first as though they had struck a reef or simply foundered with their occupants, but closer inspection revealed that both had been evacuated in an orderly manner as there were such details as a matchbox on a thwart and a pair of gym shoes, dry, in the stern sheets. So it was possible they had proved too unseaworthy and been cast adrift after their occupants had somehow been taken on board the towing craft.

A little later the sound of engines sent us scurrying into the jungle. A reconnaissance plane circled low over Pohm-Pohm and then our island but seemed satisfied that we could be left to whatever devices we might have and departed. He paid us a similar visit in the afternoon and twice daily thereafter, the nuisance value being considerable.

I took the two leading hands and Mackintosh the linguist, all of us armed, on a jungle exploration to see if we could discover anything edible or signs of civilisation. The going soon became hard and provided a mini-drama that did the four of us a lot of good even if it was seen as a gastronomical failure by our companions.

150

We made ten yards a minute, taking it in turn to lead the way against the clinging mass of vegetation and decayed woodwork. Straggling creepers pressed back into place behind the last man, or rotting branches fell to a bayonet stroke, to be pulped under foot and disgorge a legion of little red ants that trailed into the dusty leaves. Thin shafts of vertical sunlight fought through the trees, weaving as the branches stirred to chequer and mottle our steaming world. An oppressive mustiness stung the nostrils; there were no half measures in this life; everything was either grossly ripe or rotten.

Now and again a butterfly as big as my hand rose zig-zagging out of the undergrowth, its passage visible through the trees as successive flashes of red and blue and once, balanced on a dead trunk, I looked down horrified on to the yellow and black diamond pattern of a snake, before it raised its head slowly under my upraised foot and was gone. When an hour had passed, excuse enough for a rest, we sat down. Ahead was nothing but jungle, and it was well that we had marked our track by white gashes in the softest plants, where sap oozed frothily and trickled down the emerald stems. It would soon be time to start back to the anxious men by the battered boat and say what was written in everybody's eyes, that this was an uninhabited and foodless island.

Suddenly Brown raised a grimy hand. There was nothing but a subdued squawking in the tree tops and then, faint but quite unmistakable, a distant *tap-tap-tap*. We kept still. For perhaps a quarter of an hour we listened as it grew louder and louder. There were several possibilities. It might be natives blazing a trail, someone who had been shipwrecked on the other side of the island or the enemy exploring a new conquest.

It came on. We crouched in the undergrowth, peering ahead. *Tap-tap-tap* . . . As it grew, we could make out the rustling of feet in the leaves, and then the forceful brushing aside of foliage and dried timber. Leading Seaman Witherley, whose theatrical attitude would have put Bill Cody to shame, was just in front of me. A huge drop of sweat rolled down his cheek and plopped upon a leaf. There were four purposeful clicks as our hammers came back and the tension was electric. I imagined the ugly masklike face under a Jap bowl helmet that was about to present itself, and could almost see the expression of agony and amazement as our shots rang out. At least we could get in the first volley.

And then Mackintosh, unable to contain himself any longer, raised his head a couple of inches.

There was a raucous yell, a flurry of powerful wings, immediately repeated, and two huge turkey-like birds with red heads and beaks like cricket bats rose ponderously into the tree-tops! We were so flabbergasted that no shot was fired. There was silence for a moment and then the pent-up emotions of the last 24 hours were loosed in uncontrollable laughter*.

Less amused, however, was PO Cook Hobbs when he heard how we failed to vary the menu, now standardised at two biscuits for breakfast, a helping of the Army's tinned 'Meat and Veg' for lunch, and two biscuits for supper.

Nothing happened that night, nor, as was to be expected, the following day. Camp had been moved to where the stream broadened into a jungle pool and all hands lay about in the shade. A little after midnight there was a shout 'Boat ahoy' and, wonderful to hear, Terry's answering boom. He could not get in close but could take about 20 and I sent these splashing happily out. To their deaths as it happened. We had a few shouted words—he said that Singapore had fallen the day before—February 15—the enemy had landed in several places in Sumatra, the *Tien Kuan* had been scuttled at Pohm-Pohm to forestall further bombing, and there were still some survivors there. The launch turned, accelerated into the darkness, and he was gone.

The future appeared bleak again. Especially when there was no sign of Terry the next night, nor the one after that. It looked as if he had been captured, or perhaps the launch had broken down. There was now only three days' supply of food left and the ugly prospect of starvation loomed closer. Anxiety gnawed at our vitals and the ration was cut. It was then that I realised what a treasure we possessed in Hobbs. The cook branch in the Navy, though vital, is not usually productive of leaders but Hobbs was a marvel as a morale booster; the worse the situation the more cheerful he became. 'What shall we have today sir?' he would say. 'There's M & V, M & V, or M & V.' I would reply solemnly 'I think we'll have M & V' 'Then M & V it is, Sir!' Needless to say we had nothing to eat it with and made use of shells (I still have mine).

During the day one could not but admire our surroundings, beautiful near-white sand, the warm turquoise sea as clear as glass, the different greens of the vegetation and, of course, the sky, as often as not blue. Why, pre-war millionaires paid thousands for less! But they would not have had to endure the mosquitoes at night. These tormented us without respite. Most of us had the Army issue tropical shorts, really short trousers turned up to button on the thigh; let down and tucked into socks at night they were quite effective but one's face and hands suffered dreadfully. And the hermit crabs continued to be a confounded nuisance.

We had made one of the boats about seaworthy and I was just offshore in it on a trial trip with a signalman and a boy seaman called Jones,

*The birds were almost certainly Sumatran Toucans.

when there was a roar and our daily aircraft came over very low from behind the trees. We were caught napping and could do absolutely nothing. The aircraft banked sharply and came back straight for us. Waiting for the inevitable burst of gunfire I knew intense fear. The signalman threw himself into the bottom of the boat and squirmed under a thwart; I was in half a mind to do the same when I caught the expression on Jones' face and stayed where I was. He was sitting quite impassive, just looking up at the approaching death. In my division in the *Prince of Wales*, he had been something of a skate (bad-hat) in a light-hearted sort of way. He was obviously fearless as well. To our astonishment the aircraft merely screamed overhead and made off, I suppose thinking we would starve anyway so why waste ammunition. The feeling came to me that I had experienced this all before and suddenly remembered the Air Defence Position of the *Nelson* with the German bomber diving and Whitting gazing up at it with the same disdain. The signalman got up from the floorboards looking rather silly and we pulled back as the others began to come out of hiding.

That night we were sure we heard noises at Pohm-Pohm but nothing more materialised and as another morning broke even Hobbs was less ebullient. We could hardly cut the rations again. I was sitting on a dead trunk thinking of nothing in particular, except how hungry I was, when a lookout shouted. He was pointing towards a speck which turned into a man in a kolek (canoe); moreover he, now clearly a Malay, was making for our beach. A 'clear lower deck' reception committee ran his little craft up the sand and out stepped a small man of about 40 in horn-rimmed spectacles, stripped to the waist but wearing smart khaki shorts and sandals. 'How do you do?' he said. Unfortunately I soon forgot his name but he said he was—if I remember right—a minister in the Johore State government. He had escaped, 'island hopping' from Singapore, hoping to pass as a fisherman and was bound for somewhere further south.

We told him our story and that it looked as if Terry had been taken prisoner. He said he knew where there might be junks not far off and if we could provide money he would hire some and send them back for us and those still on Pohm-Pohm. He would offer half a reasonable amount, the other half to be handed over by us on completion of the hire. We had a whip-round and after some food he pushed off, paddling steadily, and was soon lost to sight. 'Well, that's the last we shall see of *him*!' said someone to a chorus of assent, but money was no good to us here and he might just be telling the truth. He certainly spoke perfect English and I for one went to sleep that night with some hope.

The following morning, our seventh on the island, there was, glory be, almost a repeat performance. Again a shout brought us running to the water's edge, and there was a largish sailing kolek, threading its way

153

in among the mangroves, grey-green bushes with twisted stems that grew in the water at one point. In it were three khaki-clad Europeans, one of whom in a Naval cap set at a rakish angle was standing in the bows directing the coxswain along the green channels of sand which wound among coral.

Willing hands helped the boat in and out stepped a blond and very sunburnt young man with an engaging smile. The sun sparkling on the sea, the sail, and his flashing teeth, made it almost too like an Errol Flynn epic to be real. But real he was, with news of the outside world, and he was listened to with more attention than any Chancellor on budget day. Sub-Lieutenant Cunyngham-Brown, Malayan RNVR, he had been sunk leaving Singapore and managed to get to the main island of this particular group which was called Sinkep, about 80 miles to the south. Commander Alexander (of Penang and our last muster at the Oranje Hotel) was there; he had been sunk in the minesweeper *Trang* (or had had to leave her after beaching) and as senior officer present had assumed command of the two or three hundred British personnel who had all been sunk in the last week and made this island. Sinkep was a civilised place with a Dutch controleur (sort of district commissioner; this group of islands known as the Rhiu Archipelago, being part of the Dutch East Indies) who was most helpful, housing refugees at Dabo, the one town on the island. There were tin mines at Sinkep and other kampongs. Dabo boasted a wireless station in contact with Batavia, the main Dutch base in Java, 400 miles away. There were hopes that a rescue ship might brave the passage from there. But the best news of all was that Cunyngham-Brown had seen four junks anchored out of sight from where we were. The effect of this can be imagined. Hearing that we intended to make for Sumatra, he strongly advised us to go to Sinkep instead, as it would be sensible to make contact with Alexander rather than play an entirely lone hand. Monro and I talked it over and decided to do this.

The other two in the kolek were Engine Room Artificers, the trio being engaged in searching out shipwrecked mariners like ourselves. Thompson said he would join them and gave me a precious .22 rifle. As they would be leaving in the direction of the junks I decided to come too, pick out which ones would go to which party and bring ours back. It was a contented crowd that shoved the kolek off and then went to collect what little that remained of our provisions.

The four junks were clustered in a little bay—I think of a third island—and choosing the smallest I climbed onboard. Brown spoke to the skipper, we wished each other luck, the kolek shoved off and they were away. I admired Brown a lot. It seemed obvious that nothing would hold the Japanese down to Java or Australia and while we were thinking, pardonably, of nothing but getting to safety, here he was doing a Scarlet

Pimpernel act among the islands, losing precious time. I do not know what happened to him.

The other three junks set off for Pohm-Pohm to embark the last of the unfortunates there. (I believe two followed us to Sinkep, the other going straight to Sumatra.) Mine was about 40 feet by 15 with two masts and a large hold amidships; it seemed to be in good order. Alone with the crew of three Chinese, I began to wish I'd brought someone with me in case they changed their minds, so sat down in the stern and ostentatiously opened the flap of my holster. Their every whim would be matters of the greatest concern; in particular the attitudes of other Chinese or Malays—all very suspicious these days of bursting bombs, sinking ships and sudden death—might well depend on how this trio spoke of us, and I hoped we'd get on. I studied them as they hoisted the cumbersome brown lateen sails. The oldest had a flat, expressionless face and was nearly bald, one was young, cantankerous and sinister (he turned out to be perpetually 'high' on opium) and the third was unremarkable. The young one reminded me of a battle-scarred hunt terrier and so was nicknamed 'Tyke' on the spot. He wore a filthy blue loincloth and his ugly, cunning little face, minus most teeth, looked out from what appeared to be a sweat-sodden 'deerstalker'. It was apparent that he was 'agin' the expedition from the start.

As the junk dropped anchor off our beach the men stood looking at the vehicle of their deliverance with hands outstretched to shield the setting sun. The first boatload came out, baling furiously. Monro eventually embarked and together we looked back at the friendly island that had served us so well: the white sand, the fluttering of a roosting bird somewhere among the mass of green, the other derelict white boat lying on a nobbly bed of mangrove roots, the dead trunk by the water where we dried our clothes and a battered biscuit tin. It was almost exactly a week since we had first set foot ashore, but seemed like a lifetime. Eager backs bent to the windlass beside the rather incredulous Chinese and, as the anchor came up, the steady *tok-tok* of wooden palls seemed to symbolise our new-found progress. The settling boat was cast adrift, the stiff sails went up again and the forefoot began to chuckle to itself as they filled to an off-shore breeze.

The men settled themselves as comfortably as possible in the smelly hold and a tarpaulin was spread over it. No sardines were ever packed as tightly, but it was better after dark when the tarpaulin came off, a mouth organ miraculously appeared and we all sang. Lying on the hard deck and looking up at the rectangle of purple where myriad stars swayed gently from side to side, I wondered at the strangeness of life. What would I have said to anyone in the spotless Gunroom of the *Prince of Wales* not so many weeks back, had he told me I would soon be lying in the bottom of a Chinese junk, with the future as uncertain as

155

the then Scapa weather?

Most of the next morning we were passing islands of various sizes, all covered with thick foliage and some with thin lines of smoke ascending lazily into still air. Hobbs cooked indefatigably in the stifling bottom of the junk where a gap in the tarpaulin permitted a triangle of sunlight. What looked like one of the other junks was in sight far astern when in the early afternoon the old man pointed to a long green streak ahead and said 'Sinkep'. After much vociferous probing of the depths with long poles, anchor was dropped half a mile out, the signal for a kolek to detach itself from the shore. It proved to be manned by three native policemen, smart in green tunics and breeches with straw hats and cutlasses, who took Mackintosh, Monro and me back with them. An old car having been provided, through the good offices of the Dutch controleur, we soon found ourselves on the outskirts of Dabo approaching a sizeable building. Morose Europeans were sitting on the verandah or standing in groups outside. I went to look for whoever was in charge, with a sinking feeling that if Commander Alexander had moved on it might be me. However, as I went in the door to curious looks Alexander came out. 'Good heavens, Brooke again! We always seem to meet in adverse circumstances; and how did you get here?'

He said we were completely isolated; there was no longer communication with Batavia or anywhere else because the Dutch had prematurely destroyed the W/T station in a fit of 'scorched earth' zeal. There were three or four Naval parties here from different wrecked ships, some RAF personnel and others already arrived from, I think, Pohm-Pohm. When the junks turned up he would hold a council of war to make plans.

One of the parties was from the sunken gunboat *Dragonfly*. She and her sister *Grasshopper* had been bombed and Commander Hoffman (it will be remembered that Ian Forbes and I were under him for the causeway operation) had beached the latter. The survivors, including soldiers and civilians, had got ashore, the many wounded owing their lives to a nurse who tore up her clothes for bandages (assisted by some Japanese prisoners under escort from Singapore). Forbes—eventually to receive the DSC—and two others had swum to the next island where a Malay fisherman was persuaded to take them all to Sinkep. The controleur then provided boats in which they had left for Sumatra*.

Whilst awaiting the other junks' parties, I bought a songkok (pronounced songkoe), the black velvet pill-box hat universally worn by Malays (being brown enough to get by, the idea was disguise from the air), some unpleasant solid brilliantine made in Japan to grease my

---

*On reaching Padang some got away but all the Naval officers and men joined the destroyer *Stronghold*. On leaving Tjilajap for Australia she ran into enemy cruisers and was sunk with all hands except Forbes and a number of ratings who were taken prisoner.

automatic, a lattice sleeping mat and a whistle. The wherewithal was begged from a Lieutenant Dickinson, MRNVR, as I had no funds left after the departure of our Malay saviour from Dankau, as it turned out our island was called. Dickinson, of *Kuala*, seemed familiar and I had just remembered that it was he who had saved Monro's life by going out to the *Kung Wo*, when the sudden roar of a Japanese aircraft cleared the place in a flash. It contented itself with a good look round and shortly after this Commander Alexander called his conference. I think there were eight or nine officers present, mostly Naval. Two or three junks and a launch comprised our only links with the outside world. Because of the air menace (the enemy had set up a seaplane base quite near) Sumatra was our only possible goal. The mouth of the Indragiri River was about 50 miles west of Sinkep and should be attainable in one night. I then had a bad moment. It did not look as if the junks would take everybody and Alexander asked for volunteers to bring two back again. I was struggling with my conscience on the one hand and what I reckoned was the serious language problem on the other when Monro and Dickinson said they would do this.

We were not yet out of the wood, however, and there followed a bizarre little drama. 'Tyke' presented himself, hostile eyes smouldering, and somewhat naturally made it plain that he demanded payment. He was sat on a chair, surrounded by the rest of us and confronted with Mackintosh; wearing an expression of utter defiance he looked like an animal at bay, which he was. 'Ask him if he will take us further' said Alexander. 'Unk hooken kook ulch clook' said Mackintosh, or something like that. Tyke's eyes went metal hard. A torrent of words crackled out of his ugly mouth to the accompaniment of much gesticulation; I had the unpleasant feeling that he had the whip hand and knew it. 'He says the contract was to bring us here and no further. It has been fulfilled. He wants the money. They must get back to their village.'

'Say we will pay him well.' Further explosions. 'He says no.' I saw Alexander take a deep breath. He then played his one and only legitimate card. Producing a neat wooden box, about nine inches long, he slid off the top to reveal glass divisions. But it was Tyke's face that held our attention. His eyes were riveted on this box and his bullet head followed its every movement. 'Got this from the controleur', said Alexander. 'Opium. If he doesn't fall for this, I don't quite know what we'll do. The controleur is dead against any violence as we must sow the right seeds for the future and we ought to respect him.' He tapped the box methodically and studied the other's face. Tyke said he had not the authority to make a decision, the old man would have to decide. Accordingly someone got on the telephone to the police and a boat went out for the latter.

Presumably we would have had to take over the junks if the old fellow had declined, but fortunately he did not, and the other crews must have conformed without trouble. Someone had a chart of the area over which we all pored and with difficulty I made a copy on a piece of scrap paper. There were a few small islands west and north-west of Sinkep and then a straight run to the Indragiri. For many miles each side of the river mouth there was nothing but mangrove swamps and mudflats, backed by jungle. I was keen to get away quickly. Commander Alexander gave me a box of opium, a typed note which was a pass from the controleur and 50 guilders. We said goodbye. I never saw that fine officer again and it was three and a half years before it was learnt he had been taken prisoner, one of that select band who engineered the escape of others but left it too late themselves*.

Return to the waterside kampong brought another farewell as Monro was to go in one of the other craft. This was the third occasion of his volunteering for potentially fateful duties in ten days. He had been an object lesson to the other officers of his ship, volunteering to stay on board her after we had all left; then to stay on the island; and now to return to Sinkep. His fate too was unknown to me until discovering—after the war—that he had been taken prisoner†.

I expected another battle of wills so nothing was said to the Chinese about our exact destination. The clatter of the windlass again wound our spirits up. We had certainly wasted some hours going to Sinkep but prayed this would not matter. It was 19:00 when we got under way; a western course was indicated and to our relief accepted without demur. Occasionally I felt my haversack for the magic box and was at once conscious of covert glances. It contained little lead tubes in rows like water colour paints, about fifty of them. My instructions were to administer one every few hours. Mackintosh explained that the opium, strictly rationed by law, could only be legitimately procured with a licence. Life to any Chinese under its power, of whom there were many, my box represented some months' supply at a time when future procurement was doubtful. As if to underline this, Tyke produced a charcoal fire in a little pot that he fanned into flame, a crucible into which he poured a dark brown viscous liquid ('Opium' said Mackintosh) and a pipe with a tiny bowl but very long stem. When the liquid began to bubble he poured some into the pipe and, lying on his side with his knees drawn up, kept the bowl above the flames while he inhaled the issuing fumes. We watched with interest. After a time he offered the pipe with glazed eyes to someone else, who refused. He then offered it to me and to show willing I took a few sucks. My lungs filled

*I am glad to say he survived. See pages 278-9.
†Another of the unsung heroes of those grim days, I doubt whether he ever received any recognition. He too survived but poor Dickinson died in captivity.

158

with a poisonous-smelling smoke, I was nearly sick and Tyke cackled his delight.

The last island on the scrap of paper was in sight as darkness fell and I was faced with a decision. Though the wind was favourable we could only hope to make Sumatra about 08:00 the next morning; that would mean two or three hours of daylight in the open sea, and more if we did not hit the right spot. Also, the Jap seaplane base was only a few miles south of our route and to be well away from it by daylight was an absolute necessity. The risk was too great and I decided that 24 hours were worth losing here to time our light correctly.

Accordingly we sailed up an attractive palm-fringed channel and anchored as the stars came out opposite some lights that meant habitation. Morning revealed a few bamboo huts on stilts and cultivation behind, which proved to be the abode of two friendly little Chinese charcoal burners. Mackintosh and I landed in the kolek we carried and he gossiped with them, pulled their legs, and very soon had things on an excellent footing. Nearly everyone else came ashore and the two fed the whole 60 on rice, sweet potato, roots and cane sugar, eaten off oyster-like shells with which the shore was covered. We bathed and fooled about in the sea which lapped right under the huts, though three times I had to blow my whistle to send everyone sprawling for cover. Once it was a formation of twin-engined bombers and twice it was single planes. I was glad we were not under way. At 18:00 leave was taken of our benefactors (they received a few tubes of opium, gleefully accepted) and we set out down the channel.

Everyone was sweating below the tarpaulin at sunset when, coming into the open sea, there was a shout of 'Jap destroyer!' that sent a murmur round the hold and a cold shaft to one's heart. But coming closer we could see she was beached, and then obviously the poor old *Grasshopper*, wreckage and black stains where a bomb had burst being quite plain. When clear the skipper was given to understand that course was to be set north-west. There was considerable argument, but I think this time he was swayed as much by the determination on our faces as by display of the opium box.

There was one more excitement on that short but trying trip. 'There's a ship coming straight for us' said the lookout. Sure enough, on the horizon was a largish merchant vessel, with course set to head us off; she could only be Japanese but we were not making more than five knots and there was no point in running for it. There passed what my tutor at Dartmouth used to call 'un mauvais quart d'heure'. The ship did not waver. No one spoke. One had the feeling that a hundred eyes were inspecting us through huge telescopes. Then one of the fire officers, who had a pair of binoculars, remarked that she was very high out of the water. Then that she had a list to port and was stopped dead.

Eventually one could make out the ripple over a reef that stretched away from her side. She too was aground; yet another victim of the omnipotent Jap 'air'. A torrent of conversation greeted the news, followed by the mouth organ, drowning the monotonous sound of gently slapping water. Just before dark we sighted the island where the enemy seaplane base was and were glad to leave it astern. Night came down and those off watch curled up for sleep.

I was on until midnight and found it necessary to consult the compass second by second as Tyke on the tiller, who had 'smoked' too much, was hardly capable of holding the course. But fortunately the wind continued favourable and the hours went by in steady progress, with nothing but the creaking of the gear and occasional grunt from a sleeper below. About 05:00 I awoke with a sensation of things taking place; something had been passed a few feet off. It was still dark. All three Chinese were up forward jabbering away and peering into the murk. Their cries increased and they came padding aft, keeping abreast of a shape that was gliding by; as it came level I could make out a sort of lattice work square and something grated on the bottom of the boat. 'Fishing stakes; they are going to anchor' said Mackintosh, listening to our friends' conversation, and in a moment the anchor went rattling down to rouse anyone not already interested. There was a perpetual washing sound from nearby but we could see nothing and resigned ourselves to the wait for dawn which would reveal with cruel clarity whether the course had been right or not. Our Chinese had never been to the Indragiri before and if there was no sign of it we would not know, from featureless land, which way to go. Many hours of bright sunlight would follow. I cursed myself for not having spent time taking an accurate tracing of the chart; but there had been so many people poring over it; I had been keen to get away clear of the others . . . oh what was the use! I strained yet again into the darkness.

Then came the first paling of the sky, the forming of vague land shapes, each one as it clarified raising higher one's hopes, until at last all was clear, distinct and marvellous. We were a shade north of the centre of the river mouth, on each side of which the expected acres of mud and mangroves stretched away into the haze. The land began to close in on each side as we progressed, a large kampong came into view along the north waterfront and soon the junk was alongside a rickety pier. I stepped out under a battery of curious stares.

A little Eurasian in white suit and topee with a sort of orderly in attendance came forward and introduced himself as the headman of Piggi Rajah. He said in English that one or two food shops could produce a meal for the party, the remainder having been cleaned out by the thousand or so Europeans from Singapore, mostly soldiers, who had passed through. He then showed me a sheet of written orders tacked to the wall of a hut. Signed by a Major Campbell, they were to the effect that we should press on up river, making eventually for Padang on the west coast. There were officers at each of several staging posts who would give further instructions and it was hoped to arrange transport. The first call would be Tembilahan. This was wonderful news, an organisation ready to help us! What little I had heard about central Sumatra concerned a mass of jungle and mountain ranges and I had imagined we were in for an epic foot slog as soon as the river gave out. The idea of this with 60 sailors who probably had not walked two consecutive miles since the war began was not my idea of a skylark. Padang I knew to be a big place facing across the Indian Ocean to Ceylon, whence we would surely be taken off provided we got there before the enemy.

There was more good news: the headman said that he could provide a small steam launch to tow the junk up the winding river. The other junks had not arrived; we had expected to be behind them on account of the day's delay and feared they might have run into trouble.

After the first proper meal since Singapore, much refilling of water bottles and collecting of wanderers who were mostly amusing themselves watching some repulsive mud-fish, we said a grateful goodbye to the village of Piggi Rajah, distributed a little largesse and re-embarked. The steamboat took the junk in tow and puffing indignantly started up river.

Thick jungle crowded the water's edge where various birds of the crane variety made dignified retreats at our approach or flapped ponderously off on vast wings. Small groups of wild pig were visible from time to time rooting about on mud stretches and once we thought we saw a fair sized crocodile. The sun went down with the usual tropical suddenness, making black filigree work of the riverside trees until the stars took over in ones and twos. Murmurings from the body of the boat died down and then ceased. All at once I felt very tired and followed suit.

It seemed five minutes later but was about 23:00 when consciousness forced its way back; the moon was up, outlining a cluster of huts and several small craft moored alongside a landing stage to which we were in the process of making fast. Stepping gingerly on to slippery planks, I was suddenly confronted by a large figure. 'Hullo' it said, 'I'm Captain Gordon, what do you consist of?' He explained that there were 200 soldiers here and more at the next stop, Rengat; others were at various places up river, all moving on by slow stages. The Dutch were being splendid, arranging somewhere to sleep, scratch meals, and most important of all a couple of motor boats; there was a landing craft from Singapore and all three were engaged up and down river, towing motorless craft full of men. 'What about money?' I said, as after paying off our junk I would have little left of Alexander's 50 guilders. 'Oh, that's more or less looked after: you'll meet Major Campbell soon, he's organising this stretch. There's Colonel Warren in charge at Padang . . . Campbell is one of his officers; there's a Lieutenant Colonel at Iyer Molek.'

'Have you seen Lieutenant Commander Terry?' I asked. 'A large, broad man with a yellow beard?' 'Oh yes, he's been doing great work with one of the motor boats, towing backwards and forwards, but he's gone on now.'

Next morning I was looking at a big junk, well over a hundred feet long, anchored downstream, when a hand slapped my shoulder and I turned to the smiling face of Norman Crawley, the RA Captain who had been at the *Norfolk*'s conference (on the projected raid across the Johore Straits) and with whom I had struck up a quick rapport. We shook each other by the hand slowly. 'It's funny, you know', he said. 'I have been thinking about you, wondering whether you got away; what happened?'

And then I heard his story which was one of the best of several outstanding tales of escape. Orders had come through to his battery to lay down their arms, at which they decided to make a break for it. Going down to the harbour, Crawley swam out to this big junk and brought back her dinghy in which the remainder of his battery pulled out. None of the soldiers but himself knew anything about sailing but they cleared the harbour successfully and made for Sumatra, passing an island outpost manned by Australians who called out to be taken along. When these had been embarked they numbered about 70, but fortunately found plenty of rice on board. With Crawley keeping to the Sumatra coast, two or three days saw them at the mouth of the Indragiri.

One of the other junks from Sinkep arrived at mid-day and it was learnt that the second had made the river mouth. What was more, everyone was off Sinkep so no return trips were necessary. Accordingly I paid off our junk to which we owed so much. The old man stowed the magic box lovingly away and we left them awaiting a tow downstream.

That evening everyone boarded Crawley's junk and another boat for a tow and some time during the early morning we came to Rengat. The anchor splashed into the yellow and now narrowing stream and a voice hailed us from the shore: 'Who's that?'. I happened to be on watch. 'Lieutenant Brooke, a big junk full.' 'This is Campbell, you can come ashore for the rest of the night or stay where you are. Probably be going on in barges tomorrow; we can't get that thing up any further.'

Daylight found him, a bustling, bullet-headed 'KOSB'* with bright

*King's Own Scottish Borderers.

blue eyes and a sandy moustache, taking details of the various parties. I was to get to know Jock Campbell very well. 'The next step up river will be in those'—he indicated some flat wooden barges moored astern of two small steamboats. 'We hope to get on this evening, but it all depends on the Dutch; they are doing wonders, but we are a damn nuisance at a very tricky time and I dare not ask too much. They only have to forget us for a few days', he paused, 'and we're finished.' He said the next step was to Iyer Molek. 'There's a lot of us there, and the transport question is getting awkward. The Dutch have something "on" but it'll probably be all right. Are there any more coming?' Someone asked if the Japs were around. 'They're not far' he said. About this time Palembang, further south, was falling to a determined attack by parachutists, but none of us knew this.

I persuaded an Australian doctor, who appeared to be in funds, to buy me a parasol, which was done to considerable laughter, but the place next to me was much prized when the sun beat down mercilessly on the barges. The troops, already embarking, were in good spirits and when I appeared in songkok with parasol up there were cheers from the soldiers and a chorus of 'All together!' 'Vast hauling!' and 'Turn up there!', echoes of the previous day when the rattan cable of the junk had parted several times. The little convoy was chugging along in the late afternoon when all of a sudden a flying fox swooped down, a large creature with dog-like face and wingspan of a goose. Shortly there was another, then another. One or two would dive down to have a look at us; more and more appeared, until they were as thick as a flight of birds, not going anywhere in particular but twisting and whirling over our heads. Further on there was a dead pole-like tree and on top a huge monkey which uncurled and stared at us. I sent a .22 bullet spitting into the wood under him, which was rather unkind, and at which he let out a foul imprecation and launched himself like a trapeze artist into the jungle. And then it began to rain. The heavens opened and a deluge began, reminiscent of Penang; everyone except the lucky few under the little stern roof was drenched, and when at 22:00 we bumped alongside a grass verge at Iyer Molek, it was still raining. A little man was waiting with a torch, reflected in enormous puddles. We stumbled out, were led off to some large barns, part of an evacuated rubber factory—and left to sleep.

The CO of this makeshift camp was Lieutenant Colonel F.J. Dillon, IASC. Always calm and tactful but firm, he sat at a table facing the entrance of the place and wrestled with all manner of problems, assisted by a Major Nicholson—it had been he with the torch. There were several hundred men in the camp, mostly in small parties. One strange little band consisted of a British intelligence officer called Clarke and a handful of Japanese prisoners whom he was escorting, he hoped, to

India. I only had a close look at one of them, a fighter pilot who had been shot down (and probably taken unconscious as the Japanese were not allowed to surrender), a pleasant enough, thoughtful young fellow, in contrast to what one had come to expect. None of them gave any trouble. Clarke, nicknamed 'Tojo', looked very oriental himself and was another I was to get to know well. (His mother was Japanese; the family had had to leave Japan when the attentions of the secret police had become unbearable, Clarke to join up in Singapore.)

The last of the Sinkep junk parties arrived that afternoon, bringing the number at the camp up to 600. They had missed the river mouth and spent six hours looking for it in broad daylight. Enemy aircraft had spotted the junk and given the occupants a nasty time investigating but eventually flown off.

The river had started to flood and navigation further up was considered impracticable. Road transport had been found for our predecessors, who were taken to the railhead at Sawalunto and thence to Padang. There had been no difficulty about this, some dozen lorries being at British disposal, until the day before we arrived when Colonel Dillon had been politely informed that they were required elsewhere. A vague promise of some in the future had been made, and the matter left at that. He looked worried. Rumour of the state of affairs was already round the camp and faces were long. Though there was a large kampong nearby, prices were going up (native boys wanted five guilders, about 3s 6d [17½p], for a duck's egg) and there was little to occupy the men.

Word came that the Japs were pushing on to cut the mountain road at a place between us and Padang; the Dutch had decided to withdraw into Fort de Kok about 200 miles north-west and every available vehicle was to be used for the troops and ammunition, particularly the latter, of which they were very short. All local lorries had been commandeered. Colonel Dillon's load was now heavier than ever, especially as further supplies of food became doubtful. He put me in charge of the cookhouse, which meant the entire food situation. Camp life centred round the cookhouse and it took a little handling. Many unscrupulous individuals came round two and three times so that I arranged for a strict routine: incomplete parties waited until last and any man coming up by himself was usually turned away. This system took time and there was grumbling against the Navy, especially among the Australians who would rather have scrummed. I had words with one officer which ended in his going before the Colonel.

The third day some lorries arrived and took off the fortunate few at the top of the roster. By the fourth day there was considerable talk among the soldiers that we were wasting vital time and would do better pushing on individually or in very small parties. That afternoon Petty

Officer Pickard came to me and reported that about half of the camp had decided to depart that night. I immediately told the Colonel who ordered a parade and made a convincing speech on the necessity, in view of the terrain, to stick together and trust to the Dutch. His words went down well and all except a handful resigned themselves to waiting. I did lose one Able Seaman, a wiry, dark fellow called Armstrong—as it happens he had given me his wallet to keep the party funds in—who decamped that night. We never heard of him again.

The following day I was put to the test indeed. Some lorries turned up and being now at the top of the list we were preparing to leave when Colonel Dillon said the Naval party could not be spared. Another left in our stead and the men got into an ugly mood, not without reason. They were unimpressed when told it was an honour and I was more than relieved when the situation was grudgingly accepted. There were no lorries the next day. The inaction was very trying and nerves began to fray. I amused myself watching some giant toads in a ditch. The Colonel decided that something had to be done. The river was in flood at about five knots, but any movement would be good for morale and it was arranged with the Dutch for an old steamboat (and the landing craft) to tow the two barges. Accordingly half the camp, which included my party, set off, making good about one knot. The bank could just be seen to be going past! Conditions were even worse than before, there being more bodies to fit in. The river wound and twisted and by night-fall we had probably come four miles in a straight line. The little steam-boat sent a shower of sparks high into the air, and we hoped the enemy had no aircraft up. But at least we were on the move.

Next day we reached a place called Basrha and could hardly believe our eyes; recognised khaki figures were wandering about at the water's edge. The news was unbelievably good. Several buses had turned up and transported the entire second half of the camp. Some had been taken on already to the next place, Tolek. Iyer Molek camp had been closed. Six hundred men take a lot of moving and another 24 hours slipped by, including a hideous mosquito-ridden night sleeping on stalls in the market place. Hobbs and a soldier cook, who had joined us permanently, set up in the back of a coffee shop, the proprietor of which, a fat Malay, was most affable. His Chinese cook shook with laughter at Royal Naval methods of cooking and relations were of the best. Later I had some request to make of the headman and, trying to walk on projecting roots, fell into the yellow water, with the humid heat and state of my clothes no bad thing.

Eventually we were allocated two small open lorries and after much handshaking and thanking the headman, climbed aboard to start a 24-hour drive which for stark, nightmarish madness will never be equalled, at least for me, and I sat in the front with the smallest Ordinary Seaman we had. Those in the back were pulverised, but of course we were going in the right direction, and at some pace. The driver was a well-built though very young Malay—he looked about 16—wearing only a filthy pair of dark blue shorts; and the road nothing but rubble and stones. After some hours, and aching in every limb, I became aware that we were entering the outskirts of a small town and in a numbed dream, climbed down on to the road when we stopped in the main square. This must have been Tolek. The usual line of wooden shops stretched away to the left; on the right was a grey stone building surrounded with grass and trees. Through the open verandah I could see Major Nicholson sitting at a table and went up to him. He smiled. 'Not so good Brooke, I'm afraid', he said, pointing to a big lorry ahead of mine which was half full of green wooden boxes. A line of green-uniformed Dutch soldiers and several natives were busy carrying more boxes from the house to a pile in the garden, and from there to the lorry and others out of sight. 'That's ammunition going up to Fort de Kok; they've got to get it all there tonight, and want our transport. Your two are the only lorries available. There is just a chance, of course, that it will all go into their own, but not much, and there's no getting by the controleur; he's the hell of an autocrat—that's him over there.' I saw a tall, fair-haired man in a blue silk dressing gown pointing at a pile of ammunition and at the house.

For an hour we waited, watching the ammunition coming out. There seemed no end to it; but at last the final boxes were stacked on the grass, a formidable pile. There was one lorry left. The pile dwindled and I gauged the remaining space in the back. The controleur was watching too—a fine looking chap at close quarters—as was the officer in charge, to whom I had been addressing ingratiating remarks. I foresaw a few boxes left over, which might or might not need our vehicles. To lose our transport now might mean never to regain it, especially since the Japanese might be close. Nicholson said something to the controleur who nodded. Nicholson nodded to me and we were off.

That was the last I saw of him. I understand he was taken prisoner. I heard nothing of Colonel Dillon either (until after the war, when I learned that he was also taken prisoner). They were two more who organised the escape of hundreds in their unselfishness, remaining behind themselves until it was too late.

The sun went down and on went a pair of deep yellow lamps that threw a soft glow about ten yards in front. Speed was not slackened. Then the moon came out and, as the lorry topped a rise, revealed the most beautiful sight of my eastern experience. The road wound away to the left along the edge of a cliff, and for miles and miles below us there was jungle and mountain and more jungle. It looked soft and feathery in undulating rolls, losing detail as it receded until coming up against a long mountain chain; here and there a jagged hilltop thrust its head up and to the right was a streak of silver that looked like a lake. The road began to twist and drop down as it clung to the mountainside and then I realised we had stopped. The driver was already down and gesticulating to a hut off the road. We stumbled in to find it a coffee house full of British soldiers. There was also fish to eat. The coffee was bitter and the fish dried miserables that stared forlornly in the candle light, but both tasted like the Berkeley's best. Then on again. The road became smooth and at about 04:00 we saw the lights of a small town immediately below. A few minutes later the lorry had stopped beside Sawalunto station. Climbing slowly down, we thanked our Jehu suitably, at which he refuelled the old bus, turned her round and with a cheery wave, drove straight back to Basrha!

An hour later there was general commotion; a train for Padang was coming in; it would take all of us. Padang, our goal! It was almost too good to be true. For the n'th time CERA Roper mustered the party, who were in high spirits. There had never been any question of difficulty after Padang. Dawn was outside, streaky and chill, showing us the sombre mountains around. The train came in, a tall ancient thing, and we climbed up to the carriages. There was a puff and a jerk, the grey stone station began to recede and I settled back with a Squadron Leader Farquharson on to the comfortable cushions. We watched, relaxed and content, the attractive countryside go past as the line twisted round mountains, lakes and terraces of paddy; after a pretty trying few weeks we had surely made it.

At mid-day the train drew into Padang to be met by two British Army officers. They explained that all British 'refugees' were billeted in two evacuated schools, the Malay School and the Chinese School, both virtually empty as our predecessors had been taken off by ships. Being somewhat junior I was surprised to be informed that I was in charge of the Malay School. A Major Rowley-Conwy was i/c the Chinese School. My new responsibility would comprise about 100 sailors and 300 soldiers, nearly all Australians. Having marched them there and settled in, I was taken to the British Officer in Charge, Padang.

He was Lieutenant Colonel A.G. Warren, Royal Marines, who had his headquarters in the Oranje Hotel, a modern building in the middle of town. All the officers of the new 'draft' were gathered there and went into his room. He was a fine figure of a man who seemed vaguely familiar, very dark with a black moustache, and great force of personality. Our hearts sank at his words.

'The situation at the moment is not good. We have about a fifty-fifty chance. I have wireless communication with Colombo, but cannot get anything through *from* them, as the consul burnt his cypher books the other day, which was of course premature. Ships have been in fairly regularly since the fall of Singapore, taking off refugees as they arrived, but nothing has been here for five days now. We do know that one was sent from Colombo, but she is two days overdue, and I have just had a report from further down the coast that the last one to leave, which was for Java, has been torpedoed. There is daily Japanese air reconnaissance here and it looks as if they have pretty well sealed off this port either from the air or by submarines or both. The enemy are about 60 miles away by road, though not yet in strength, and the length of time we are left unmolested depends entirely on whether the early reduction of Padang is included in their strategy. So you see we are in rather a poor way.' He smiled at our rueful faces and I could not help feeling that here was a man equal to anything.

Then he got down to administrative details. Rowley-Conwy and I received our orders (only half the men to be absent at a time; always at five minutes notice to go) plus a few guilders for expenses, and then went our different ways. The loud clop-clop of the pony in front of me (transport was mainly by gharrie, an enclosed and highly decorated little trap) was only half heard, and I was too preoccupied to notice anything outside. The whole thing had been a race against time, and presumably we had lost. It was hard. We might wake up to find the town in possession of the little yellow soldiers tomorrow morning and there was nothing we could do about it. Though the Dutch Army was in position in the hills around Fort de Kok, it was their tactics to leave Padang undefended (they had made those of us who had arms hand them in at the station, though personally I had managed to avoid this). It was not going to be easy telling the troops, and doubtless the majority would take to the hills rather than capitulate, but for my sailors at any rate there could be little logic in this. The gharrie stopped and I looked out on to a sea of faces. Telling them the situation as optimistically as possible I did not exaggerate as experience had shown that nothing but the truth was much good. They went off in groups to discuss it.

The Malay School was a white stone building built round a grass courtyard with a big tree in the middle, under which a couple of native barbers were already hard at work. The large rooms lent themselves readily to the various parties, which were soon organised and set to cleaning up, as much to keep the men occupied as anything else. Good food, brought in a Dutch van, the opportunity to wash myself and my clothes properly and the feeling that the future was somewhat out of my hands, went some way to counteracting the nasty taste produced by our prospects. A night on hard boards was no hardship now and next morning Warren produced enough money for officers to have eight and men five guilders each to refit what was left of their uniforms.

Padang proved to be a large straggling port, very well laid out with avenues, trees and gardens. The European houses looked quite modern, cafés abounded and a large market sold everything one could think of. Hobbs and I went shopping for domestic requirements of the camp, to a refrain in Cockney, West Country, Scottish and Australian accents as soldiers and sailors bargained with gesticulating shopkeepers; the scene was so reminiscent of 'Gib', 'Alex', 'Honkers' or a hundred other places that it took an effort to realise that the underlying atmosphere was not so carefree. There was a Dutch barracks at which I had arranged to go and listen to the news, bending over an old radio with the orderly officer who translated with anxious features; the purport was then given out at the school. The news got worse and worse; Palembang in the south had fallen to parachutists; the fighting in Java (the centre of the Dutch East Indies) was clearly going badly. Nearer home the enemy, somewhere in the hills we had crossed, were taking this and that place and coming closer and closer. One seemed to have heard it all before.

It was an antidote to have lunch at the Oranje Hotel, stood by Alex Lind, a hefty young Dutch- and Malay-speaking Lieutenant MRNVR. He was on Warren's staff and told me something of the Colonel. He had been a senior member of the Special Operations Executive (SOE) in Malaya, as the name implies a secret organisation (of mixed regulars and ex-planters) that had been very active behind the Japanese lines, organising raids, sabotage and subversive activities generally. I had had a hint of this already as the Colonel had told me in the course of conversation about the Japanese that he was not going to let them take him alive if he could help it. He said he was well known to the enemy who had put a big price on his head—Malaya being full of cheques and sabotage orders signed by him behind their lines—and 'they know how to make people talk'. Warren had been at Penang when it was evacuated and I suddenly remembered it had been he who had come up in a white steamer and shouted a change of destination.

In Sumatra to arrange subversive activities with the Dutch when Singapore fell, he had sent one of his SOE men to set up the escape route that had served so well. (Major Campbell, whom I had already come across, was another of these.) Warren had voluntarily assumed command of the British forces at Padang though several more senior officers had passed through with no inclination to take over. He was, however, hoping to escape as soon as he could turn over his responsibilities to Colonel Dillon, expected the very next day.

Terry, I discovered, had left Padang in a ship not long before we had arrived. No-one knew for certain but it looked as if it was the one that had been torpedoed. I returned to the school with a heavy heart. Surely the end had not come at last for that indomitable spirit. Perhaps he was all right and would turn up yet again.

Time hanging heavy during the afternoon, I went for a walk. Happening on a photographer I went in and a solemn Chinese took a picture, sideface, to give the rather straggly beard—standard among us refugees—every chance. It was to be ready in 24 hours. In the evening we learnt from the radio that Java had fallen. After supper I went to an hotel for a beer with a most likeable subaltern called Fairfax, an RAF Flight Lieutenant and an Australian subaltern. I had with me my knapsack which contained my pistol and a few oddments. After we had been talking some time a boy came up and asked for Lieutenant Brooke.

I said I was Lieutenant Brooke. He said I was wanted on the telephone. It was Major Waller, on Warren's staff at HQ. He said I was to come to the Colonel's quarters at once. I told Fairfax and the others that this might be the big getaway and if I rang and told them to have a beer on me (secrecy might well be necessary) they were to go at once and get the men ready. I went outside and with some difficulty secured a gharrie in the pouring rain.

At the address given were Rowley-Conwy, Clarke (the Intelligence Officer) and two other officers I had not come across before, in addition to Lind, Waller and Davis, late of the Straits Settlement Police, who had helped me with some problem at the school. More arrived until there were eight of us refugee officers, all having had the same summons. The air was electric. Warren was nowhere about. His lieutenants ordered drinks and we sat like opposing teams before a match, every questioning eyebrow being answered with a commonplace. All at once Campbell came in and said we were to make our way unobtrusively to an upstairs room.

Warren stood there and we made a semi-circle round him. I could feel my heart thumping. He looked at each of us as we came in. When there was silence he spoke. 'I have decided', he said 'with the help of information received, that if any of you are to escape, it is useless to leave it until after tonight. The Japs can be expected at any time, and there is no chance that a ship will get through at this eleventh hour; still less that she would get away. It is likely that all personnel here will be made prisoners of war. There is just a chance for some of you. The other day I authorised the purchase of a prauw* which is provisioned and has been lying up the coast so as not to attract attention. I had intended to sail for Ceylon in her, with my officers, having turned over the responsibility here to Colonel Dillon. But the latter has not arrived; I fear he may have been captured, and I am staying.

'I have got you eight here because there is room for you in this boat. You have been selected as the most useful to the war effort in other theatres, and I am ordering you to go.

'You will sail tonight. It is a very long way and there is considerable risk. This is just the end of the suitable monsoon weather. You may

*Pronounced 'prow'.

170

make it before the south-west monsoon breaks or you may not. Personally, I think you have a sporting chance. Has anyone got anything to say?'

For a moment there was stunned silence and then Clarke said he had promised Singapore Intelligence that above all things he must stick by the Japanese prisoners. Colonel Warren said 'I over-rule that. You are to go'. I said I did not see how I could possibly leave my men at this juncture and he said 'I'll talk to you in a minute', or words to that effect. I went on to the verandah, my mind in a turmoil, and one of Warren's officers—I think it was Lind—tried to persuade me not to be foolish. Then Warren appeared. 'I'm ordering you to go!' he said. Then: 'Anyhow, they'll segregate the officers from the men, so you wouldn't be any use to them'. I had been steeling myself to disobey him but his last remark—almost an aside—suddenly decided me. It would be pointless to go into captivity to no avail and rightly or wrongly I said I would go. 'Good', he said. 'Campbell', turning to the latter, 'everything in order? Right, get going. Absolute secrecy; we don't know what orders the Dutch authorities may have had from Java which has just fallen, and it is quite possible that the surrender terms, if there are any, include the handing over of all allied nationals, so keep away from everybody.

'Goodbye; good luck to you all!': And that was the last we saw of Colonel Alan Warren, Royal Marines.

I thought of various new clothes assembled and the little rifle but any idea of trying to get them was banished. I could not possibly go back among those men to collect my gear, saying nothing. Outside were seven gharries, already hired, into which we piled. 'You come in this one with me' said Campbell. I suddenly remembered poor Fairfax and the others waiting patiently for a telephone call and asked if I could go and put them off. 'No, no time now' was the answer. 'Anyway, a slip of any sort at this juncture might wreck the whole show.' The door in the back slammed shut, the gharrie tilted, sending a shower of water off its roof, and we went clopping after the little red lights in front. The last and longest lap of the journey from Singapore had begun, but I felt like a deserter and it was to be three long years before (having received many letters from them) I ceased to see the faces of my men at the Malay school, when they woke up on that next Sumatra morning to find that the place where I slept was empty.

7

Sederhana Djohanis

On went the cavalcade through the pitch-black night. Occasional showers made the rear lights hard to see, collisions causing a volume of Malay and grunts as an unwilling beast was goaded to new effort. Doors opened in kampongs in question of such weird doings at midnight. Shouts were answered by the drivers. A long convoy of ox wagons was encountered and once we lost the way. Every delay was a nervous business, especially as it had been heard in the town that the British had a boat secreted up the coast and Campbell's official car had been withdrawn that morning. We seemed to be going on forever when at last the leader turned off the road into a rutted lane. The few stars became obscured by nodding palms and soon we could hear surf breaking on the shore. Then the foliage thinned and we came out on to a beach, lit, to our surprise, by a rising moon. There were shadowy huts around and the silver line of the sea beyond.

Everyone disembarked stiffly and Davis paid off the drivers. Their voices, arguing about something, had only just died away when three forms materialised hauling a large kolek across the sand. Half the party embarked and the rest of us sat down on a log bench in front of one of the houses. Its inmates left their trestle beds and lit an oil lamp that threw flickering yellow shafts onto our faces. Davis introduced himself and we were all given a cup of water which was most acceptable. What they thought of this sudden influx of ill-assorted *tuans* is hard to guess; for my part I expected yet again to wake up and find it all a dream.

'What on earth is a prauw?' asked a shadowy form beside me. I said I hadn't the vaguest idea but thought it sounded like an oversize canoe, probably with triangular sail and outrigger. We both fell silent, probably with much the same thoughts. Was it one or two thousand miles? I was glad that I had a knowledge of the sea and then on second thoughts felt it might be one of those occasions where ignorance is bliss.

The moon was well up by now and entertained us with a fairy scene. Surf broke on the sand in a wide arc fringed by rustling coconut palms whose long shadows crossed and bent among the knobbly trunks and squares of attap roof. The sea looked like molten metal and just before a fleeting rain cloud obscured the moon we made out the returning kolek

The author aboard the MV Anglo-Canadian.

Above *HMS* Bermuda *at Scapa Flow after hoisting Walrus flying boats aboard.*

Left Bermuda *alongside at Bona, firing a blind barrage.*

Below *Covering the North Africa landings:* Renown *and* Victorious *from* Bermuda.

Above *Captain Back watching fall of shot.*

Above right *6-in bombardment of Fort d'Estrée, Algiers.*

Right *The author in 'Arctic issue' en route to Russia.*

Below *Chipping ice off one of* Bermuda's *paravanes in the Arctic.*

Air attack by 150 'planes of the BPF on Palembang, Sumatra, January 24, 1945. See pages 226-228.

Opposite *A Corsair's wheel collapses. The running figure is the author.*

176

not far away. It was a relief to move out of the mosquitoes and pile in.

The prauw was further out than expected but on grating alongside I was agreeably surprised as two substantial masts traced slow arcs across the stars and to climb on board was quite an effort; moreover there was a pointed attap roof amidships. Ducking through a small opening into the lantern-lit interior I found a dozen forms asleep on the bottom or on half decks at each end, was given something to lie on and went out like a light.

Waking to the gurgling and creaking of fair speed I watched perplexed as a line of suspended garments, mostly khaki, swayed overhead. Then a voice roared 'Breakfast!' and the immediate past rushed back. In typical British fashion no-one was introduced to anyone else and we new arrivals ascertained the nature of our shipmates by furtive enquiry.

In overall charge was R.N. Broome, a spare, obviously capable Malay Civil Service member of Warren's SOE team. A man of few unnecessary words, he now divided us into two watches (one always on deck, of course, and one normally below, in the usual four-hour stints) with some excused on special duties. The starboard watch was to be under himself and the port watch under I. Lyon, a sandy-haired Gordon Highlander Captain; also an SOE man, he proved to have set up the Indragiri escape route. 'Jock' Campbell, yet another, was to be in charge of provisions, abetted by L.E.C. (Doc) Davies, an RAMC Major. I was in Lyon's watch with A.J. Gorham, a swarthy RNVR Lieutenant whom I did not recognise with his new black beard but turned out to be the *Kung Wo*'s second officer; H.E. Holwell and R. Cox, both MRNVR Lieutenants ex the minesweeper *Trang*; G.J.C. Spanton, a cheery, freckled little Captain, 1st Manchesters; and H.M. 'Tojo' Clarke whom I knew. I had also run across most of Broome's watch before; the gunner Major G.H. Rowley-Conwy (known to all as Rowley); his 'shadow' Lieutenant D.C.A. Fraser; Major W.R. Waller, who had been on General Percival's staff; J. Davis, a Malay Police Superintendent, and A.V. Lind, Lieutenant MRNVR (both SOE). The one not met before was B.A. Passmore, a tall dark Lieutenant RNVR— also SOE. John Davis had insisted on bringing his Malay orderly with him, Jamal Bin Daim; remembering Norman Crawley and other unfortunate claimants left behind, this seemed at first a strange move, but he was to prove his worth. Similarly Broome had brought a Chinese, Lo Gnap Soon, who did such cooking as there was. In all we numbered 18 of whom eight were SOE and the rest 'guests' (all but Gorham being last minute arrivals).

From Broome we gleaned the general plan. This was to work up the coast some two hundred miles to a latitude about that of Ceylon and then sail straight across the Indian Ocean using the north-east monsoon, a steady favourable wind which did not, however, extend far enough south to allow us to start westward right away. If all went well the voyage might take three weeks, but two factors were likely to extend this. First, the notorious character of the west coast of Sumatra and second, the change of monsoon from north-east to south-west in April. As will be seen, south-west was no use to us and the date being March 9 there was a danger that if precious days were spent off Sumatra early on, we might find ourselves halfway across the Indian ocean being blown towards Burma, (in the process of falling into Japanese hands). In fact the whole thing was a gamble.

It was necessary to learn as much as possible about the prauw and her gear before getting rid of the original native crew, an old jurangan and two boys who were still onboard. The idea was that they would give us a 'crash course', and this is just what it turned out to be! I can still see the wizened old man in sarong and orange straw hat squatting by the tiller, keen eyes concentrating on the middle distance, and lips, between squirts of scarlet betel nut, pursed in a low whistle to coax the wind.

The boat herself came deceptively well out of a first inspection. *Sederhana Djohanis* (variously translated as 'Lucky John' or 'The Good Ship Johnny') whose function had been general trading, was a sailing ketch with masts of about 50 ft and 25 ft, carrying a very large head of sail (with main, mizzen, fore and jib). She was roughly 45 ft at the waterline, with a beam of 16 ft and draught of 4 ft; with no keel the result was very saucer-shaped. There was a tremendous bowsprit. The hull was well found, most of her bottom being copper-plated, though it was to peel off badly in heavy seas. The central roof sloped down each side at a steep angle, so that the only flat exterior route from one end of the boat to the other was along the nine-inch top of the gunwhale. A large triangular platform was superimposed on the stern, extending the already rising line of the hull and when I came to take the tiller it was to find that this gave the helmsman a commanding view and welcome release from embroilment in a crisis.

But one did not have to be at the helm to realise that the keelless prauw's sailing ability was very limited. She would not sail nearer than some 80° to the wind and made the most devastating leeway close-hauled. This factor alone nearly put paid to us in the long run as it decimated westerly progress. But with the wind abaft the beam, which seemed to be the only method really favoured by Malays, she went well and to make six knots goose-winged (sails out on both sides) was not unusual.

The wind was fair that first morning as *Djohanis* sailed in bright sunshine past the palm-covered and mostly uninhabited islands that dotted the coast. Going below for the mid-day meal, the newcomers in my watch satisfied their lively curiosity on the subject of resources. As always on such occasions, the main problem would be water. There were two large drums and some petrol tins which worked out at a pint a head for 42 days, with a little left over for cooking the odd hot meal. This did not allow for evaporation or accident but no-one thought that, if successful at all, 42 days would be anywhere near the mark. Food consisted of a supply of bully beef and tinned salmon (I cannot now touch either!), biscuits, and a limited amount of extras such as tea, coffee, sugar and rice. There were a few bottles of whiskey (for medicinal purposes!), mattresses, blankets, two Lewis guns and several rifles. Most important, as was soon to be revealed, there was also a supply of sailcloth with palms and needles for sewing. One unfortunate deficiency was fishing gear; some makeshift tackle was to be contrived but we never caught anything.

'Garth' Gorham told me that Anthony Terry had been back to the island but found us gone, it would seem on the very night we got away. I wondered again whether the poor old boy had survived his sixth sinking. It struck me that that nail-biting delay at Iyer Molek had probably saved the rest of us from going in the same ship. This set me thinking of my men at the Malay school. Had the Japanese arrived yet? Had I done the right thing? What would Terry have done? A wave of depression was infinitely increased, when, rummaging in the knapsack, I came across to my horror the black leather wallet that contained the remains of my party's communal funds. The only good thing was that it also contained a list of their names; if we got through I would make good use of that.

With an effort I turned back to Gorham with a question about our chances. I think he said the first part of the trip would be the worst, indicating with dirty thumb a passage in the Sumatra Pilot book—'NW squalls, variable baffling winds, calms and S currents may be experienced close to land . . . it (our route!) should seldom be chosen by sailing vessels bound N in either monsoon'. Gorham had a sextant (presumably saved from the *Kung Wo*) and when about to board a ship for India had been held back by Warren to navigate the prauw. In the ensuing period he had copied out the necessary pages of navigational tables on board a destroyer and amassed some other rudiments of the trade in the form of a chart of the coast of Sumatra (it did not, of course, extend far out) and a wind map of the Indian Ocean, torn from a pocket dictionary. Sights need very accurate timing and Brian Passmore had procured a dilapidated radio and two batteries, most important for the time signal. (He also had a Leica and was to lend it to me occasionally to take some of the pictures that exist of our ship.)

We had come some 40 miles by mid-afternoon; an offshore breeze continued to blow fresh, enabling a short cut to be taken, and the Pilot's author appeared a pessimist. Not for long however. Islands were

179

coming thick and fast towards evening and Bapa (Father), the old jurangan, conned us through a narrow gap between two of them that kept the breaking surf but a hundred yards on each side of the boat and its new owners' hearts in their mouths. Unfortunately, or perhaps fortunately—he did not keep it up. Further navigation began to look very doubtful as darkness fell and it was regretfully decided (it was, of course, necessary to put as much between us and Padang as possible) to anchor off an island called Paryang. A little later, Bapa lost his nerve near some large rocks and dithered so much that we dropped anchor without further ado, concluding the first and altogether encouraging day's run.

Broome had not wanted to waste time like this but was probably trying Bapa—at least according to his lights (*Djohanis* had none!) unreasonably. Original insistence on continuing after dark had upset the old man badly and the log was to show that in fact the prauw had seldom been under way at night.

Another limitation, somewhat basic under the circumstances, that had dawned on a few of us was that *Djohanis* was not meant to go out of sight of land! With her huge sail area and flattish bottom she was designed for shore breezes and the traditional Malay 'tidak apa' (swing it till Monday) philosophy. An inability to sail close-hauled had already been appreciated but yet another serious weakness was clearly demonstrated at 04:30 when sail was made to an easterly wind. Probably we were clumsy in the half light, but the mainsail tore on something, drawing attention to the shocking state of the canvas and rigging. To begin with the sails were made of very thin, cheap canvas, now rotting, that tore if poked hard with the finger! At night stars could be seen through the mainsail, which was the worst though closely contested offender. Much of the cordage was on its last legs; it was four-stranded and corresponded to tarred sisal. There was hardly any spare. Only the 'essential services' such as throat halliards boasted real blocks (these being rough native affairs), other locations having merely a piece of wood with a hole in it. The resulting wear and tear was appalling.

It was obvious that what would just do for pottering around the coast was quite different to that required for an ocean passage at the change of monsoon. It was also evident that our existence would be one of the finest judgement as to when to reduce sail, rehoisting, and eternally refitting. This may sound but the yachtman's fare, but when carried out on the Equator on a little meat, biscuits and a pint of water per 24 hours, turned out to be tough.

The first confirmation of these forebodings was not long in coming. We could never make much of the old Malay's methods and it was evident that cries of 'Lee-oh!' or 'Let draw' (the Naval equivalent) awoke no Cowes or Malta memories for him. International co-operation

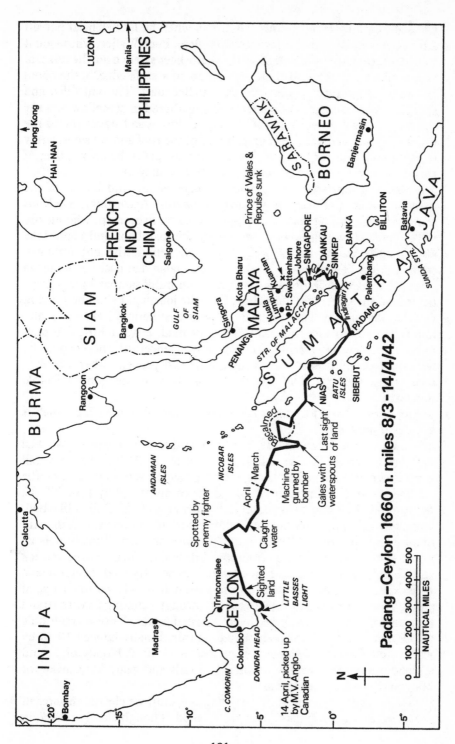

Padang–Ceylon 1660 n. miles 8/3–14/4/42

was sadly lacking and the final fiasco was when he let her head pay off after a gybe, before operations were complete. Poor Waller, whose job it was to stand on the roof and steer the mainsheet safely over the mizzen, failed sadly ('well what the hell can you do on a knife edge?'), the boom becoming temporarily secured to the smaller mast. The sail filled and *CRACK* went the boom. The debris was gathered in somehow and the three Malays set to work on the boom, binding wood staves round the break. The sail had been torn on a corner of the roof and we sat in a row to sew a long rent for the first of a hundred times (as the only splicer of rope I came to be excused sewing, no great advantage.)

It was now important to procure a spare boom, and be rid of the native crew in readiness for striking westwards. Accordingly *Djohanis* came to anchor off a small island only visited by fishermen, who luckily were there, provided us with two reasonable bamboos and could take Bapa to the mainland. Shaking hands all round, the old jurangan pronounced a benediction—'Tuan! Salamat Jalan dan nasib baik sahaya mintar Tuan Allah lindong semua tuan, lagi bulik sampai ka'lain nagri dengan salamat'. ('Tuan! good luck for your journey. I shall be praying to Allah that you will arrive safely at your destination.') He was really touched and I am sure thought us all quite mad. It was a little damping to see the old seaman being paddled away. Henceforth there would be no Bapa to enquire from, even though he had proved rather a broken reed, as to the craft's idiosyncracies or those of her unpredictable homeland.

The rest of that 24 hours is taken direct from Broome's log which is graphic if not formal:

'Under way again about 17:00 on starboard tack with wind NW. The night was bloody. We were beating up N about 21:00 when a squall came down and we had to lower mainsail, which was well done by the starboard watch. Wind went all round the compass and by a.m. fell to a flat calm, and we had to lower all sail to prevent chafe. Rolled like hell. Nearly lost all our water but eventually saved all but one tin. Wind still non-existent at dawn. All sails required work on them. Finally hoisted jib and got away for a short time to south wind. Then hoisted mizzen and found mizzen halliard one strand gone. Hoisted nevertheless. Hoisted main starboard side and immediately had to lower to change of wind. Tore a large hole while lowering, through catching in wire strand on starboard runner. Mended this. Hoisted again. Tore a large hole through catching under boom. Repaired this. Finally hoisted 10:30 by which time no wind. Onshore breeze began 11:30. A bloody night and a bloody morning. Seriously worried re sails and gear. May make for Nias and see what we can do.'

This proved to be typical of the conditions until we cleared the area of *sumatras*, as these vicious squalls were called. Though clearly related in devilment to the *gregale* of Malta, its twin at Gib (which would sweep down the Rock to flatten unsuspecting naval whalers) and Portland's speciality, *sumatras* took the palm for surprise. In the middle of a sultry calm a long black shadow would suddenly appear, racing towards us over the water; seconds later the boat would heel right over as if struck and go tearing off, usually to the accompaniment of ripping canvas. Sometimes the squalls would veer 360° and then die as suddenly as they had come.

As little progress was made against a contrary wind, it was decided to put in at the inhabited island of Tamang for a concentrated attack on the sails. As luck would have it a small Dutch tug appeared and gave us a tow to another island 70 miles further up, which was as far north as we needed to go. A perfect little tropical island—dark green palms, white sand and still blue water—Pulau Ilir was a fitting last contact with the Sumatra to which we owed so much, but our thoughts were less on this than on the miles and miles of sea to come. Would they deal kindly with our rough and hardly ready conveyance? We did not know. Striking west for Ceylon (about 1,000 miles as the seagull flies) contact with terra firma was severed for the last time at 17:00 (on March 12), nor did *Sederhana Djohanis* ever drop anchor again.

She had made 180 miles from the starting point so we felt moderately safe from that direction. It would be nice to record that we hurtled westwards with songs on our lips, but the wind proved unfavourable and we tacked back and forth making no progress at all. There were still some islands to be cleared and one dawn found us in a light wind off Bansalan, an unusual plateau-like coral formation about a mile square. Approaching this we could see the emerald green streaks over a reef, but decided with our shallow draft to try a passage rather than the alternative long detour, and held on. A sudden shout from forward proved discretion the better part of valour and we gybed without delay, to return as we had come. It was none to soon for one could see great coral shelves and clusters a few feet under the boat, with pale sand and multi-coloured fish weaving in and out of sea plants as clearly as in an aquarium. Even as we watched they scattered in a flash, and a long grey shape glided into view. It came up under the hull as if in silent warning to the potential survivors of a holed boat, kept us company for a while, and then disappeared with two lashes of an ugly sickle tail.

Not long after this a fresh south-westerly breeze came off the land and showed signs of blowing up strong. The mainsail was already down, being patched where the topping-lift had rent it in two places, and we sacrificed the mizzen. In spite of preparation, the jib downhaul jammed when the storm arrived with a rush to tear the sail right down one cloth. The foresail was soon lowered too, the wind reaching about force seven. In two and a half hours we covered 26 miles under bare poles; no mean performance and a very thrilling, though uncomfortably runaway sensation. This was the first of several experiences of 'penthouse sailing' and was fortunately in a westerly direction. The prauw steered quite well within limits, but heaven knows what would have happened if the direction or terrain had been otherwise. The wind dropped almost as suddenly as it had arisen and was followed by a horribly short swell. The boat was extremely 'tender' due to her shallow draught, lack of keel and big masts, and in this case her motion exactly fitted the wave interval, making her very lively. Those on deck hung on like limpets and those below, keeping their feet only by willpower bred of the vital importance of their task, were employed holding the precious water drums in place. They looked for all the world like the followers of some ancient rite, thrown into alternate gloom and relief by the light of the swinging lantern. In the end it jumped to a sudden buffet and crashed to the deck, leaving the performers in the dark and unfettered use of their vocabulary. The stowed mainsail projecting astern was rolled under, as was a canoe, lashed between shrouds and the penthouse roof. If there had been no roof or even if it had not been strong we would have been swamped. It was most unpleasant and I, the only regular Naval officer onboard, was very sick; there were ribald comments at this, though for the record I was not the only one!

After a day's near-calm the setting sun saw the prauw racing under bare poles again for a group of islands and those who could conjure up enough fatalism went to sleep with their fortunes in the lap of the gods. Navigation was impossible; we just sped along hoping for the best while the land loomed up all round. This blind rush went on until daylight when we found ourselves clear of the islands and out at sea, having passed clean through the lot! Someone remarked that he now knew why sailors are superstitious. So far we had done 300 miles in the first week. This was up to schedule and, given the steady monsoon without too much being asked of the gear, our chances appeared good.

Looking around I thought how lucky we were (though it must have been good management) in the large proportion who had knowledge of sailing. Broome was very much at home and extremely active (he would lend a hand on the bowsprit when necessary and was to shoot up the mainmast like a lamplighter when the peak halliard broke in a gale), but Ivan Lyon in particular gave one the comfortable feeling that he knew exactly what he was doing. Which he did. It came about in conversation during the long night watches that sailing, preferably single-handed, was his ruling passion. He had several outstanding voyages under his belt, solos in Malaysian waters including Singora to Singapore and Mersing to Saigon in a three-tonner and Singapore to Australia in a 12-tonner. When I asked him why he had not joined the Navy he said because he knew he could get more sailing in the Army! Ivan was worried about his wife and little son; he had sent them to Australia from Singapore but had heard nothing and feared he might have left it till too late.

The quiet-spoken but infinitely resourceful Brian Passmore was a seasoned yachtsman and a member of the Ocean Racing Club. I, of course, had sailed on and off for years, the rough justice meted out by a naval cutter not being bad preparation for *Sederhana Djohanis*, and some of the others had taken their yachting seriously at Singapore. It was not long before 'Doc' Davies was talking about starboard and port and Soon, the cook, was even tending the foresheets when his blowpipe and little wooden galley did not call. Jamal, like all good Malays, was above most menial tasks. Everyone got on extremely well (Jock Campbell was as much as anyone the avuncular architect of this, though one was hardly needed), there being only one serious disagreement the whole voyage. At this time it was a long way ahead.

Suddenly we were surrounded by barracuda jumping in dozens, like bayonets twinkling, rival theories insisting that they were being chased by sharks or that they heralded a breeze. The former appeared more likely for it soon fell calm again and very hot. With the continuous sail-making and hoisting, mostly unmentioned here for fear of boring repetition, the one pint of water—taken in thirds—was proving a minimum. For a few days the results of currents and unfavourable northerly or southerly beatings took us back to the north-west of the last island and it began to look as if we might be chained to the land after all. This was fortunately not to be as March 18 found us bowling along again in the right direction. The navigator announced that we had done 96 miles in the last 24 hours. The words were hardly out of his mouth when the drone of aircraft engines sent us all below except Jamal, who took the tiller, an unfortunate but logical procedure as our one hope of immunity was to be taken for a trading prauw about her lawful occasions. This seemed to work as the big Japanese 'Army 87' reconnaissance bomber flew steadily past and did nothing.

A period of several days sweltering calm now set in. Everyone, suffering acutely from the shortage of water, was listless and inclined to be short; the feeling of helplessness was depressing to a degree. The sails hung motionless and the masts creaked to a minute swell with a regularity that made one want to scream. All the while precious time was slipping away. There were still some 900 miles—in a straight line—to do. With April 1 only nine days off, we would have to do 90 miles a day, when the average to date was not 45. Looking at the deep blue sky which seemed to end only under the boat where little black and yellow fishes revelled in the only shade for miles, it did not seem as if we would ever move. Of some slight recompense were the wonderful Turner sunsets, long streaks of orange, crimson and gold firing stray clouds into banks of billowing pink. Some would sit and admire the sight as if held in its ill-boding spell, but the more practical would pick out lager, gin-sling, or burgundy from the vast salt stretch that mirrored it all with tantalising fidelity. Later the moon would be reproduced as a perfect circle.

Eventually, marvel of marvels, a steady breeze arrived. The little fish gave way to the glinting darts of their flying kin and, as the air began to circulate through the penthouse again, its cheechak lizards (pronounced 'cheecha'—an apt description of their intermittent cries) resumed their scampering about the deckhead; occasionally they would drop on to a surprised sleeper, himself bitten with ever more audacity by rejuvenated cockroaches. (Some of the latter had achieved a length of two inches and were the bane of life, burrowing into one's longish hair to browse on the scalp or whatever they found there.)

The horizon began to sprout isolated black clouds and course was shaped for the nearest of these in the hopes of collecting water; but it passed ahead and it then looked as if we would be involved in a storm coming down from the north. This turned out to be a small cyclone which approached at high speed. The mizzen and jib had just been lowered in record time when someone shouted 'Waterspout!' And there, sure enough, was our first sight of one, a few miles away. The sea at its base was whipped into a whirling cone that dwindled to a stalk about 30 yards in diameter. This rose drunkenly to the angry clouds above which stretched down to meet it. The apparition, new to most of us, made good progress in our direction and all eyes watched with some interest. A discussion ensued as to whether the water went up or down but fortunately we did not have the chance to prove either as the spout sidled off, bending and swaying like a sleepy reptile, before dwindling to an hourglass and disintegrating in the middle.

When the storm hit us the boat heeled and moved forward as if a clutch had been engaged, accelerating like a machine. She flew in its grip for a short time and then was relinquished as abruptly. The wind then settled at west. A clumsy gybe to a later shift cost us the foot of the mainsail which blew out for a third of its length, providing a long job at daylight. The wind then headed us and an exasperating 24 hours was spent sailing NNE with our destination abaft the port beam. The navigator's announcement that we had done two miles in the opposite direction to Ceylon brought morale back down to rock bottom. It was March 24 and a pang of real apprehension made itself felt.

On this and similar occasions Jock Campbell would come out with a carefully hoarded tit-bit. Marmite on the breakfast biscuits, marge, or greatest of all treats, a *nasi goreng* of rice and bully beef. It was an education to watch as well as feel the effect. There is nothing like hard work and short rations on a doubtful venture to clear a man's mind and reorganise his sense of values. Here were 18 grown men savouring every sip, or gobbling the first issue so as to be in the running for any possible 'buckshee', according to inclination. Or the officer accustomed to thinking nothing of a few whiskies, going to a shady corner to suck a third of a pint of water through his closed front teeth, discovered to be an excellent method of refrigeration. Extra rations were also issued after occasions of exceptional exertion, for which the burly quartermaster was always parrying jocular demands.

By this time most of us had gravitated both into habitual 'cruising stations' and specific jobs about the boat. The watch on deck was inevitably divided by the awkward design of the prauw into a group forward and another aft. I usually joined the after group, partly because taking the tiller passed the time, partly because I liked to be at the decision-making end (not that I took much part in decisions myself) and partly because I was tremendously drawn to Ivan Lyon.

As to be expected, some opinions aired were somewhat naive and one had to be on one's guard against damping rejoinders. But with Gorham (who also was a bit of a pessimist), and particularly Ivan, one could discuss matters without any inhibitions. A man of few words, the latter was always cool and deliberate. An account of his later exploits I was to read implied that he was aloof and somewhat unapproachable. I did not find this at all; he may have taken some time getting to know, but sitting cheek by jowl every alternate four hours, and many other hours too, cut this period drastically and it was not long before I had for him not only professional respect but considerable affection. In the very worst moments, when asked his opinion he would always say, 'I keep an open mind', and this is how I shall always remember Ivan Lyon, with the ghost of a smile puckering the edges of very blue eyes.

But the forward end of the boat was undoubtedly the jollier with the ebullient Rowley-Conwy in a dreadful old 'deerstalker' usually the centre of a story-telling ring, from which appreciative guffaws would be wafted aft from time to time. He was by no means all banter, however, having got his battery away from Singapore in a junk—just like Crawley—to some islands where it had run aground. Splitting up he, Fraser and the others had pushed on separately, Rowley eventually securing a motor boat with which he picked up his men and a lot of other refugees as well, before finally making Padang a little before I had. Fraser, a big, bespectacled, cheery young ex-planter and member of the Malayan Volunteer Air Force until it ceased to exist, had been taken on strength by Rowley just before the end. 'Holly' Holwell was yet another in demand for'ard as a raconteur. Though not more than 40, he had a white beard. On first acquaintance I had taken him to be about 60 and solicitously helped him through the bulkhead door, much to his and Richard Cox's amusement. Holwell, from the Naval Offices at Fort Canning, had originally worked on a plantation and Cox in a shipping company. Both had spent ten days in two of *Trang*'s lifeboats—Cox was her First Lieutenant—before getting to Sinkep and then the Indragiri.

As my specific job was setting or shortening sail I chose the bowsprit, from which the jib was handled. One ran out along the frayed wire footrope that was suspended by 'stirrups' beneath, one arm over the thick spar. Being by nature pretty agile I enjoyed it, not too different from manning one's boat over a boom or other naval antics. Rowley did the same in the starboard watch, a little more sedately at first.

A new trouble arose when everyone began to go 'busok' as Jamal called it, coming out in sores, and it was well that we had the Doc and his small stock of medical equipment. Two enthusiasts jumped into the water as an advance on the dipper bucket, but that was the last time anyone did; a 12-foot shark was on the scene in seconds though he may have been there unobserved all the time. We were visited by an exhausted swallow, considered a sign of luck; he proved quite tame, eating out of the hand. Yet another natural history lesson was provided by two immense blue-nosed whales, rolling and spouting in concert. They came straight at us and rifle bolts had begun to chatter nervously before they passed close astern.

By now we had got the measure of the prauw's and our own capabilities. Nevertheless, seven minutes was considered a good time for getting off all sail! This was mainly due to the care necessarily lavished on the mainsail, with spare hands stationed at notorious tearing points as the canvas descended. With the penthouse roof at an angle of 45°, this had taken a lot of getting used to, especially in heavy weather. In the end everyone discarded footwear and developed toes with the tenacity of crabs. A complication was that the main boom was so long that, when going about or gybing, it was necessary to hoist it over the mizzen by a topping lift from the mainmast head, a full-time job for two men and one which seemed to get heavier as the days wore on. If a sea was expected that would not permit the main boom to be projecting astern, its 'tack' had to be unrove (a bight of rope securing the boom to the mast) which, when eased away, allowed the boom to slide forward, becoming more and more unwieldy for those cursing and slithering on the sloping roof. The jib also provided rare entertainment since the bowsprit was nearly as long as the boat and in heavy weather the locus of its end would have defied any mathematician.

At last, on March 28 a steady breeze arrived. The north-east monsoon at last? And then from the heights of hope we were shot to the depths of gloom. 'Aircraft!' We dived below and Jamal took the tiller as usual. The bomber approached slowly from astern but with any luck . . . *Ratatat . . . ratatatat!*

188

The bullets crackled on the water, on the hull and penthouse roof, and a few smacked around inside. There was a pause while we got to our feet, swearing volubly, and quickly piled any useful material against the side. Then someone remembered Jamal and Soon and called them in. They had sat still at the tiller while bullets sent wood slivvers flying and lashed the surrounding water for seconds. 'Jaga biak! Tuan, dia balek!' And sure enough, it was back again. We got down feeling bloody. To have to lie and take it like this was infuriating as well as frightening, and one was much tempted to be up and doing.

He circled the boat three times, giving us in all five long bursts. A heartfelt oath brought an agitated 'Anyone hurt?' from the doctor, but it was only someone who had been missed by inches, the bullet splitting one of the big ballast stones. A bomb could be expected at any second and the suspense of waiting blind while the noise of those engines approached was indescribable. But no bomb came and when the droning eventually died away it seemed too good to be true—no one had been hit. Nor had the hull been punctured below the waterline or any of the water containers damaged. The sails suffered considerably, one theory being that their large expanse had drawn the gunner's fire high.

The next day was a test of nerves indeed, as doubtless the blighter was on patrol and would come back for another look. By astonishing chance there was low cloud overall. When the dreaded engines were heard we froze to a man, as if it could help. He flew back and forth unseen and eventually went away, *Sederhana Djohanis* sending up a long corporate sigh. For a period only one man was allowed in the open, to prevent surprise, the congestion below adding to our discomforts. I was never more thankful to be a non-smoker. Proper cigarettes had given out, the most addicted unfortunates relieving their nervous cravings with some dreadful native tobacco, rolled in lavatory paper.

'Easter Day' I heard with surprise; only three days short of a month out of Padang. The watch on deck were entertained by a big swordfish jumping, its great silver body flashing like a torpedo and tapering to a gnarled spike with which they fervently hoped to have no closer acquaintance. Jotted notes about this time read 'Night, squall to squall. 12:00 calm after big squalls. Rolling. Exhausted and seasick. G's wireless check on the time put us back 110 miles. Bad!' That was worse than being shot at, wrecking the gear, or suffocating in calms. As mentioned, the navigator had to know the time exactly and while the old radio gave the time signal this was all right. Then the battery began to fail so that the radio only worked for a few seconds and a wristwatch pool was set up to help him switch on as near as possible at the right moment. He had had no luck for days until hearing on this occasion 'Colombo had its first air raid yesterday'. This was bad enough but anxious calculations, based on the fact that the announcer was well on with the news, revealed that the watch time was minutes out, putting us back 110 miles. However, we were spared the shock of arriving at the estimated position of land with none in sight.

The breeze varied for a few days, though coming mostly from the right direction. It was exciting when frigate birds wheeled overhead, their split tails forming encouraging 'V's, but as usual the fates did not permit anything on the credit side for long. The shout of 'Aircraft!' produced, for the first time, a thrill of delight. We were 250 miles from Ceylon (based on a snatch of 'Roll out the barrel' which always preceded the time signal; when carefully resung it indicated a minute before and proved a good guess). There was a scramble for something to wave at this single-engined and obviously friendly aircraft; but as it banked to come at us, the sun caught the ugly red blob on its side. Down again, cursing, among the ballast. He roared down in a shallow dive, pulled out, flew round a few times and then disappeared westwards. The solution to the air raid announcement, he was clearly from a Jap carrier. Unless Ceylon had fallen to the enemy!

It was decided that the time and place were more suited by a decoy helmsman of Indian appearance. We were all dark brown and a plain sarong plus the best beard left little to be desired; for the first time there was little rivalry for the latter distinction, and I do not remember that this particular beauty contest was actually accorded a winner. To ensure our return to practicalities the peak halliard parted when hoisting the mainsail one evening, with the result that the gaff fell from half way up the mast, to be brought up just short of three cowering members of the fo'c's'le party. The halliard was spliced, turned end for end, found rotting and spliced again. Looking round one had to smile: here was a rare copy for Heath Robinson. Both booms were broken and mended; the spare bamboos still reclined on the penthouse roof, getting entangled with main and foresheets at every opportunity. The sails were mosaics of patches and stitches: hardly a rope could not boast a splice or join. The fishing line had been sacrificed to do its bit in a more productive capacity and was in evidence here and there. A little 'squaring off' would have to be done before sailing into Trincomalee under the White Ensign!

All at once the question arose whether, shipshape or not, we could count on the White Ensign being received with the respect expected. The distinct rumble and crump of gunfire and bombs was heard, just over the horizon. It went on for an appreciable time. Obviously a naval battle was in progress, perhaps the prelude to invasion.

I caught my wrist on a rusty nail and the next day felt a bit off colour. This was followed by dizziness and the surprising discovery of a red line running from the small cut up to my armpit. It was shown to 'Doc' whose eyes widened momentarily before he reached for a bottle of pills.

190

'You must have a course of these', he said in a matter-of-fact tone and I started in on them. The next 48 hours were not pleasant, the effects of M & B seeming worse than the ailment. But after about the third day I woke up with a clear head. Having gone well and truly septic I do not know what would have happened without the Doc and his M & B (then fairly new). Ivan Lyon was also under him about this time but it was a measure of the man that one did not know this till later.

Davies was soon to have another patient. One night Douglas Fraser, leaning out to free the foresheets from the cathead, slipped on a rope's end and somersaulted over the side. He managed to grab the cathead *en passant* but caught his jaw on a fluke of the anchor and hung there pouring blood until help arrived. Fortunately he remained conscious, or perhaps unfortunately, because having been hauled back with a very bad gash he had to be sewn up with sailmaker's twine and needle (dipped, as an antiseptic, in eau de cologne). The scene in the darkened penthouse was like another ancient rite: Jock Campbell kneeling with the patient's hand in one fist and the lantern in the other, Rowley administering outsize 'drams' non-stop (including one to himself as a steadier!) and the doctor's concentrating profile as he applied needle to the gory triangle of upthrust beard.

More troubled weather brought surprise squalls, but though pretty weak—everyone had lost several stone—we were well drilled by this time and bungling would produce a bellow from the helmsman. Waterspouts towered up on the horizon, after which the wind blew steadily and the boat skimmed before it. This period of a few days ending on April 11 was the only one which could boast the north-east monsoon in the steady form expected. Had we not been favoured with this dying effort, the story might even then have ended very differently.

The wind then alternately died and came fitfully back again, bringing all the 'opposite monsoon' calculations to the fore, but it served to push *Djohanis* slowly westwards until there was but some 80 miles to go. For chart we had only the wind map from a pocket dictionary and a new set of problems could now be expected; the wind dropped sometimes to calm, and it was found that a current was sweeping us south. Nothing was known about these waters and we feared it might take us too far. Next stop Durban! Morale plumetted again. Originally we had been trying to get north into the monsoon, then having gone too far needed to come down and here we were about to overshoot Ceylon. 'For those dependant on the wind' there seemed to be no 'set of rules' at all, and there were heartfelt oaths about never going to sea in anything without an engine again.

And then something happened.

It was not pronounced as one might expect by the lookout screaming 'Land!' with a hysterical bellow, or someone croaking the magic word through parched and swollen lips. Gorham, who had been scanning the horizon through glasses for some time, said 'I don't think you'll all be disappointed if you come up here and see what I see'.

But it was not quite as bad as that. There was a tremor of excitement in his voice that had the penthouse cleared in seconds, those with sores and bandages scrambling bravely in the wake of those more agile, each to give vent to his particular type of yell at sight of that thrilling purple line. Had he been there, the old jurangan might well have thought that after all the strain had proved too great. Perhaps he really had prayed for us as promised, before his house in the Sumatra sun. How long ago it seemed! That cynical horizon was broken at last. Land! In every eye was a light. In some the reflection of soft beds, bacon and eggs or beer, in others clean clothes, music, or just a sense of security and, certainly for all, an absence of cockroaches burrowing into one's hair.

A tribute to The Day was the sudden appearance of a few more-or-less shaved chins, having indulged in the incredible luxury of fresh water. At sunset the air was heavy with the most intoxicating scent. Ceylon. We turned in very happy.

Early next morning there were, to our excitement, two big tankers in sight. A distress signal was constructed and frantically waved, but they either could not or would not take any notice. Gorham affected a dislike of the Royal Navy (though not, I think, the *Djohanis* members in particular) and often made caustic remarks about it. With the exception of Soon, the Chinese cook, I had been the most seasick and this, of course, was a huge joke. One did not lose, therefore, this opportunity of pulling his leg about the merchant service keeping a poor lookout. We cursed the tankers but at least felt reassured by their presence. A light breeze had got up and *Djohanis* continued south-west, closing the land all day, which passed unnoticed as the thirteenth. For the next 24 hours we stood down the coast.

Then followed the only serious disagreement of the whole voyage, whether to land almost anywhere as soon as possible or continue on for a state arrival between lines of astonished warships, even if it did mean extra days and the return of reduced rations. Lyon, all the sailors, Rowley ('Damn it man, we can't sail all this way and then turn up like tramps!') and, I think, Broome, were for the latter, the remainder for *terra firma* and the 'touter the sweeter!' Being outnumbered, we capitulated and set course straight in. One could hardly blame the opposition. There had been so many dashed hopes, hostile aircraft, inaccurate watches and above all calms . . . and we would look damn silly if the south-west monsoon did settle in and drive us away at the eleventh hour.

But the wind backed and, there being no moon that night, we did not dare go too close to the shore. As a result daybreak on April 14 found

Djohanis, after a night's south-easting, out of sight of land. There were justifiably angry looks from the *terra firma* faction and we turned through 180°, resolved to find the first possible anchorage and get ashore.

A ship was seen on the horizon which was encouraging but as the land approached its desirability receded; an almost unending line of white breakers beat on scrubby sand dunes with a background of wild bush and mountains. Brown rocks were soon visible and the water changed colour alarmingly. It was evident that this might prove the most dangerous experience yet, but Ivan, who was at the helm, said nothing, going in at an angle to the beach. A shout from the fo'c's'le 'mine on the port bow!' added insult to impending injury, but an added 'Sorry; turtle!' made amends. There was not a soul below now. The fore part of the prauw was packed. Nobody spoke, but the nearer we got the clearer came the growling of the breakers, and the more often the *terra firma* soldiers turned anxiously to the stern. Ivan had been annoyed at the decision to go in and was enjoying their discomfiture. However, the wind was right for a getaway and as usual he knew what he was doing. With about 200 yards to go someone shouted 'OK! You win, for God's sake let's get out of it', and without waiting for more, Lyon swung the tiller over. This sent us up the coast roughly north-east and opened up a pleasant cove with palms in sight behind, possibly denoting habitation. (It was discovered later to be a game preserve, hardly hospitable asylum for distressed mariners!)

Things then happened quickly. A ship was sighted to the north coming straight in our direction, and to provide sea room while the shore was studied we went about. As so often before, the gaff caught foul of the shrouds; the sail was half lowered to clear, filled in a rebellious balloon, strained for a second and then split for 14 feet. This was the last straw.

Either the proximity of land sapped our determination to sit down at once and sew for hours, or the easy way out was accepted by all as too good to miss. By common consent we stood out and lowered mainsail right in the path of the approaching ship, a freighter in ballast of some 5,000 tons. The distress signal went up at the main, the ensign upside down, the flashlamp died in a last effort, and I mounted the roof semaphoring 'Sixteen British officers from Singapore, request assistance please' while everyone waved and shouted. To our dismay the ship altered hard to port and began to make a wide detour; as she turned a large gun in the stern was seen to be covering us. We redoubled our efforts, and to our delight were rewarded. She stopped a long way off. I semaphored for them to send a boat and got the obvious reply 'Come alongside'. She circled right round making a lee, and we secured alongside amidships; it was well that our last manoeuvre should be decently performed.

By now the ship's side was lined with inquisitive faces and a queer sight they must have seen. A strange native craft with stranger crew, some in rags, some in sarongs, and some in uniform; the latter carefully kept since our departure and quickly donned; Naval officers, Army officers, Civil officers, a Malay and a Chinese.

There were shouts of 'Where are you from?'

'Sumatra.'

'When did you leave?'

'March 8.'

'Crikey, they've been five bloody weeks!' And for the first time we felt rather pleased.

There was no time to lose as no master likes to stop for long in submarine waters. Lines were sent down for treasures and minimum requirements, while two Jacob's ladders clattered over the side. We went up one after the other, those at the end of the queue having a last forage down below. A moment of farce was greeted uproariously by the spectators when Alec Lind's sarong—he was wearing nothing else—parted company and he came up starko. I grabbed the throat halliard block as a keepsake; it had come down from the mainmast head in the mêlée. There was a considerable lop on the sea, and the long bowsprit grunted and snarled up and down the ship's side as if expressing the little boat's opinion of our infidelity. The headrope parted when there were still three or four to come up, and she drifted out, refusing to be left alone. But she relinquished them in the end and was cast off as the last man was helped, beaming, over the rail. Sandwiches and tea were waiting and to walk six consecutive paces on a flat surface was heaven. One looked round at a row of new faces, and could hardly credit that it was all over, when such a little time before there was no change.

The telegraph clanged. The prauw drifted astern as the steel deck of the *Anglo-Canadian* pulsated under our feet. *Djohanis* was a desolate sight bobbing unguided to the sea and we noticed from above what really pleasant lines she had. Part of the foresail was trailing in the water where the lash-up had been too hurried, like a soldier's boots reversed.

The events of the last few minutes had been almost too quick to take in. I would surely wake up to an abrupt shake, and the gruff 'Port Watch.' Yet safety was around us, the luxuries of civilisation but a few days away.

It was only this realisation that softened the lump in my throat as the little prauw grew smaller. We had hated and cursed her, her obstinacy and waywardness, her bugs, her smells, and her unfathomable ways. Her successes had been taken for granted or forgotten; she had come to the aid of 18 desperate men and had brought them through, carried them 1,660 miles, baulked by their foreign methods, mishandled and misunderstood. Who were we to be pleased with the achievement?

It was a silent group that watched from the stern rail, where the wake seemed to push her towards the horizon. The ship's officers kept away, realising it was not their moment. I did not see Campbell conferring with the Captain, who rightly considered the prauw a danger to shipping. There was a bang. 'That's good', said someone. The first shot sent up a fountain that subsided to reveal her still bobbing courageously, but the second and third went home in the penthouse and waterline so that when the debris cleared we saw a stricken thing. She took several more hits, retaining the tenacity of an Amazon to the end. But the range was now opening fast, we could not dawdle and the cease fire was ordered before anyone could swear to her sinking. But in a while I saw in my mind's eye the little red letters under her counter:

Sederhana Djohanis
Sasak

surrender with Malayan grace to an otherwise cheated sea.

8

Operation 'Torch' and Arctic convoy

The *Anglo-Canadian* was bound for Bombay. She had had a rough time recently, having been continually bombed. All British shipping had had a rough time, not excluding the Royal Navy. A vastly superior Japanese task force that included five carriers and four battleships (under Nagumo, the Pearl Harbor Admiral) had been rampaging with impunity, its aircraft having attacked Colombo and sunk the 8-inch cruisers *Dorsetshire* and *Cornwall* and the carrier *Hermes*, with their attendant destroyers. The *Anglo-Canadian* had recently steamed through the debris of the *Hermes* and, on checking positions, I realised it was her end we had heard just over the horizon. The escort destroyer was the poor old *Vampire*, last seen disgorging survivors from the *Prince of Wales* and *Repulse*. But this was not the worst part. The Captain of the *Hermes* was Dick Onslow (a great friend of ours and my popular Commander at Dartmouth) and as all the ships had been quickly overwhelmed by dive bombing I feared—rightly as it turned out—the worst.

Another item of riveting intelligence was that the tankers we had seen, done our best to attract, and been exasperated by the lack of interest shown, were Japanese, on hand to refuel their fleet! We had come within an ace of being caught, right at the gates of deliverance*.

The four days to Bombay were bliss with clean sheets, baths, rest, food and drink, though the ever watchful Doc warned us against too sudden an onslaught on the last two. Some listened and some did not. I held back for three days and then let go, suffering appalling indigestion. Lazing about in clean clothes or strolling up and down the spacious decks, it was quite difficult to get used to the idea that it did not matter a damn where the wind was coming from!

Looking out of my scuttle early on April 19 I saw that we had arrived, and to some tune. The ship was at anchor in Bombay Roads and not only were there dozens of merchant ships but the entire Eastern Fleet,

*Quite how narrowly we escaped was not discovered until after the war. Another prauw which must have left the Padang area soon after us and had Colonel Dillon of Iyer Molek on board, was stopped off Ceylon by one of these tankers (or her escort) and all on board taken prisoner. The bad luck of this hardly bears thinking about.

including a battleship and two carriers. Our presence was signalled to the nearest, which happened to be HMS *Formidable*, and she replied that a boat would be sent for the Naval contingent. So, after heartfelt farewells to Captain Williams and his officers, Cox, Holwell, Lind and I (Gorham and Passmore did not come for some reason) found ourselves climbing the long gangway to the carrier's quarterdeck.

We were entertained by the Captain, who made us sign his Distinguished Visitor's Book, and by the Wardroom. Both questions and gin were being dealt with non-stop, when the slightly sobering intelligence was received that the Commander-in-Chief's barge was on its way to take us to his flagship, the battleship *Warspite*.

Though under his command for operation 'Halberd' (the convoy to Malta in September), I had never seen Admiral Sir James Somerville, one of the most successful and popular Admirals of the war*. Genial, florid and welcoming, he was amused at our beachcomber appearance (though of course cleaned up, we still had beards and lean and hungry looks) and we had to recount the whole story, which gained, I fear, from the alcoholic lubrication. As we were the last out of enemy waters by a long way, he was particularly interested in the Japanese air patrols. More gins followed and, speaking for myself, I was relieved to get ashore to the Taj Mahal Hotel still walking fairly steadily.

Though we knew he had made a signal to the Admiralty which would be repeated to our families, the next thing was to send a cable home. Rather bombastically, mine read 'Okay thinner thirsty thankful escaped Singapore but sunk crossed Sumatra then sixteen hundred miles Malay dhow thirty seven days picked up off Ceylon fourteenth future uncertain.' I had been posted missing (as, presumably, had all the others) and these two communications were well received at home.

From my mother:

Harts Gorse
Beddingham
30/4/42

The night I heard the news Daddy was away in Scotland and Kitty Tennant†
was staying the night with me. We had been out until about 7:30 doing a farm job and had only just got in when the telephone rang and it was Admiralty Casualty Dept to speak to Captain Brooke. I said he was away so they said 'Then can I speak to Mrs Brooke?' I said I was Mrs Brooke and then a voice said 'I have some good news for you of your son' and then he told me! I clung to the bannisters!! and tried not to become quite dotty! Kitty and I then celebrated in gin and champagne (I had both but she only had champagne!) and we spent

---

*His KCB on top of a KBE was to be saluted by a brother Admiral with the famous signal 'Fancy! Twice a knight and at your age . . .'
†Wife of Captain Tennant of the *Repulse*.

the rest of the evening in the hall—she sitting on the floor by the stairs—with her head on the third stair! And I sat propped up against the radiator—because the telephone, with telegrams and telephone messages simply never stopped! Oh what a night! Kitty was afraid I was getting a little drunk. I was but it was joy and not the champagne.

John* is now an officer in the Rifle Brigade. Smart, spick and span and quite keen. Getting his cap at just the right angle! And his little cane under his arm! . . .

Lind, Holwell, Cox and I were sent straight home in a troopship. We all had a last get-together that evening and said goodbye on the ample steps of the Taj Mahal. It was quite an emotional moment. And so the *Sederhana Djohanis'* crew split up, we fortunate four going home, most of the others to renew their argument with the Jap.

Eventually, after a six-week fattening process that could hardly have been bettered, I walked into the drawing room at home and said 'Well *am* I lucky to be here!' The casualty department asked my father (at the Admiralty) if I could visit them as they were so used to sending out the dreadful 'regret to inform you . . . missing', or 'killed in action' telegrams that it would give them a great fillip to meet someone posted missing who had come back. Accordingly I passed a happy half hour with the mostly middle-aged ladies there.

But the most important duty was to write to the nexts of kin of my party. None of them had heard anything (I think I am right in saying most of them never did) and their replies were both heartrending and a little gratifying in that my escape had at least done a modicum of good.

I had nothing to tell poor Colonel and Mrs Terry. They knew that their son had left Padang but that was all. Later it was confirmed that there was only one survivor from his ship that had sailed about March 5. His great work among the islands and up and down the Indragiri was now recognised by the DSC, as was that of Surgeon Commander Stephenson who was with him. The DSC is not given posthumously, which kept hope alive, but he was never heard of again.

After a month my appointment to HMS *Bermuda* arrived. She was a brand new, 9,000-ton cruiser of the *Colony* Class (twelve 6-inch, eight twin 4-inch pom-poms, torpedo tubes, one Walrus Seaplane) and, remembering my stupid stomach, she seemed a satisfactory halfway house between a stable platform and the better life of a destroyer. (Actually she proved a pig in heavy seas and extracted the inevitable toll.) Except that the weather was pleasanter, arrival at John Brown's yard was a repeat performance of Birkenhead 17 months before.

*This referred to John Persse and another cousin who I did not even know was at Singapore. Unfortunately he was taken prisoner.

I had a good journey up with two other NOs, one of whom was a submarine Captain of 23*. The ship is first class. I am Mate of the Upper Deck, Quarterdeck Officer, after Control Officer ('X' turret) and 2nd Catapult Officer. We commission in a couple of weeks and you can imagine there is a hell of a lot to do. Our messman was Captain Leach's valet, a useful thing. There are survivors here among the officers (and probably lots more among the men) from *Prince of Wales, Royal Oak, Fiji, Trinidad, Edinburgh,* and *Ark Royal.* In fact non-survivors are rather mere!

Have had a letter from John who is "under canvas and water" near Sheriff Hutton.

The officers were a particularly decent bunch. Our Captain was Terence Back, a tall and very cultivated man, being interesting on almost any subject; the Commander (R.W. Griffith) was small and, I was glad to find, easy to get on with—I was his right-hand man regarding what went on in the open air—and together they epitomised the long and the short of it! Both were concerned of course to start the *Bermuda* off on the right foot and at first my return to this sort of life after months a fairly free agent took a little getting used to.

The Gunnery Officer (Lieutenant Commander Hugh Cartwright), the Torpedo Officer (Lieutenant Sam Hesselgrave) and I lived in a cluster of cabins just forward of my turret, into which I could project myself in ten seconds if need be. Both were recently and rapturously married so I was odd man out. Guns' photograph showed a pretty blonde sitting on a gate and Torps' a smouldering brunette; but there had just been a tempestuous encounter with a beautiful girl to whom I lost my heart but not quite my head (there were those who thought I should have done that too) and I was able to keep my end up with a large Lenare portrait, the subject of much appreciative comment.

Guns himself was tall, dark and smooth, with, fortunately as it was to turn out, the chest of a guardsman. Torps was also dark but in a hairily saturnine sort of way. I still have a cartoon I did of him wearing a shako, called 'Count von Hesselerughe of the Chausseurs Torpilles' which made him look like a Latin desperado, but in fact he, like Guns, was a very friendly fellow. Both were most efficient and I learnt a lot from them. Our cabin flat became a happy club, though possibly not on the day when Hugh Cartwright, suggesting we take the whaler away, enquired if I had ever done any sailing before!

Though cruiser casualties had been heavy enough, the demand for new ones was not quite what it had been for battleships pre-*Bismarck* and our gunnery work-up was a shade more deliberate. It was still hard going—'X' turret occupied most of my waking thoughts—but it was

---

*J.C.Y. Roxburgh, a future Flag Officer Submarines.

rewarding; progress could more or less be measured by the stopwatch. There were perhaps eight of us regulars among the entire turret's crew of 30, and this included myself, a Petty Officer and the Ordnance Artificer who lurked in the depths ready to make running repairs. Most of the rest were straight off the beach; about my age, they came from every walk of life, their only uniformity a blank and sometimes apprehensive expression as this strange new world unfolded about them. Faced with the three gleaming guns, all their pristine machinery which went down three decks and a no less alarming drill-book for the '6 in.Mark XXIII', I must have had a pretty blank look myself.

Gun drill was a tough business with a steady levy of minor injuries, but generally popular. (The Marines had a dummy 4-inch gun for practice and, passing it one day, I saw what I thought was a white sausage on the deck. They were standing about, seemingly at rest and I asked jokingly whose finger it was. 'Marine Robertson's, Sir', said one casually. 'Just lost it.') Once confidence had been gained the stopwatch was produced to promote competition among the three crews. Eventually a loading cycle of four and a half to five seconds was attained at low elevation, another two to three seconds being required with the guns elevated for long range. The time would lengthen as fatigue set in but was creditable.

Ever since my first day as a Midshipman in the *Nelson* I had been concerned with fire control as opposed to gun drill and now began to feel a certain lack of involvement. Partly to overcome this and partly as a piece of fairly intelligent anticipation, I contrived a method of local control against torpedo bombers, which were committed to a period of low, level flight as I very well knew. The 6-inch guns did not normally take any part in AA fire, being too cumbersome, but I reckoned that using the high gear designed for slewing the turret on to a target and pre-set fuzes for barrage fire, there were possibilities. The result of a huddle with the Ordnance Artificer was a special voicepipe from the turret trainer to the small hatch in the roof of the turret just above my position; it ended in flexible piping so that on opening the hatch I could climb out and sit on its rim with the voicepipe in one hand. The other held a bell-push to a small bell in front of each gun layer (one ring for 10°, two for 20°, three for 30°). Ready-use shells in racks on the turret walls had fuzes set (and painted) to burst at 4,000 yards (red) 2,000 yards (white) and 1,000 yards (blue). The trainer was conned down the voicepipe and repeated the fuze colour to the loading numbers, the guns being elevated according to the bells. The idea was to pick a spot in the sky well ahead of the aircraft and, if all went well, loose off three broadsides at decreasing ranges. It seemed to work surprisingly well and we usually ended up a regulation practice with a 'repel torpedo bombers'. Guns viewed the departure from the drill book with tolerance though little enthusiasm. ('I suppose if it amuses the lads it's OK.')

It was a relief to find that Sam, the other Catapult Officer, knew all about launching and recovering the Walrus flying boat. Recovery could be quite a 'white-knuckle' operation if the ship was rolling, a matter of teamwork between me, the aircrew, the party tending lines to the latter and the crane driver; but eventually we got to using hand signals only. Launching, merely a matter of timing so that the Walrus left on an upward roll, was normally straightforward but I made one frightening miscalculation. At the fall of my flag the catapult trigger was pressed and the Walrus roared off, but instead of climbing steadily it headed straight for the sea. In a split second of mental agony I thought I'd killed the two occupants. The pilot either kept his head very well or was still in a state of temporary blackout because he waited until the hull hit the water (with a smack that could be heard above the engine) and then, catching her half volley with a jerk on the stick, bounced the sturdy machine into the air. Now only a knot or two above stalling speed, she came down again in a long swoop only inches above the sea, to gather way and extract full recompense from the horrified perpetrator of her antics.

When the pilot returned I expected some well deserved verbal blood-letting and hurried him to the Wardroom bar, but he laughed it off and pretended that it was all in the day's work. It was not to be the last time that this fish head (Fleet Air Arm slang for a seaman officer) was grateful for the forbearance of a naval aviator.

At the end of August the radio, followed by the Press, was full of a major raid on Dieppe. Most of the soldiers concerned had been Canadian, landed for some hours of heavy fighting and then with-drawn. Reading between the lines the operation had not been a success; there was little about achievements, the accent being all on experience gained for combined operations of the future. We realised that there must have been a strong naval escort and that it would have seen a lot of action.

On August 30 the *Bermuda* returned to the Flow after a practice firing and for the second time since the war began an innocent-looking letter in my pigeon hole outside the Wardroom knocked a major hole in my world. Edward Egerton had been killed. There had been a direct hit on the bridge of his chasseur at Dieppe. He had died almost at once. I took the letter down to my cabin and sat there for a long time. The awfulness of it assailed me in waves. His poor mother, probably alone, with Uncle Jack in Freetown and Kit, Ed's younger brother, sure to be in training somewhere. I could only imagine what they would all be going through. Poor Uncle Jack, always rather hearty and down to earth but a great family man beneath it all.

Until the war the lives of Ed and I, from sharing a pre-school governess at seven to Sub's courses in 1940, had hardly diverged. I had had a letter from him a fortnight before. I got it out and read it again. It said he was bored, nothing much seemed to be going on. I felt grossly unworthy; the luck of the devil seemed to attend me and here was Ed with none at all when it really mattered. He had two other close friends and a girl. They must all be feeling the same as me, that their lives would never be quite the same again, but none more so than his poor mother. I felt sure she was taking it well, because she was that sort of woman, but inside she would be partly destroyed, because she was that sort of woman too. A letter to her brought the following reply:

Sheriff Hutton
11/9

Having landed their share of the troops earlier in the morning at about 11 am the Chasseurs were ordered in as near as they could get to take the troops off once more. (I do not know what happened during the interval.) The senior one of the three was put out of action quite early on, and that left Edward in command of the other two, altogether they went in five times to pick up people, the first three times they were helped by the smoke screen, their own and the destroyers', but they ran out of their own smoke by the fourth time, and went in uncovered, and each time the fire from the shore was getting hotter and hotter, with a mass of machine-guns in the houses and gun batteries in the cliffs; on the fourth run they picked up everyone they could see, went back out with them and transferred them, but then Edward said, so as to be *absolutely* certain that they *HAD* left no one swimming about, they would go in just once more. This they did, found no one, and had just turned to go out for the last time, when a shell came and struck the bridge behind Edward, pierced the deck and exploded below. The First Lieutenant was, mercifully, not on the bridge at the time, but on the deck below it, he was knocked out by the concussion for a few minutes, but then rushed up on the bridge to see what had happened, and found the signalman and a seaman very badly wounded (one has since had his leg off, and the other has a piece of shrapnel in his lung) and Edward also laid out, but he was completely conscious and his mind working clearly and he handed the ship over to the 1st Lieut, telling him exactly what do do next, for about five minutes and then he quite suddenly and peacefully faded out, and they thought at first he had fainted.

After about ¾ of an hour when they had managed to get well out of the firing Edward, and all the wounded, were transferred to a bigger ship that had medical services on board, and Edward was buried at sea on the way home.

It would be just like him to go back once more, just to make sure; always fearless on the rugger field, fearless in the hunting field, and now fearless under fire.

Shortly afterwards his mother sent me Ed's uniform and the news that he had left me his horse and point-to-point racing kit. The thought was typical of him and I was very touched—in happier circumstances it would have been a big thrill. But it was 20 months before I put a leg across 'Fore Royal.

On September 13 *Bermuda* received a signal from the Fleet Gunnery Officer congratulating us on the high standard of our passing out firings and shortly afterwards she became a fully worked-up member of the 3rd Cruiser Squadron. Though not thrown into action at once like the *Prince of Wales*, we did not have long to wait for interesting occupation. On October 25 the ship found herself, a hotbed of inaccurate surmise, bound south for Plymouth, whence she sailed southward immediately after embarking a full Admiral's staff, and some strange black boxes which were stowed in the torpedo flat. Our destination proved to be Gibraltar, where the passengers disembarked in an atmosphere of great secrecy.

A good deal was revealed to us on November 5, a date very suited to the name of the operation—Torch—because we rendezvoused in the Atlantic with the spearhead of the great mass of invasion convoys which had been coming steadily and secretively out from England. Their task was the landing in North Africa of General Anderson's 1st Army, destined in time to link up with Montgomery's 8th Army which had begun the battle of Alamein a fortnight earlier. The basic plan was for three initial landings to take place simultaneously at Algiers, Oran and Casablanca, the first two a British responsibility covered by the Royal Navy and the third—in Morocco outside the Mediterannean—being entirely by American forces* (their European baptism of fire). The naval forces of both countries were under Admiral Sir Andrew Cunningham (the famous 'ABC') who had just hoisted his flag (not too literally as he was to be found in a tunnel in the Rock with General Eisenhower) as Naval Commander Allied Expeditionary Force. It turned out to be his staff that we had brought out. The secret of the black boxes was also revealed; they were stuffed with Algerian currency, presumably for the payment of friends and bribery of others.

Retracing our steps in company with the two advance Med-bound convoys—about 50 ships—and their cruisers, destroyers and escort carriers, we all passed through the Straits of Gibraltar on the night of November 6. *Bermuda* then became part of the well-remembered Force H.

The coast of Algeria was closed next day, the first wave taking to their landing craft before dawn on the 8th to be led in by a carefully planned organisation of submarines and collapsible boats. The duty of Force H was to stand off and bar the way to French or Italian intervention from seaward and so we saw nothing. It was soon learnt, however, that there was not much resistance at Algiers but considerable trouble at Oran.

*The American Admiral (Rear-Admiral M.K. Hewitt, USN) was flying his flag in the cruiser *Augusta* of Placentia memories.

The destroyer *Zetland* bombarded Fort d'Estrées on Cape Matifou, just to the east of Algiers. Only temporarily silenced, its battery began to drop shells uncomfortably close to a waiting carrier and at 14:00 next day *Bermuda* was detached from Force H to bombard. She went in to about 8,000 yards. There was no opposition and our shooting seemed to be good, the 6-inch salvoes sending up heavy mushroom-like fountains of brown earth and debris where gun emplacements showed up against the rocky hillside. Aircraft from one of the carriers also bombed this fort, which surrendered to American troops some time later.

When enemy reconnaissance had reported the convoys it was thought they were going for Malta, as so often before, and preparations made to attack later. Thus excellent opportunities were lost and the first German air attack did not come until dusk. Even so several ships were damaged and *Bermuda* and *Sheffield* were very lucky to come off scot-free, particularly the former. The two of us were in company that evening, somewhere off Algiers. The sun had just gone down when our radar picked up a considerable body of aircraft—there proved to be 23—flying low and closing rapidly. The two ships separated and were increasing to full speed when twin-engined torpedo bombers were sighted coming in over the water. They were met by a barrage as we turned hard towards and thereafter it was every man for himself on both sides. The enemy—familiar cigar-shaped Heinkel 111s—split up to operate independently and we lost visual contact with *Sheffield*, as both ships twisted and turned in the gathering gloom. For *Bermuda*'s part a thrilling duel ensued, the Captain hurling the ship about at 33 knots in a seemingly permanent convulsion. The 4-inch banged and the pom-poms thumped as the fleeting shapes were sighted first on one side and then on the other. The speed of things and the low visibility precluded director control of the 6-inch, but I requested and received, with infinite satisfaction, permission to implement 'repel torpedo bombers' and my maligned but much-practised local system came into its own in a way I had never dreamed of.

For half an hour I sat on top of 'X' turret, wearing concussion ear-pads, holding the flexible voice-pipe and bell-push, and loosing a broadside whenever opportunity arose. As described earlier, the relative slowness in training meant that I had to select a spot in the air several seconds ahead of the aircraft; if it changed course radically in the mean-time it was just too bad. Thus I would pick a target, wait until its approach course was evident and say something like 'Train right, train right. Blue (for the fuze setting). Train left. (Two toots on the bells for 20°.) Train left. Well. FIRE!' This necessitated doubling up and shutting my eyes before being engulfed in a scorching blast but I would be up again to see the result; if this was anywhere in front of the aircraft he was usually put off, as the end product exploded in an impressive triple eruption. There was no time to look for torpedo tracks, but apparently they were all about, one missing the stern by yards.

Once the ship rolled very heavily towards the enemy just as I said fire and the shells went into the water about a cricket pitch away! On another occasion three aircraft were coming in more or less together. I had ordered 10° and the roll of the ship sent the broadside into the sea just in front of the foremost aircraft and correct for line. The ensuing splash went up about 150 feet, blocking out the planes. Two reappeared round the side but to my delight there was no sign of the other. I did not claim anything as the light was so bad, but wondered . . .*

Such a 'Harry Tate' system required perfect response from the trainer and layers but this I got and it was the greatest fun despatching three 112-lb projectiles at will using the gun barrels as sights†. *Sheffield* was not so hard pressed and on completion of action—with no damage to either of us—she closed and signalled that we were showing a light. The Bo's'n's face was very red when the door of his upper deck store was found to be open with the light on inside. No wonder our friends had been so tenacious. Assuming that they carried the normal two torpedoes each they probably aimed 20 torpedoes at each ship and were plain unlucky. I am deaf enough for a small disability pension as a result of gunfire and reckon it can be put down to the Bo's'n's door as much as anything else. At the time a buzzer sounded in my ears, to the exclusion of all else, for days. *Sheffield* also said that some shell splinters had landed aboard; I was secretly grateful that no mention was made of calibre!‡

The *Bermuda* was ordered in to Algiers a little later, I think to provide AA and radar support until these had been landed. The big concrete jetties and wharves of the modern harbour contrasted with a picturesque backdrop of cascading Moorish houses giving way in turn to larger blocks behind, reminiscent of Oran but on a larger scale. As things turned out we were only there for a short time but it was not without incident, especially for me.

As the ship approached an apparently deserted jetty, sand-coloured and shimmering in the African sun, it was not known how friendly the

---

Bismarck fired her 15-inch at the *Victorious'* torpedo bombers so that the splashes rose up in front of them. One of the Swordfish (Lieutenant P.D. Gick) was lifted 30 feet, the water bursting through the bottom of the aircraft (*Naval Review*, January 1979).

†I was reminded of these words when, going through my father's effects recently, I came upon a letter from his brother, my Uncle Arthur, written from Gallipoli in the thick of the fighting in 1915. He had been sitting on a parapet of the front-line trench with a field telephone to his guns some way back, calling down fire on every Turk that moved. 'I never had so much fun in my life' he wrote.

‡*The History of the War at Sea*, Vol 4, says 'The cruisers *Sheffield* and *Bermuda* were heavily attacked, but came to no harm. Of three German aircraft destroyed that day, two fell in the Algiers area, probably during this raid.'

natives would be. In the event no-one appeared and I was slipped in a whaler with a berthing party, to land ahead and secure our hawsers to the bollards ashore. A heaving line thrown from the fo'c's'le was missed by the berthing party and fell back. The next was caught and the perspiring seamen ran away with it, dragging the big 6-inch manilla headrope to which it was attached, through the water from the approaching bow. The end appeared like a brown serpent out of the oily scum and reared slowly up to a bollard on the quay as the men strained. It caught on the lip of the quay. Hands reached down but could not get a purchase. A swell began to take the ship's bow out.

Supplementing my own exhortations, a frustrated bellow from the First Lieutenant on the fo'c's'le rubbed it in that seconds were now worth a guinea a time. Encouraging the men with all the eloquence I possessed, I became vaguely conscious of a similar commotion going on further down the jetty. Half my mind continued to query who on earth it might be; we certainly had not landed a second party. The head rope capitulated with a rush and leapt up to embrace the bollard, depositing half a dozen men in a blasphemous heap. I turned to look down the quay.

A very tall British Army officer and four soldiers in full battle kit had nearly got a wire on abreast the stern. 'Heave! Heave! Heave!' came the cry and then the peculiar Naval terminology: 'One, two, six—Now!' On went the wire.

The officer straightened up and rubbed his hands on his thighs as I advanced. He pushed back his tin hat and grinned at my look of amazement. It was Whitting, who had been a Midshipman in the *Nelson* and with me in the Air Defence Position when the bomber had attacked the *Ark Royal*. Of course he came aboard and told me how he had worked the oracle (he always wished he had joined the Army) and obtained a transfer to the Royal Artillery. The story has a sad ending as I heard not long afterwards that he had been killed, possibly in an early engagement with the Germans from Tunisia who were not slow to react to Torch.

Next stop was Bône, 300 miles to the east of Algiers. It fell to an assault from the sea the next day and thence we were ordered to support the small force concerned, securing alongside a mole. The *Bermuda* had two days' uncomfortable sojourn in this inhospitable harbour, roasted by the hot sun and nearly by man-made combustion as well. The Luftwaffe had begun to make up for lost time and was attacking targets both ashore and afloat without respite. Being only 250 miles from Sicily and 150 from Sardinia, it was not surprising that we at Bône were bombed continuously while alongside. Without the ability to manoeuvre this was unpleasant.

During one attack someone indicated a Ju 88 dive bomber right over us that appeared to have escaped attention. At the same moment the sun flashed on its wings as it tipped over and came down. The Captain was walking about on the quarterdeck. As I watched from the top of my turret a large black bomb separated in leisurely fashion from the aircraft which then pulled out and away. Feeling instinctively for the edge of the little hatch and easing my legs through, I satisfied myself that the bomb was in fact coming straight for us and then yelled to the Captain to take cover. He dived under the overhang of 'Y' turret and I retired into my own, closing the hatch. After 15 seconds nothing had happened. Only our 4-inch and close range weapons continued in a cacophony of constant noise. I waited another five seconds and then climbed up again. All was well. Below, the Captain crawled out and dusted his trousers. He looked up at me with a look that would have frozen an iceberg but I was busy scanning the horizon . . . The bomb was either a dud or it had overshot and landed in the water the other side of the mole.

The nights were fine with a bright moon which brought intensification of the attacks. Our tormentors could see us fairly easily but we could seldom see them. Guns was equal to this, however. He gave every gun in the ship a special position of elevation and training so that virtually no area of the sky was left uncovered. At the words 'blind barrage' they opened up and continued to fire at the highest possible rate until he pressed the cease-fire gong. The result was most impressive, probably not least when seen from the air, as twelve 6-inch, eight 4-inch (firing every three seconds) and a dozen pom-poms and machine-guns started up. The 4-inch and 6-inch kept up a continuous pattern of bursts above the ship, towards which tracer from the lighter guns ascended in a fan of animated light. Expenditure of ammunition being heavy, the 'Bona blind barrage' was not unleashed unthinkingly, but it was good for morale in frustrating circumstances and we certainly never got hit.

Guns went about in a sort of ecstacy during this entertainment.

Not so happy at first was the PMO, who, as Wardroom wine caterer, suffered acute exasperation because there was plenty of wine ashore but no bottles. However, every empty he could find was pressed into service and we eventually left well replenished.

By this time many German and some Italian submarines had been concentrated on both sides of the Straits of Gibraltar and were having considerable success among all the targets coming and going (including the unfortunate escort carrier *Avenger* which blew up with almost total loss). But with all the Torch troops ashore and no sign of the Italian Navy, it must have been decided that the original Force H was again sufficient in the western Mediterranean, because the ships on loan from the Home Fleet, including *Bermuda*, now started regretfully back for their northern mists.

The ship's North African foray had been a success. Hazardous experiences shared and suitably dealt with always knit a ship's company together better than months of less active occupation and, although our actions had been minor and brief, all in *Bermuda* now had their tails well up. In particular the Captain's handling of the dangerous torpedo attacks were very telling.

There was a pause at Gibraltar and I went for a leg-stretch to the new airfield. What a lot had happened since the days of Pierrot and Rocambole (among other things Madagascar had just fallen to the Marine General Sir Robert Sturges, my original patron.) It seldom pays to revisit places of happy memory; there was not one familiar object among the huts and piles of stores, only the rook-like birds still circled from the crevices high above. But my eyes were on the distant Spanish hills. The dust rising in the foreground seemed to come from a multicoloured group of men and horses as they pounded into the last turn and the sudden roar that went up came from a thousand frenzied throats . . .

We were back at Scapa by the end of November. Paravanes (PVs) were often streamed when the water was sufficiently shallow for mines, usually leaving or approaching the Flow. One such occasion was memorable. I was in charge on the fo'c's'le and we were recovering PVs, torpedo-like obejcts that, towed on wires from the bow, steered outwards each side. (If this arrowhead configuration fouled a mine the latter's mooring wire would slide out to be severed by cutters on the PV; the mine would rise to the surface and be sunk by rifle fire.) Recovery necessitated raising the towing point to within about 15 feet of the deck for a man to lean over the side and fish for the wire with a hook dangling on another wire. This could be tricky as the hook would revolve and was seldom pointing the right way at the crucial moment. I had a most experienced leading hand on the job, but there was a lot of motion on the ship and he was having no luck. After several attempts the PCO (Principal Control Officer, a Lieutenant Commander in operational control) on the bridge shouted out to hurry up. Moments later there was no success and another shout. I ignored it as chivvying only had a bad effect and there was nothing to be done but contain oneself in patience while the unfortunate man did his best. When there was a third and louder exhortation from the bridge I lost my temper— not a thing I am prone to. I turned and yelled 'Why not come down here and bloody well do it yourself!'

There were gasps of admiration (or possibly anticipation!) from the men around, but the words were hardly out of my mouth before I realised what I had said. Leaning over the side a minute later I felt a tap on my back and the PCO, having accepted my invitation, said 'Go to your cabin—you are under arrest!'

There followed an unpleasant hour or so, awaiting my fate.

Flight deck incidents.

Above *Too high and too fast.*

Left *Through the barrier.*

Below *Tragedy only days before the end of the war. Lieutenant (A) Anderson ran out of fuel only yards from the ship.*

Above *Author, on left, helps fit a strop before towing a damaged Corsair away.*

Below *'Just a horrible line' (see page 252).*

Above Formidable *seen from a destroyer shortly after the first kamikaze.*

Below *Seen from* Indomitable *after the second hit.*

Eventually the Captain's messenger arrived with a bit of folded paper. It said 'Lieutenant Brooke resume your duties' and I never heard another word about it. Later I apologised to the 'two and a half' concerned and formed the impression that someone had endorsed the sentiment, though not of course the substance, of my remark.

As already discovered in the *Nelson, Douglas* and *Prince of Wales*, life ashore at Scapa was not noted for its night spots. For the first 24 hours after a spell at sea one was glad to relax off duty; thereafter, though there was the odd film or live show in a capital ship and personally I was lucky with fencing or drawing, boredom inevitably set in. In these conditions various excesses and pranks all helped to keep one sane. Two or three stick in my mind.

It was a rare guest-night, meaning boiled shirts, the Marine band and a special menu. I was Officer of the Day; in the bad weather prevailing this usually meant eschewing the festivities to await morosely in one's cabin a call to deal with some emergency, but there was a second anchor down and I had taken a chance. 'Some hope' said Sam Hesselgrave with mock malice.

The padre's opening grace was hardly done when I became aware of a glistening oilskinned presence behind my chair. It was the Bo's'n's Mate. 'The Officer of the Watch says the wind's veering, Sir, and would you weigh the second anchor? There's power on the capstan, the cable party's been warned' and, with a glance at my bow tie, 'It's blowin' a gale.' Torps said acidly 'Counted your chickens!' but I ignored him and retired with a scowl.

A few minutes later, a pale cone of torchlight took in a pair of boots and a few dripping links of the cable as it grumbled home with interminable slowness. I stood with shoulders hunched against the rain except when sudden gusts made me grab at the rail or put a steadying hand on the steel deck. Rivulets of rusty water chased the slope of the fo'c's'le. Nobody spoke. Now and again came a clank from far below as a coil subsided in the cable locker. There was a brief tussle when the cable quivered, giving inch by inch, and then sagging surrender, accompanied by a curious 'flop'; the anchor was aweigh. I moved my torch. A yellow starfish lay on its back, small suckers contracting and expanding. The toe of a seaboot made towards it. 'Wait', I said, and to everyone's surprise bent down and put the starfish in my pocket. The men glanced at me curiously and left it at that.

Dinner had reached the savoury stage when I sat down again.

'Special for you, Sir.'

Sam viewed the oddity set before him with mixed feelings, of which distrust was uppermost. Some joke or a galley masterpiece? Mounted on a piece of toast, it presented a not unpleasant coppery top that might well have been owed to culinary art. Conversation had died and all eyes were upon him; for better or worse he made his decision. At the touch of a fork in the middle of its spineless back the starfish gave a convulsive heave and twined one feeler round the implement. Torps recoiled and what he said was fortunately drowned in a roar of laughter.

The gale increased during the night with attendant complications, and I did not peel off my sodden uniform until 02:00. Saluting the end of a rotten day with a long sigh, I put my hands on the pipe running along the deckhead and with practised ease swung up and into my bunk. Stretching luxuriously into its welcoming depths, I suddenly withdrew my legs and leapt out with a cry. A cold, clammy something had writhed at my touch. Throwing off the bedclothes, I was nearly sick, for still reposing on a piece of toast, but in a spreading pool of its own creation, sat the starfish.

For many days the ship was at sea which meant an accumulation of mail on return. Everyone was to be seen calling names, cursing their lot, or threading their way triumphantly out of the throng. The Chief Engineer had four letters, though two were bills; the Bo's'n a package from his wife, and the Marine subaltern retired to a corner with three blue envelopes and a pink face. Torps attacked his parcel with undisguised enthusiasm. What could she have sent him? Interest was universal. Two coverings of brown and three of tissue paper were unfolded in silence except for the breathing of spectators. A layer of felt was revealed and everyone craned forward. It was lifted to produce sudden anxiety for the PMO, who thought Torps was going to have a stroke, for there at the bottom of the box, looking very depressed, was the starfish.

But Sam had the last laugh. I entered the Wardroom to see him confiding in a grinning group and to catch '. . . his cabin, he'll never find it and it's going to smell *awful*!' They dispersed guiltily and the doubts started there. Every time I went into my cabin I sniffed; the habit grew and I began to sniff everywhere. It was a low blow to have retrieved the brown paper from Torp's wastepaper basket to use again, but he was getting his own back. With the technicians at his disposal he could have done anything with wooden panels, deck covering . . . or had he done nothing? I never knew.

Another incident concerned Dickie Griffiths, the 'Major' of Marines, and Reg Harper-Smith, a young Paymaster Lieutenant. They would do a turn on guest nights which was invariably demanded as soon as the feats of physical prowess had begun to pall. It was of no profound wit, but a firm favourite due to the undoubted talent with which they carried it off. Portrayed were two exiles in 'white man's grave' surroundings. One of them would describe his downfall, which turned out to have been caused by the other. The heart of the performance was that every so often a handclap would summon a well versed steward with a double

214

gin. This, in reality only water, was lowered in one gulp, the actors becoming more and more 'inebriated' in the most hilarious fashion.

On the occasion in question, however, someone went 'back stage' and to the terror of the steward, substituted the real thing, neat, for the water which was ready ranged in a dozen glasses. It was expensive, but worth it.

The scene began. The first handclap heralded the first glass. When both had recovered from the ensuing spasms there was just the hint of a pause, as they realised what was in store. One cocked an eyebrow at the other, signalling 'Does the show go on?' To their credit, at least most agreed so, it did; handclap after handclap, gin after gin. The consternation of the steward was pitiful to see as he bore in salver after lethal salver, but among the audience there was only one who realised that the antics which were keeping us speechless with laughter were only too genuine—until both passed out.

The 'Major' was all right, but poor Harper-Smith became quite ill, with, presumably, alcoholic poisoning. It was ten years before I found myself again with Dickie Griffiths, and owned up to being the perpetrator of their predicament.

Another of the redoubtable Major's party tricks was eating glass. He would take a tumbler in his teeth, bite off a largish section and chew it with no apparent ill effects. I saw this done by someone else later— with no possibility of fraud—and am still astonished by it.

'No 1' (The First Lieutenant, Lieutenant Commander R.P.S. Grant) also had a trick which was equally popular though unfortunately he only did it once. The object was to jerk the table cloth out from under a mass of cutlery, china and glass, without disturbing same. He gripped the cloth, took an almighty heave and projected the whole lot into a corner of the Wardroom with a sound like our shells bursting on Fort d'Estrée!

All that could be said for Christmas 1942 at Scapa was that it was better than its Malayan predecessor. The last day of the old year saw us make a rush departure from the Flow in company with the C-in-C in *KG V* and the latter's new sister *Howe*. Admiral Tovey had just received reports of a highly successful action in defence of the eastbound Russian convoy JW51A but was hurrying to provide heavy support should the German ships return to the attack.

Two or three major warships could annihilate a number of merchant vessels in minutes, yet to keep an adequate defending force at sea on the offchance was to risk it running out of fuel when most wanted. With the progress of the slow convoys predictable to the enemy once sighted by his aircraft or U-boats, Admiral Tovey's was no easy task. The *Tirpitz* had stepped into the massive seaboots of her dead twin *Bismarck* and resuscitated the latter's power to threaten; so much so that in July an erroneous belief that the *Tirpitz* was at sea had caused the First Sea Lord to scatter convoy PQ17, with the result that 23 out of 36 ships were lost to U-boats or aircraft attacks. Success or failure was a finely balanced matter indeed. I think it was to underline this before our first proper convoy operation that the cruiser Admiral came on board from his flagship *Kent*, when we returned to Scapa after cruising uneventfully a thousand miles to the north. He was Rear-Admiral 'Turtle' Hamilton, my first Captain in the *Prince of Wales*. Standing on the quarterdeck capstan—he was very small—to promise 'blood, toil, tears and sweat' he was sure there would be a repetition of the last attack. Certainly everything pointed to it when we sailed on about January 20 to cover convoy JW52 to Russia.

This had left Loch Ewe, where the *Nelson* had been mined exactly three years before, and following the usual winter route steered north until reaching about latitude 71°. Then shaping parallel to the Norwegian coast it kept 600 miles off to give the Luftwaffe as little chance as possible. 'Turtle' Hamilton's responsibility was to cover the convoy across the top of Norway while it gradually closed the coast— past the enemy's lair at Altenfiord—to arrive at a point whence it could drop due south to Kola Inlet in Russia. Of course the convoy was keeping W/T silence and when it was located the three cruisers found themselves a little astern, exactly where U-boats tended to congregate before attack. Most of us in *Bermuda* were unaware of this latter gem of intelligence as we sped across behind the lines of squat, stoical ships, in company with, I think, *Glasgow*. But we nearly learnt the hard way because, when German records eventually became available, it was found that *U-625* had fired a salvo of torpedoes—with every prospect of success—at both of us.

With good radar showing up ships for many miles one was not as blind as previously in these waters; but against this there were only some three hours of darkness. The long periods of watchfulness provided an added strain, and though the enemy obliged, surprisingly, by doing nothing unpleasant, the thermometer hardly conformed.

The cold was intense and became steadily worse until we reached our zenith of 73° 30' N (950 miles from the North Pole). There had been an issue of good arctic clothing, including a Russian-type hat with descending flaps, but one's face had to be in evidence. The cold of my *Douglas'* experience was nothing to this, as ice appeared all over the ship's upperworks. It transfigured rigging and boat's falls to fairy-like trails, jammed the smaller guns which had to be perpetually freed with low pressure steam jets, made walking dangerous and life generally miserable. Poorly protected against cold by nature, and not being long out of the tropics, I felt the conditions more than most. The temptation to crowd round an electric fire on coming off watch was irresistible and gave everyone terrible chilblains.

Instead of the usual about-turn when the convoy had reached a safe position, we went right through to its destination. The white hills of Russia were to starboard on January 27 as a posse of Soviet destroyers came out to shepherd us in to Vaenga, a small port on the Kola Inlet, not far from Murmansk. A Russian liaison officer came on board as soon as we had anchored and remained for our three-day stay. He was a smart, upstanding fellow who spoke good English and had a sense of humour. I asked him where he came from and he said Siberia. Rather facetiously and regretting it at once I said 'I thought that's only where people are sent to', but he smiled, 'Oh, we do come from there sometimes!'

There were two macabre incidents. A British submarine was in and one of her officers told us, apparently truthfully, that they had been berthed alongside a Russian boat and had invited her Wardroom over for what ended up as a very convivial party indeed. One of the Russians somewhat disgraced himself. Next morning both boats were waiting to slip and the British CO shouted across to the Russian conning tower asking how the miscreant was. There was no response but when he persisted the other CO replied grimly 'We shoot him'. The general impression was that indeed they had.

The other incident concerned the hospital ashore, whence a party of us repaired to borrow skis from the resident RNVR doctor, lent to deal with casualties from convoys. The hospital, bare stone inside and out, was spartan in the extreme. As we toiled up a spiral staircase laid with straw, bloodcurdling screams came from nearby. Someone asked the doctor, who had taken no notice, what on earth it was. 'Oh, a minor operation' was the casual reply, 'they are short of anaesthetics.'

He duly provided several pairs of skis and we took them through the snow to a gentle slope on the outskirts of the town, passing log houses and lines of disembarked Martin Maryland bombers and Hurricane fighters. Some of the locals wore snow-shoes but not skis and when we started fooling about under a Canadian expert in the party, a curious crowd of flat-nosed Eskimo-like peasants gathered to watch with deadpan expressions. We enjoyed ourselves hugely, roaring with laughter and of course falling all over the place, while the spectators surveyed the mad foreigners without the flicker of a smile. There were no contacts that I remember, nothing to be bought and a generally depressing atmosphere ashore so that we were not sorry to depart.

The next westbound convoy was picked up and covered on its return voyage. Again there was surprising lack of enemy action, only one ship being lost to U-boat attack. Instead, as far as the *Bermuda* was concerned, there were undoubtedly friendly encounters. En route for Scapa we put in to Hvalfiord in Iceland; making oneself understood to the blonde shop girls of Reykjavik was in hilarious contrast to our Russian experience.

HMS *Bermuda*
6/1/43

We are back again after quite a good trip. A Colonel Kennedy wrote to me about Colonel Warren saying would I go and see him when convenient as they wanted to make some recommendation for him. Mrs Warren has been officially informed that he is a prisoner of war. I will thank Aunt Emily for the sheepskin cuffs; I needn't say they're too small. Perhaps they will fit better on another part of my anatomy! The cold is certainly no respecter of locality. The temperature on the last trip was 29°F.

When I did visit Colonel Kennedy in Baker Street it was to find a number of Army officers in a nondescript house and somewhat clan-destine atmosphere, discovered later to be the Special Operations Executive HQ (the SOE, to which Warren, Lyon, Campbell and the others belonged). Surprised to learn this was the first they had heard of the Sumatran operations, I wrote reports on Colonel Warren, Colonel Dillon and Major Nicholson (all survived and I was to meet the latter eventually). Warren (actually Ferguson-Warren, I found) ended up with the CBE and DSC; I hope I was able to repay him in some measure by having a small part in one of these.

Meanwhile misfortune had struck the ship a dreadful blow:

HMS *Bermuda*
1/4/43

... We had an awful tragedy last week. The Commander and Gunnery Officer were washed overboard in a gale. The Gunnery Officer was picked up all right but not the Commander. The saddest part about it was that he was due to be relieved on the very day he was lost, and his relief was waiting when we got back. He was an awfully nice man and it is so dreadful for his wife.

This came about when recovering paravanes. The sea was rough with a short, steep swell coming from right ahead. The Commander, who was not happy about the conditions, went down on to the fo'c's'le to give moral support. The work was virtually complete—they were 'stopping' the paravane towing wires to the guardrails—when the ship went ahead and turned back into the sea. The Gunnery Officer, who was in charge, was just abaft the port hawse pipe, the Commander and the ratings on the other side a little further aft.

As she gathered speed the ship's bow rose and fell two or three times and then suddenly dropped right into a mass of oncoming water. This surged 'green' over the fo'c's'le. Most were able to hang on to some-thing but the Commander, Guns, a Petty Officer and, I think, another, were washed over the side. The last two were swept back again

218

at once—as sometimes happens—but to everyone's horror the Commander and Guns were seen to be struggling in the rough water and dropping quickly astern. A Petty Officer called Scott, who happened to be painting a carley float in the waist with a couple of men, quickly threw it over the side. The Captain brought the ship round in a 360° turn and thanks to the float—visible from time to time on the crest of a wave—was able to bring the ship back to the exact spot, skilfully putting her across the sea to make a lee for the luckless two. The Commander was just visible for a short time floating face down and then he disappeared. It was much too rough to lower a boat. A scrambling net had been thrown over the side but stopped well short of the water.

Guns, who had been shouting to the Commander to keep him going, was now in a bad state himself. Thrown a heaving line he grabbed it, wound it round himself and tried to tie a bowline, but his fingers were frozen and all he could do was to take a turn and hang on to the end. He was pulled towards the ship through huge waves and they lowered a lifebelt to him on a light grass hawswer. Managing to get into the lifebelt, he was hauled up and lifted over the guardrail—unable to take any part himself—and collapsed on the deck. Under a cloud of depression—hundreds were on deck by now—the ship got under way again. The water was icy cold and Guns frozen stiff when taken down to the Sick Bay; if he had not been of powerful physique he would probably have succumbed. He owed his life to this, the quick thinking of Petty Officer Scott, and the actions of the First Lieutenant—he was directing those on the spot at the culmination of this sad affair. With hindsight it is easy enough to conclude that the accident was caused by an error of judgement on the part of Captain Back. But one should remember that things are not so easy in the stress of the moment and the Captain was responsible for the safety of the ship and for every life on board; we were at the time a sitting target for a submarine and it was his duty to be on a steady course and at reduced speed for the minimum time possible.

We learnt later that Commander Griffith was considered in high places to be a near certainty for flag rank. There was one satisfactory postscript in that Petty Officer Scott received the DCM for his vital action.

A remarkably sudden and unpleasant development for me was a bad attack of haemorrhoids. Doctors in the hospital ship where I was sent for a second opinion insisted on the knife and it was decided that I should be landed at the next mainland port of call. The operation was no picnic in those days, but there would be sick leave to follow and I looked forward eagerly to reunion with John Persse and combined operations concerning the London night-life in which I knew he revelled. Leaving *Bermuda* when she put in to Plymouth after escorting an Atlantic convoy, I was sorry to say goodbye to Guns, Torps and other friends, not forgetting my 6-inch turret. The Captain thoughtfully discharged me to HMS *President* (London) as this would mean a hospital nearer my home, but arrival was marred by the news that John had in fact sailed for the Middle East only a few days before. Our monumental 'run ashore' was not to be.

From North Africa his letters became, if anything, more full of fun than ever. Always seeing the humorous side, he enjoyed regimental soldiering and must, I knew, be a wonderful 'shipmate' to his brother officers of the Rifle Brigade and without doubt the men too. Our circumstances were now reversed, he was roughing it and I, if not in the lap of luxury, was at least getting all night in.

Brand new, the Royal Masonic Hospital was under a famous surgeon who practised the excellent principle that young men convalesce best surrounded by pretty faces. This was explained by the three other inmates of my ward as I arrived, goggle-eyed at the VAD pulchritude passed in the passage. 'Ours is a redhead' said one, 'but it's no use trying anything on, she's got a boyfriend in the RAF.' The redhead came in, well up to scratch, and exclaimed on the cleanliness of my feet as I was getting into bed. 'Oh we wash our feet in the Navy' I said, 'not like the RAF,' which took some time to live down.

When the hour for the operation arrived there was no sign of the offending piles, reduced by the unaccustomed rest. 'Now you're here', said the surgeon, 'is there anything else the matter with you?', and without an inkling that it would keep me ashore for many months I admitted to a painful knee. This was diagnosed as cartilage trouble and an operation performed. After sick leave over-eating with relatives in Ireland the piles returned with a vengeance and I was back in hospital again. Appointment to HMS *St George* in the Isle of Man followed. This, the RN Boys Training Establishment (evacuated from those at Shotley and Gosport), was enjoyable except for the invariably rough crossing from Fleetwood (spent by me in ignominious solitude lest my seasickness should be observed by my 16-year-old charges, not all of whom were afflicted!) and an incident shared with another divisional officer, a young Lieutenant Commander called Errol Bruce.

We took away the establishment's entire complement of cutters and whalers for a weekend's circumnavigation of the island, got into trouble off a lee shore and wrote off the lot on breaker-lashed rocks. No one was killed but on return the two 'admirals'—we were divided into fleets for exercise purposes—were most apprehensive as to how the Captain was going to take this. Actually he just laughed ('Hooky' Bell of the *Exeter*, he was no stranger to misfortune himself, having conned the ship from aft with a boat's compass when the *Graf Spee* wrecked his bridge).

We had a very good show last night and I took care to look after the blonde acrobatic dancer when they came into the Wardroom afterwards. The Commander is an expert billiard player and is usually to be seen with some other expert studying the line of a shot. I got a life out of him by asking if it would be in order for the dancer to do the splits for us on the billiard table.

Why don't you take on the Chairmanship? I think it would be a jolly good idea. Nobody deserves it more than you or knows more about it so why hold back, as Uncle Atty would say?

Well done Henry getting the MC. What a good show. Uncle Basil and Aunt Essex must be pleased. I hope to goodness Bill Buckhurst wasn't one of the Arnhem group was he?

How annoying about the ducks, the drake had better be run in for failure in execution of his duty! The invasion seems to be going extraordinarily easily, it must have been wonderfully planned. I went to a big "Salute the Soldier" dance and in the scrum for coats and hats at the end a two badge AB came up to me wreathed in smiles and said 'You're Lieutenant Brooke, aren't you, Sir? The last time I saw you was in the *Prince of Wales* just before it sank and you sang out to some of us to stand up and not be such damn fools, it was only a few small bombs dropping—I've always remembered that, Sir, I've always remembered that!' and, giving me a hearty handshake, disappeared into the crowd before I could open my mouth!

It would suit me to leave at the end of this term, but I must say I hope not before as everything is going OK.

PS. Such a big bomb landed in Hyde Park the other day that it blew all the 'ats off the American soldiers!*

Having run a large part of the Sussex Women's Land Army since the war began, my mother had received feelers about her taking over the whole from Lady De la Warr, who had done a long stint. She did, in fact, take over and run the county with distinction until the WLA was disbanded. Bill Buckhurst was the De la Warr's eldest son, a parachute officer. He survived the war but at this time it was one of the strains on his parents that their second son, Harry, was missing. Slight and fair, he was a most attractive character—not unlike John—who could charm anyone and anything; we had been on several evenings together and I still have an evocative piece of paper that introduced me to the 'private parties' held at the 400 Club on the recommendation of the Hon Harry Sackville. I had last seen him on a recent leave, when he came over with his mother and we strolled about in the garden. The outlook was black at the time and I said so. 'Oh, I don't let it bother me,' he replied with his quick smile; 'I ignore the radio and the papers and just get on with my job.' I marvelled at the steel core that had been just beneath the

*Readers of the present generation may have to ask their elders about this!

rather playboy exterior all the time. His job was flying the new American Mustang fighter at zero feet on sweeps across France. One day he simply did not come back. There never was any news of him, which was, I think, the hardest form of tragedy for families, and sorrowing friends, to bear.

Meanwhile, my knee was behaving no better than it had before and, after X-rays and acrimonious messages had been exchanged between our PMO and the Royal Masonic Hospital, I found myself being ushered into a ward yet again. This time it was the naval hospital at Sherborne. One day an entire aircrew came in, all bad, and one of them died. I felt a terrible impostor with my miserable knee.

All this took time and it was mid-1944 before I was back in circulation, plus a stick. On June 26 I ended a letter home: 'John is evidently seeing a good deal of fighting. I see his regiment and the 16th Lancers were the first into Perugia'. It was only too true that John had been seeing a good deal of fighting. It never entered my head that anything was wrong when I was told there was a telegram for me. It said he had been killed on the 20th.

I could not believe it, staring at the form quite numb. Surely there must be some mistake; other people got killed but not John. I told myself I would not see him again, but it just did not seem possible, his laughing face kept coming between me and anything I did. The thought of him lying buried in some Italian hillside was just a bad dream that would somehow come right and, clutching at any straw, I read again his last letter, full of life if ever a letter was. Soon I began to receive letters from others in the family and these seemed to really bring it home. Then, crowning misery, there arrived one from John himself, written a few days before he was killed. It said 'The going is hard' and I knew it must have been very hard.

A light seemed to go out of my life from that day.

Enquiries to Keith Egleston, who I know was a great friend in the Regiment, eventually brought the following reply:

The attack that Johnnie was killed in was a memorable one, for the Battalion captured that night a hill that dominated the whole of the ground north of Perugia, and held it against all counter attacks. We were personally congratulated by the Army, and Corps Commander, and unlike so many casualties that happen in war, through odd stray shells, mines, etc, Johnnie's was met in the most gallant fashion possible, and was not in vain. His Platoon was attacking a house that was held by German snipers, and they had to cross a flat piece of ground to approach it. The Germans brought down very heavy mortar fire and wounded several men in his Platoon.

During this very critical stage he was quite magnificent and kept the Platoon together. They got the house, and were pushing on past it, when a bomb wounded one of his men close to him; he immediately went to help him, and render first aid, and whilst doing this, a bomb landed right on top of him; he was killed outright. After his death, the Platoon went completely to pieces, so much so that they had to be disbanded and split up amongst the rest of the company, which shows what a tremendous influence he had on them.

I managed to get his body in, two days later; it was not, unfortunately, possible before owing to accursed snipers from neighbouring hills, and he is now buried in Perugia . . .

His parents received over 600 letters of sympathy from Generals to Privates and the equivalent in civilian life. There is, I think, a tendency to eulogise about someone who has died; at least to give the benefit of the doubt. This did not apply to letters about John. All were straight from the heart and anyway there was not a doubt to be considered. His Commanding Officer, Lieutenant Colonel D.L. Darling wrote:

'He was loved by all of us and his Platoon absolutely worshipped him. He was as brave as a lion in action and had all those qualities of initiative, daring, resource and the knack of getting people to do what he wanted, which are the hallmark of good leadership . . .'

From his Company Commander, Major Charles Mott-Radclyffe:

'I am writing to you with a very heavy heart . . . His death has cast a gloom amongst us, and nowhere greater than with me ... I always used to go over to his tent or truck and gossip about home and racing and other unwarlike things with him. He was always cheerful and never failed to see the funny side.'

From Colonel Charles McGregor, from whom he received his commission:

'. . . I had about a thousand young officers through my hands during the time I commanded, out of which about ten or a dozen were outstanding, and he was one of them. He had an amazing control of men for a boy of his age.'

There was a long one from Surgeon Lieutenant Commander Maurice Partridge, RNVR, with whom he had struck up on the way out:

'. . . I was particularly glad when Johnnie would come into Alexandria and see me. Sometimes he would ring me up and (quite imperiously) bid me out to dine, it was a long way and nearly always inconvenient but I always went . . .

'All those talents, I noticed made him an obvious favourite even in his outstanding Regiment, and it was striking how batmen, drivers, orderlies and so on would do things for him, for which others sighed in vain . . .'

There is a wealth of meaning in 'it was a long way and nearly always inconvenient but I always went'. It takes me back to a hundred boyhood incidents. Where John was concerned there was never any question of not having a go; he was not unreasonably forceful but afterwards you realised it had never entered your head to refuse. But the words John himself would have liked best were from his Platoon Sergeant, P.G. Wright, 'A' Coy, 7th RB:

'He was a great leader and an example to us all in his courage, endurance and cheerfulness. I cannot express what I feel at your and our irreplaceable loss, sufficient to say, the whole platoon knows we can never have another officer quite like J.H.P.'

John would now be grey, I suppose, lined and probably putting on weight; but all I see is a slim, freckled, sunburnt young man, with thick hair and laughing eyes that in some magnetic way put all around at rights with the world.

His death, and a letter from a cousin of Colonel Warren's (enclosing one from a Japanese prison camp, which said simply 'Well'), reminded me I had been ashore too long and that—remembering Warren's parting words 'to be useful to the war effort in other theatres'—I had an eastern debt to pay. With the *Tirpitz* and the *Scharnhorst* sunk and the Italian fleet surrendered, they were refitting ships for the Pacific and there might not be much more time. So I had myself passed fit and volunteered for a ship in the Far East.

An appointment came almost by return and was something of a shock. It was to HMS *Formidable*, the large fleet carrier last seen during the 'Torch' landings in North Africa. A shock because carriers were not usually popular ships with their seaman complement, being physically awkward to operate and suffering from a split personality. The Air Arm were inclined to look on a ship as a floating runway and its seamen as chauffeurs; the latter resented both this and the aviators' nautical ignorance. So this appointment was not altogether good news, even if a carrier was sure to see a lot of action. There was certainly nothing to indicate that *Formidable* was going to provide about the most satisfying commission of my career.

While en route for India in a troopship towards the end of 1944, my destination was changed to another carrier, HMS *Indomitable*, no reason being given. Deposited on a hot concrete waterfront at Trincomalee with nothing on hand except a very large lizard that was losing a battle with a sort of crow, I experienced considerable deflation; the carrier element of the British Pacific Fleet (BPF) had just left on a sortie eastwards. Venturing, on their return, among my new messmates in the *Indomitable*'s Wardroom was to register further if highly personal disappointment. Flying the flag of Vice-Admiral Aircraft Carriers, Vice Admiral Sir Phillip Vian of Narvik, *Bismarck* and much Mediterranean fame, they had been to Sumatra and actually cruised up and down just north of Padang, trailing their coats and despatching aircraft to bomb oilfields inland. (Departure had been between the islands of Simalur and Nias, the latter well remembered for alternate *sumatras* and calms.) There had been little Japanese reaction. What a change from April

1942! It would have been quite something to have returned to the very spot I had set out from and in such a way.

The other carriers were *Indefatigable* (fairly new), *Victorious* (personally remembered for her *Bismarck* and 'Torch' participations) and *Illustrious*, of Malta and many other battles. Of course, *Indomitable* was the one which could have made so much difference to *Prince of Wales* and *Repulse*.

Apart from the near-miss described, the timing of my arrival was not too bad. The BPF had only been formed—under its C-in-C, Admiral Sir Bruce Fraser—in the last few weeks from the more powerful elements of Admiral Somerville's Eastern Fleet (he had been at its head ever since *Djohanis'* naval members had drunk his gin in the *Warspite*) plus some additions from home. These included the battleships *KG V* and *Howe*, the former becoming the flagship of Admiral Fraser's Second in Command, Vice Admiral Sir Bernard Rawlings.

The BPF would be using Sydney as a rear base, looking in there before being placed at the disposal of the US Navy's C-in-C Pacific Ocean Area, Admiral Nimitz. It would rank as but one of his task forces, whose Admirals were junior to Fraser; partly to avoid this but mainly because of the vast amount of organisation on his plate, the latter had decided to remain ashore at Sydney, leaving Vice-Admiral Rawlings in charge at sea. This command structure seemed at first rather complicated, but one soon found—as a carrier officer—that one looked to Vian, and frankly only thought of his seniors at rare moments. I had never seen Admiral Vian before. With a tremendous reputation as a fighter, he was said to be a bit of a tiger all round, and as quarterdeck officer I was glad to have had considerable experience of the foibles of Admirals. Living, of course, immediately under my domain in harbour, he was of medium height, spare with ginger hair, craggy features ending in a firm jaw, and a direct look from under bushy eyebrows that was rather disconcerting.

The fleet put to sea on January 13 for the four carriers to exercise a full scale air attack on Colombo in the morning with fighter sweeps on Trincomalee and another place in the afternoon. I joined the 'goofers' in a special walkway alongside the flight deck right aft and was thrilled as the heavy Avengers and tubby Hellcat fighters roared down the deck, to return later with a thump and squeal of tyres only feet away. It was surprising to find that most of the fleet's aircraft were American. Each carrier had around 20 Grumman Avengers, deep-bellied torpedo-spotter-reconnaissance-bombers topped with distinctive 'glasshouses' through which the heads and shoulders of the three-man crew could be clearly seen, and some 36 fighters of various types.

These numbers were about half what equivalent American carriers had. The reason related to a basic design decision. Our ships had heavily armoured flight-decks and theirs did not, the weight saved going into the additional aircraft. At this time, the US Pacific Fleet, quadrupled since Pearl Harbor by prodigious building efforts, had reaped and was continuing to enjoy ferocious revenge, particularly in the Marianas. The Japanese Navy had lost hundreds of aircraft with, more importantly, their trained crews, and was turning to the desperate solution of the Special Attack Corps of suicide planes. Though the additional aircraft of a US carrier were most valuable, the ships themselves were proving highly vulnerable to the diving kamikazes (meaning 'divine wind') which went straight through to create havoc below. We did not know about the American decks at this time and as word of the new menace came through we could only wonder what it was like to be on the receiving end.

The activity over Ceylon turned out to be a dummy run for a big attack (it proved to be the biggest Fleet Air Arm operation of the war so far, with nearly 150 aircraft engaged) on the important Japanese oil refineries at Palembang, specially requested by Admiral Nimitz. (Palembang, near the east coast of Southern Sumatra, was the place taken by parachutists when I was at Iyer Molek.) A force of oilers had been sent on ahead and on January 16 we sailed to rendezvous with them and replenish. The equator was soon crossed and of course the heat was terrific. I soon found that a carrier—its thick steel flight deck acting as a sort of cauldron—was undoubtedly the hottest type of ship afloat. Tropical uniform made the most of any breeze, forced draft and fans large and small did their best, but one went about below in a perpetual sweat that soaked three shirts a day. An allied and unpleasant development for me was that for the second half of a four-hour watch on the bridge I found my legs becoming very painful from varicose veins, not an entirely new experience but never serious before.

The ship's main gun armament consisted of a battery of two twin 4.5-inch turrets at each corner of the flight deck. I found I was in charge of the two forward batteries and so for the first time ever was below decks. In the early hours of January 24 1945, the fleet was in the flying off position and at 06:15 Admiral Vian gave the go-ahead. It was a flight of 220 miles to the target, of which 150 were over land.

The aircraft thundered down the deck overhead at regular intervals but, at action stations, I saw nothing and spent the time strolling between the two batteries looking as competent as possible. After some hours the aircraft began to land on again. It all seemed rather impersonal until, after the fleet had withdrawn and relaxation in the Wardroom was the order of the day, I listened and watched for the first time while pilots and observers relived their doings with pithy and sometimes hilarious descriptions, plus much graphic gesticulation with both hands. Every now and again there was a pause as a name was mentioned and I knew that behind the scenes there was melancholy activity in the cabins of those who had not come back.

Four days later there was a repeat performance against Palembang. Again the tantalising roars overhead. Silence descended on the last one away, but there was no long wait this time. The CAP (Combat Air Patrol) of Seafires was prowling round overhead when suddenly a 'tally ho' report from one of them indicated that he had a 'Tojo' fighter in sight*. It duly escaped into cloud but we had been spotted and could expect attention soon. In fact for some time there were intermittent sightings and brief encounters in the lowering, watery sky that occasionally emptied into dense rainstorms. A Japanese fighter was shot down, but so was a Seafire, a Corsair patrol returned one short from a brush with an enemy group and yet another was detected probing from the southward.

The air strike then began to land on. Six badly damaged Avengers ditched near various ships, but only one aircrew was not picked up. All who were going to do so had returned by about 11:30. Not long after, seven 'bogies' were detected 25 miles to the south-east; soon they were in sight from *Illustrious*, the nearest carrier, and proved to be 'Sally' twin-engined bombers. Two Corsairs were put on to them and one shot down a Sally eight miles from the fleet. The various alarms had kept us on our toes, but the effect was beginning to wear off when suddenly the 'Alarm port! Follow director!' that I had not heard for too long sent the guns of the port battery slewing round, motors humming and hydraulics squelching as the layers and trainers picked up their pointers.

The barrels were at a lowish elevation and only traversing slowly when the guns went off, the smoking, empty cases bouncing on to the deck behind. Firing every few seconds, this continued until the barrels dropped ominously. 'Barrage Red!' yelled the communication number and up went shells from the rack. Presumably we were firing at torpedo bombers which had dived to sea level and were coming in on their final run. *Crash!* 'Barrage White.' *Crash!* A slight vibration, allied to a familiar, rhythmic thudding indicated that the pom-poms had taken up the running; then silence. 'Return to lookout bearing' and the loading numbers climbed down to manhandle the brass empties into a corner of the gun-bay.

Apparently there had been a pretty sharp action, all over in less than five minutes. The fleet had turned away to starboard, after which four of the remaining six aircraft went for *Illustrious* and *Indefatigable* on the port side of the circular formation, the other two working round the rear towards *KG V, Victorious* and ourselves, to come under general fire

*Japanese fighters were given boys' names, other aircraft girls'.

as they approached. By this time *Indom* had 'scrambled' three Hellcats; one shot down a Sally immediately and went on to share another with *KG V*. *Indefat*'s Seafires, in their element, chased one Sally through the fleet's barrage until it crashed into the sea only 300 yards off their parent ship. Also chased by Seafires, another had come at *Illustrious* very low and was shot down just off her bow. Yet another was shot down by gunfire astern of her and the last of the seven succumbed, off *KG V*'s starboard beam, to one of her pom-poms. There had been no damage at the hands of the enemy, but on the debit side some of them had been allowed to get too close for comfort, one of our Hellcats returned badly peppered, and worse, two shells from a cruiser had hit *Illustrious*, causing a number of casualties.

The strike—on a different refinery at Palembang—had gone well, but the enemy were expecting us (they may have got information out of captives) and the cost had been greater. Losses from all causes for the two attacks were 41 out of 378 sorties, bad enough at nearly one in ten, with 30 aircrew missing. It was not known of course at the time, but of these, nine poor devils were taken alive, one being a Sub-Lieutenant from *Indomitable*. They were brought to Singapore and eventually beheaded by the chivalrous knights of 'bushido', the Japanese code of honour. (Some time later an American magazine most irresponsibly came out with a large picture of a bearded British Sub-Lieutenant, kneeling, with a Japanese soldier alongside, sword high in the air. It may have been carefully planted as propaganda, but I fear was authentic enough.)

The enemy lost 68 aircraft, 38 on the ground and 30 in the air, with another seven probables. Production at the last refinery attacked proved to be nil until the end of March, when both were producing at one third capacity; this was increased only to half by the end of May and full production was never regained during the war. Our Captain, J.A.S. Eccles, was a Japanese interpreter and put out to the fleet translations of statements he heard on the enemy radio. These spoke of enormous British losses and of the fact that our attackers had been suicide planes, all of which had crashed on their targets!

Three weeks later the fleet entered Sydney's beautiful harbour, the *Indomitable* turning short of the famous bridge to come alongside in a naval dock area with the extraordinary name of Woolloomooloo ('Wuller'm'loo').

Robin Buller, Sandy's younger brother, was now a two-striper in the destroyer *Ursa* and we had several pleasant runs ashore together, particularly to Sydney races.

HMS *Indomitable*
22/2/45

. . . On Sunday we went bathing at a well-known surf beach called Bondi with a

228

girl I had met at a dance. We ended up showing them (there was a girl friend of hers too) round *Indom* . . .

Whether I realised it or not, the 'Battle of Sydney' had in fact begun. The hospitality was so overwhelming that after a spell one was to be almost (but not quite!) glad to go to sea for the sterner but hardly less exhausting struggle. My father had been in Australian waters as a young Lieutenant in 1912 and I was particularly lucky with an introduction to a charming, middle-aged lady called Nell Knox. We clicked and she gave me a room for myself in her large house overlooking Elizabeth Bay.

I had come to think I knew most of my way round the *Indomitable* when a signal arrived reappointing me to HMS *Formidable*. She was held up somewhere and not expected for two or three weeks. The PMO had said I needed an operation on my legs and this seemed an excellent chance. The fleet had sailed for the forward area when I came out of hospital but there was not long to wait for my new ship.

9

Kamikaze

When HMS *Formidable* approached the jetty at Woolloomoolloo on March 10 I stood looking up at her great grey bulk with understandably mixed feelings. She looked much like the *Indomitable*, but in fact as a sister of *Illustrious* and *Victorious* was a couple of years older.

Having said my traditional joining piece to the Officer of the Watch I repaired to the spacious Wardroom and was musing on the last occasion of being there—bearded and somewhat lighter in weight from *Sederhana Djohanis*—when a large hand descended on my shoulder and a pleasant Canadian voice said 'My relief I believe?' I turned to find an immensely tall Lieutenant—he made my six feet look diminutive—who introduced himself as McPhee. After a few pleasantries, 'What's the job?' I asked. 'You're Fire and Crash Officer and Chief Flight Deck Director.' 'I'm *what*?' He laughed. 'Yes, it's a bit unusual; you are part of the flying organisation when at sea, not allowed below the flight deck in fact. In harbour, you're the Commander's Assistant.' 'But what on earth is a Flight Deck Director?' He explained that, when taxiing, the nose of an aircraft stuck up in the air so that the pilot could not see his way ahead and relied on hand signals from a Director to one side. The half dozen Flight Deck Directors were all 'fish-heads'—seamen officers—including the Captain of Marines.

Some time back the Fleet Air Arm officers so employed had indulged in a number of prangs until the Captain, fuming, had said 'Bring on the seamen officers, it's only common sense!' The 'A' boys had stood back and waited for the inevitable smash-ups, but there weren't any and to their chagrin the system had become permanent. 'It's an excellent idea anyway', said McPhee (who I soon learnt was called 'Moose'; with a large proboscis and equally prominent adam's apple, he did look rather like one), 'because it gives the ship's company a stake in the flightdeck. There's none of the "them and us" you so often get and she runs like clockwork.'

Responsible for action at all flight-deck fires and crashes, I would have a large specialist fire party and live entirely in the island at sea. A full turnout of the other ship's officers would only be required for operating a good number of aircraft—so I was the Chief Flight Deck

Director. I must have looked a bit rueful. 'It's not very difficult really', said McPhee. 'Only common sense; just like the Captain said.' He went on to indicate that the Captain (Philip Ruck-Keene) was a ball of fire, adding rather ominously that I would find that out soon enough anyway. It struck me that Moose was something of a ball of fire himself and might be a hard man to follow.

'Come and meet the Captain and the Commander; then we'll have a good look round.' Both were naturally preoccupied with the business of arrival; the Captain shot me a steely look, the Commander (D.H. Fuller, very good looking with curly grey hair) indicated a discussion later and I was soon following my leader, who stopped to introduce me from time to time on the tortuous route to a hangar. Its central fire-curtain being up, this stretched nearly the whole length of the ship and held a conglomeration of Corsairs and Avengers which were being worked on by their ground crews, oily near-naked bodies dripping with sweat. Throughout was the distinctive aroma of 'dope', that most evocative of all smells to anyone who has served in a carrier. A strident bell pealed its warning at which we ran for the after lift—a cut-out section of the deck operated by huge 'bicycle chains' at the sides—that wafted us, in company with an Avenger with its wings folded back, to the welcome breezes of the flight-deck.

The fire-fighting equipment of this near 800-foot expanse was headed by eight red machines, strategically placed around the perimeter just below deck level. They looked basic but were apparently efficient enough, big open coffers into which were poured the contents of adjacent drums of a stinking glutinous liquid, 'I believe its mainly blood from slaughter houses', said my mentor. 'Terrible stuff, you mustn't get it on your clothes.' A fire hose extended from one end with a special five foot nozzle and usual handwheel. On switching on, the water sucked the liquid up a pipe from the coffer and on passing through the nozzle the mixture became foam much like the top of a glass of Guinness; this settled on the flames from burning oil or petrol and put them out. Looking at the contraption with some interest I wished I could remember more of my Midshipman's fire-fighting course; something told me I was going to need it.

There were a number of hand 'foamites', water-spraying versions, an asbestos suit which allowed a man to go right into a fire and various gadgets (including a CO_2 machine, a cylinder on wheels with a long rubber pipe) for fighting fires in confined spaces such as the cockpit of an aircraft. These were kept at the foot of the island, through the main door of which we passed to climb several ladders. 'The Bridge Mess—your home from home.' I looked into a small room where a table and chairs took up most of the space not occupied by surrounding bunks. 'A round dozen live here' said McPhee. 'Most of the junior officers with essential jobs.' We had a look at the bridge which was straightforward, at the Aircraft Direction Room (ADR) which was not (I had never been in *Indomitable*'s and a large perspex screen, facing several complicated looking control consoles, meant very little) and descended to the Wardroom for a mass of further introductions.

The CO of the Avenger squadron proved to be 'Pablo' Percy, a prematurely balding two-and-a-half whom I remembered from Dartmouth, but most of the other aviators, including both Corsair squadron COs (Lieutenant Commanders A.M. 'Judy' Garland and R.L. Bigg-Wither) were RNVRs whom I had never met before. One of the Fighter Direction Officers—Philip O'Rorke—had been at Dartmouth with me and I had been shipmates with a Lieutenant Berger before, but that was the sum of known faces. Joining a new ship, especially a big one, is always something of a trial and doing it twice in two months a bit hard. However, the spirit of this particular one was almost tangible and the good luck of dropping into such an unusual and challenging job too good to be true. In any case, being up to the eyes learning the ways of the Commander's Office (mainly planning the next day's routine under his aegis), making the most of Moose before he left, and keeping the Battle of Sydney boiling out of working hours, hardly left time for consecutive thought.

The few days before we sailed for the forward area were crammed with last minute preparations, mostly topping up with minor stores that had been overlooked or hearsay suggested would be needed. In the latter connection I was most fortunate.

We were shown a US Navy film called *Fighting Lady*, a magnificent record—several cameramen died in the making—of a carrier's recent experiences in the Pacific (though actually made up from several different ships). Kamikazes screamed down to crash yards away, blow up just beyond the muzzles of belching guns or plummet on to the next ship. Appalling fires raged, aircraft landed on to skirt smoking holes in the deck and all in all we were very impressed. I noted in particular the plethora of excellent fire-fighting equipment deployed, some of it unfamiliar.

The *Illustrious* was to go home—she had engine trouble—as soon as we joined the fleet and her gunnery officer materialised to give us an equally graphic account of what to expect. I came to the unpalatable conclusion that our firefighting equipment was totally inadequate and was shocked to discover that there was no more left in the dockyard store; it had all been drawn by our predecessors. In some trepidation I went and bearded Captain Ruck-Keene who, hardly looking up from his papers, said 'Are you sure? Then buy some; buy some!' Knowing better than to ask how, I took myself off to the largest store in Sydney and asked for the firefighting department. To my surprise there was an excellent one, full of the latest American gear. I ordered a variety on approval, had a field day testing them on the flight deck and invited the skipper to witness a demonstration of the chosen items. On completion he said 'Come ashore with me in half an hour' and I found myself the rather embarrassed third party to a verbal meal, with much table thumping, of the unfortunate Captain of the Dockyard. By the end of it he was only too glad to get rid of us by underwriting the expenditure of many thousands of pounds.

This proved to be typical of 'Ruckers', as the Captain was affectionately called. A lock of grey hair over a round face gave him an engaging boyish air that could be in considerable contrast to the fireworks exuding from it. Inclined to speak in staccato bursts, he was a mass of energy and drive. His gimlet look approved or withered with equal intensity and a dressing down—known by the 'A' boys as 'the full nausea', shortened to 'the full'—was something to avoid. (A minor rebuke was 'My *twelve year old daughter* could do better than that!' and most of us developed an almost manic curiosity to meet this paragon.) As can be imagined fools were not suffered at all—officers who did not measure up were inclined quietly to disappear—but at the same time one knew exactly where one was with him and it was soon apparent to me that anyone who at least tried hard was not likely to come to too much harm. Though feared, Ruckers was very popular, not least because his ferocious energy made sense. Also it was catching. To be highly motivated is, to go one better than Napoleon, three quarters of the battle—and it makes one feel good.

A submariner by trade, the Captain had, on appointment, immediately learnt to fly and two recent tours de force had been the replacement (by dint, one understood, of much postal table thumping) of the ship's British aircraft by American ones more suited to the Pacific; and also the *Formidable*'s unprecedented do-it-yourself repair at Gibraltar. On the way out from England after a long refit and much working-up of aircrews, she had stripped the 12-foot, 45-ton centre engine gearwheel, located deep in the bowels. This pointed to a return home with additional time lost but the Captain thought otherwise. The edict went forth that the job would be tackled by ship's staff with local assistance, and it was, the first move being round the clock digging through many decks by the whole ship's company working in shifts!

In short, nothing was impossible to Ruckers and such was his personality that the ship was very soon to demonstrate that this went for her too.

Of 23,000 tons, she was 740 feet long, capable of 32 knots and had the same gun armament as the *Indomitable*. Some 20 Avengers were carried (848 Squadron) and 36 Corsairs (1841 and 1842), four night fighters being added later. The total number of officers and men was about

1,800. Few of them could have been feeling as apprehensive as I when we put to sea for concentrated flying exercises on March 21. Moose having left, I was on my own with a vengence, rather self-conscious and hot in a yellow jacket and red skull cap on top of overalls (the standard khaki shorts and short-sleeved shirt being no rig for fire-fighting) as I waited at the foot of the island with the remainder of the fire party—including an unfortunate in the heavy asbestos suit—for a dash into action. My first duty would be to get the pilot out before the aircraft went up in flames, to which end there was the standard aircrew knife with blunt end for cutting free if necessary. I went over the various connections for the umpteenth time (it was best to assume that the pilot would be knocked out or at least dazed)—parachute harness (twist to the right and bang in), safety harness (a variety of methods of release), r/t lead, oxygen tube—cravenly hoping I would not be called upon too soon.

Seen properly for the first time, the dark blue Corsairs did nothing to slow the adrenalin. 'Jolie laide', they were beautiful and brutish at the same time with incredibly long snouts that had the pilot sitting near the base of the very large tail, with kinked gull wings that combined to give a curiously reptilian air. I have read that one pilot on first introduction went straight off and made his will and can quite believe it*. The view forward was even worse than usual and enforced a method of landing on that kept my heart in my mouth to begin with. They came skidding in at a sharp angle with nose up and flaps down but seemingly pretty fast, until straightening up at the last moment. At first I found it difficult to tell whether they were making a good or bad approach, except that the 'batsman', a lonely figure right aft on the port side, would in the latter case be gesticulating frantically with his two circular red bats. In a hopeless case he would wave the pilot round for another go, 18-cylinder engine roaring with the sudden full throttle. After a satisfactory approach the batsman would cross the bats in front of him to signify 'Cut!' at which the pilot would cut the engine to sink—or virtually drop in the case of a Corsair—on to the deck.

There were eight wires lying across it, about ten yards apart, the object being to catch an early one with the special hook lowered for the purpose. The wire went round revolving sheaves at the sides and disappeared into hydraulic systems below. When a wire had been caught it gave enough to halt the aircraft in a few yards and then went limp, at which two aircraft handlers would run out and disengage the hook. The pilot would then taxi forward, folding his wings as he went (Avengers' were folded manually) to take instructions from a flight deck director waiting for'ard; these included a beckoning 'come on' with

*Carrier Pilot, by Norman Hanson.

234

both hands held high, clenched fists for 'stop', or one hand pointing to the side the pilot was to alter direction by pivoting on that wheel. When he came abreast you pointed at the next director and so passed the aircraft up the deck.

Both Corsairs and Avengers were very heavy and strong. Sometimes, coming in a little too high but still catching a late wire, they would be clawed down to land with bone-shaking force, but none the worse. Beyond the wires were two vertical barriers, made of three heavy wires slung between large steel uprights and held apart by vertical pieces. These, one just abaft the island and the other a few yards forward, were to prevent aircraft that had missed all the wires from crashing into others manoeuvring or already parked forward. On an aircraft catching a wire the barriers were lowered for taxying over and then raised again for the next customer.

That first day one Corsair came in right over on the port side; the batsman jumped for his life into the escape net but was caught by a wing tip *en passant*, fortunately not badly damaged. And an Avenger requested an emergency landing for some reason. This was broadcast by Commander (Flying) from his position overlooking the flight deck and of course we were all keyed up, but it landed safely. To the best of my memory there were no prangs on deck; however, the nature of the world in which I now found myself, if only at its perimeter, was made starkly clear when one Corsair took off, banked sharply to its left and fell into the sea. It sank quickly and though our escorting destroyer, *Nizam*, rushed to the scene the pilot was not recovered.

The pale green Avengers were more staid and with a good forward view, made normal approaches, but they had not the manoeuvrability or reserve of power of the more glamorous fighters and seemed to provide their share of nail-biting moments. When flying was finished for the day, we had secured to a buoy and it was all chatter in the Wardroom. I found myself both awed and determined. Awed at the existence—so much tougher than I remembered from my air course in the *Ark Royal*—that these men (mostly two or three years younger than me) looked on as their daily fare; and determined to do my best for them.

There followed two more days of concentrated exercises, DLTs (Deck Landing Trials) and practice shoots. By way of a final fling our Avengers carried out a massed torpedo attack on the ship, after which she sailed for Manus in the Admiralty Isles, 1,000 miles to the north. In company with the Canadian cruiser *Uganda* and the destroyers *Urchin* and Robin's *Ursa*, we took a week to get there, exercising hard all the way. An aircraft crashed—my first—missing all the wires and ending up in the barrier with showers of sparks and much raucous rending of metal; I got to him pretty quickly but it was a 'walk away' as far as the pilot was concerned, with no fire. Not too badly damaged, the aircraft was hauled to the forward left by Jumbo, the mobile crane, via a wire strop round the boss of the badly bent propeller.

After oiling at Manus, a very large anchorage bounded by distant grey hills, we left again for Leyte in the Philippines, anchoring in the even larger San Pedro harbour four days later. Leyte had only recently been wrested from the Japanese, in fact fighting was still going on in the north.

HMS Formidable
8/4/45

'It is Easter Day today. We had quite a nice service on the flight deck. I imagined you both in church at home although you would have been asleep at the time. Everything is going well and though working pretty hard I am thoroughly content. Have just finished writing out the orders for my responsibility which fortunately my predecessor didn't do, so the whole thing will be organised as I want it . . .

'. . . I live in a small mess on the bridge at sea which is great fun and of course cool compared to below. Am mess secretary and we are all a happy lot. I think this is certain to be the most efficient carrier in the fleet. We do things the others with better facilities don't do. There is deck hockey on the flight deck but I don't take part as it is too hot . . .

'I always think it would be rather marvellous to be able to free the actual people I was with in Sumatra, but of course am never likely to get ashore in a forward area in a thing like this . . . We get constant heavy showers which are lovely by day but infuriating at night when sleeping in the open . . . It seems incredible I have already been away four months, the time has flown so!'

The Bridge Mess was certainly a pleasant little coterie, headed by Lieutenant Commander (Flying). Known as 'Little F'—as opposed to Commander (F), the senior Air officer on board—he was Harry (B.H.) Hawkes (all Hawk(e)s in the Navy are Harry, presumably after Uncle Tom Cobbley's 'Arry 'Awk, and I never got to know his real name), a most efficient officer with a great way with him, vital in this particular job, and the pleasantest messmate possible. With a springy step and boyish face with large, laughing eyes that must have slain the girls, he was in direct charge of operational work on the flight deck, such as flying off, ranging and spotting aircraft (ie, placing them on spots painted on the deck), bombing up aircraft, maintaining barriers and so on. For this he had 60 ratings working in three watches—the whole lot were often required—known as the Aircraft Handling Party, equipped with 'dodgems' (towing trucks) and other gear. It was evident that the AHP would do anything for Little F.

Part of the huge expanse of San Pedro was given over to the British Pacific Fleet and its Fleet Train. The BPF was out operating but the latter embraced us as its only major customer and we spent the next six days getting to know it and the somewhat unappetising 'beach'. At first glance a motley collection of merchant ships, the Fleet Train was in fact a mobile dockyard and stores dispenser under its own Rear Admiral, eventually to boast 125 ships and 25,000 men.

We sailed from Leyte on April 10, those in the open air thankful for a breeze in exchange for the indescribably uncomfortable heat of this tropical Scapa Flow. The BPF's oiling force was joined two days later and, turning out on 14th, I saw that the BPF had arrived; two battleships, four carriers, five cruisers and a dozen destroyers. After they had fuelled, *Illustrious* left for home and *Formidable* took her place, Admiral Vian flying over from *Indom* to have a quick look at us and brief the Captain. The BPF, under Admiral Nimitz as his Task Force (TF) 57, was now operating in parallel (but not in close contact) with the American 58, both coming immediately under Nimitz's second in command, Admiral Spruance. The new TF 57 had arrived just in time to be in on the preliminary moves against the next objective—Okinawa. Formosa, the Sakishima Islands and Okinawa were strung out south-westerly from Japan, the first two being natural staging posts for aircraft coming to the aid of Okinawa. The BPF was given the task of interrupting these reinforcements and this had mainly meant continuous attacks on the airfields of two islands, Ishigaki and Miyako.

Our ships had not come off unscathed, as one could see from a glance at *Indefatigable*'s blackened island. A kamikaze had come vertically down on her flight deck, four officers and ten ratings being killed and 16 wounded. Equipment was damaged but her flight deck only dented—a matter of great satisfaction all round—and she was soon operating aircraft*. *Illustrious* and *Victorious* were very near-missed, in fact both were touched and suffered bomb explosions, the former losing two Corsairs and both being deluged with impedimenta and bits of Jap pilot (eyeballs and skull fragments were found on *Illustrious'* flight deck and a sliver of burnt flesh hanging from a gunsight; *Indefat* had a finger to show for hers). There were casualties in *Indomitable* from machine-gunning by a Jap fighter and the desroyer *Ulster* had a near-miss bomb that did so much damage that she had to be towed to Leyte. Eight Avengers had been lost and nearly double that number of fighters, though the crews were saved in several cases. Tragic incidents had been the shooting down of a Hellcat and a Seafire (unfortunately not the first, or indeed to be the last occasion) and the blowing up of a Corsair—the petrol tank had ignited—on board *Illustrious*. It had crashed on landing and a number of people who were swarming over it trying to free the pilot were killed with him.

Each one- or two-day strike period was numbered so that, when at

*Her USN Liaison Officer commented: 'When a kamikaze hits a US carrier it's six months repair at Pearl; in a Limey carrier it's a case of "Sweepers man your brooms!"'

about 03:30 on April 15 the strains of Flying Stations banished sleep, it was Iceberg 5 on which our boys were about to embark. The object was to keep up a rain of bombs and machine-gun attacks on the runways and nearby installations of the same two islands from 06:00 almost without a break until dark. *Formidable*'s contribution was 12 Avengers for both the first and third strikes, two strikes of eight Corsairs, each armed with two 500-lb bombs, and more Corsairs for the CAPs (Combat Air Patrols) over the fleet and targets ashore.

It is cold, dark and hostile as I step out on the hard steel deck and not for the first time feel the unfairness of things that keeps most of us safely on board while a select few roar away to an even chance of death. I test my special wand torch used for signalling to the pilots; its perspex finger, projecting from the metal cylinder, glows satisfactorily. Corsairs are coming up the lift and being manhandled, wings still folded, on to spots right aft; then the 12 Avengers in front of them, the leader on the centre line, a little in advance and wings spread. The pilots, observers and tags (telegraphist-air-gunners) emerge from their island briefings to disperse among the forest of angular shapes among which the odd shaded torch flickers like a firefly. It is getting lighter. Little F, with two flags that one can just see are red and green, materialises abreast the leading Avenger, in which Pablo Percy and his aircrew are now ready. One can just make out 'Wings' (Commander (Flying)) in an island sponson. We Flight Deck Directors, in yellow waistcoats and skull caps, who have been conversing in a group, distribute ourselves down the deck park, in a line behind Little F. Suddenly a voice comes over the loudspeakers: 'Start up, start up, start up!' The engines cough angry gouts of flame and then roar into steady life. The air reverberates and one would like to cover one's ears. Then the flight deck heels a little— we are altering into wind; in fact the whole fleet is altering into wind as, elsewhere in the vast circular formation, the scene is mirrored in three other carriers. There is a slight movement on the island at which Little F waves the two chockmen away, raised his green flag and revolves it round his head. The leading Avenger thunders as it strains against the brakes, shaking violently; Percy raises his thumb, the flag drops and the aircraft, heavy with bombs—*Formidable*'s first Pacific flight in anger— moves forward. It accelerates and is soon trundling down the deck at surprising speed—off the end, a slight dip, then up into the air and away to starboard. The next is already on the spot and roaring. Off it goes. Soon all 12 are away, formating on the leaders who are flying round. The first snarling Corsair is following them, its raven-like companions unfolding their wings and crowding forward in their turn. Each fairly rockets up the deck. They fly round too, in formation, and then suddenly all are gone and there is comparative quiet.

But no respite. The big barriers go up with a clang and the bells of the forward lift scream as it descends for the next lot of aircraft. The flight deck aft has to be clear for landing on—though everyone got away without trouble—so the newcomers will be bunched forward and then brought back to take off, towed tail first by the dodgems, as soon as the first strike is back and out of the way below. All at once it is 'Stand by to receive aircraft' and here they are. No-one requests an emergency landing and a quick count shows that they are all there. They land on, taxi forward, and—pilots handing over to their fitters—the aircrews walk back to the island for debriefing, sweating, laughing and ribbing each other about some incident. After waiting its turn (aircraft land on quicker than the lift can cope) each machine is struck down, pushed to its corner of the hangar and attacked by fitters, mechanics and armourers; they work until it is either ready or pronounced u/s (unserviceable), in which case they work even harder. Meanwhile, debriefed, dehydrated and temporarily drained of energy, the pilots and observers have only a warm shower and a hot, vibrating cabin to unwind in, the tags even less.

When the last aircraft of the first strike had disappeared below, *Howe* made to *Formidable*: 'To our now very critical eye your chaps made that land-on look very easy'. The Avengers had bombed Ishigaki airfield, scoring, in the strike leader's opinion, 90 per cent hits on the runway; the Corsairs had bombed opportunity targets including flak positions and aircraft on the ground at both Ishigaki and Miyako.

Then it was 'Start up, start up' . . . and the whole process was repeated. A few enemy aircraft were detected by radar but the only hostile act was the approach of a flying bomb, radio-controled from a parent aircraft, that came within eight miles and then dived into the sea (probably out of fuel). A decidedly unfriendly act, though not enemy inspired, followed the failure of a Corsair to release one of its two 500-lb bombs. No amount of aerobatics would shake it off and so there was no alternative but to land on and hope for the best. We watched with bated breath. The bomb came off with the shock of landing and cartwheeled down the deck towards us. Everyone dived for what cover there was but it rolled to a stop in a corner and was pounced upon. Exactly the same thing happened with another Corsair a few minutes later and the Captain, never at a loss for pithy comment, spoke for all concerned when he signalled to Admiral Vian 'It's nice to know they don't go off'.

We were beginning to think this was an auspicious first day's operating when in the late afternoon word went round the flight deck that pitched us all into gloom—'Judy' Garland, CO of 1842 Corsair Squadron, had been shot down by flak over Ishigaki. Of course, I hardly knew him but apart from the fact that to lose a squadron CO on the very first day was bad, to many this was a great personal blow. Apparently he had dived from some height, the hard-earned experience of other ships being that one should come and go at the lowest possible level.

Except that different airfields were the targets, the next day's operating was a carbon copy of the first. Getting into the routine, I was not so tense and even able to take an interest, at odd moments when there was no flying, in other things that were going on. Intrigued by the extraordinary snatches of apparent conversation (in the most matter of fact tones except on the odd occasion of high drama) that were sometimes broadcast round the ship, with talk of angels, bogies, bandits and such like, I squeezed into the ADR. This was where Philip O'Rorke or one of the other FDOs (Fighter Direction Officers) with a highly trained team of ten officers and 15 ratings, sitting in semi-darkness, watched the big perspex and other displays, listened to reports from pilots and their own staff, assessed the constantly evolving situation, as often as not projected their minds several minutes ahead and having decided what to do, instructed pilots accordingly.

Though several enemy aircraft were reported no attack developed; but there was another sharp reminder that Japanese AA fire was very accurate. One of our Avengers was shot down; the pilot and air gunner were killed but the observer, Sub-Lieutenant Gass, baled out. He came down in the sea only two miles offshore and was rescued under rifle fire by an intrepid Walrus from *Victorious*.

The fleet retired to refuel in the evening and Admiral Vian signalled 'All airfields unserviceable—Iceberg 5 completed', which was satisfactory. The next two days were spent refuelling and replenishing from the Fleet Train. A ceaseless stream of unfortunate maid-of-all-work destroyers acted as go-betweens, from whom we hoisted in stores of all kinds. Of course 1,800 men use up a lot of everything. *Formidable* took her turn to provide Avenger anti-submarine patrols and so there were several interruptions for flying. Meanwhile feverish work was going on in the hot hangar servicing aircraft and all in all this was the reverse of a rest period.

At 06:00 on the 20th flying off started again. One of our Avengers ditched on the return journey and four others were detailed to search for it. They found nothing—it must have put out an inaccurate position—and returned disconsolate. However, 24 hours later an American Mariner flying boat on rescue patrol sighted the three men and picked them up ten miles from the coast. No wonder many airmen were superstitious! Life so often hung on a few gallons of petrol, a word heard on the r/t, a glance in the right direction . . .

By this time the fleet was on its way back to Leyte, *Formidable* having received the signal from Admiral Vian 'As good a three-days operating as I have seen'. This was confirmation of what most of us had already sensed—HMS *Formidable* had no reason to have an inferiority complex about being the new girl. The ship was fighting fit, morale was sky high and, to be fair on the others, we were fresh.

Return to Leyte and expected let-up proved but a repeat of the hectic storing and making good of the days with the Fleet Train, plus even worse heat thrown in. Sitting in a pool of sweat in the Commander's Office as I wrestled with applications for special working parties, the next day's boat trips to distant store-ships, routine inspections of this and that, one could only marvel how the poor devils in the various machinery spaces kept going at all. Of course carriers were, as already described, particular heat gatherers. Another annoyance special to the breed (and the great Pacific distances) was the necessity to fill up—apt description—with drop tanks. These were the lozenge shaped, discardable aircraft petrol tanks that, carrying 176 extra gallons, provided greatly extended range. We had to stow large numbers—awkward to handle—wherever we possibly could.

The new CO of 1842 Squadron, Lieutenant Commander D.G. Parker, joined and on May 1 the fleet sailed for the same hunting ground, now becoming very familiar to our aircrews and presumably like the backs of their hands to those of *Indom*, *Indefat* and *Vic*. On the way an AA practice shoot was carried out against sleeve targets, towed at 7,000 feet. The carriers fired in turn. *Formidable* shot down two sleeves, first on one side and then on the other. The other ships had no success. Admiral Vian made 'How do you do it?' and the Captain replied 'All this and hangar too', a mild boast that was rubbed in next day, when a large combined 'Balbo' (after the Italian Marshal's air fleets) of 48 Avengers and 70 fighters—Corsairs, Hellcats, Seafires and Fireflies—exercised a mass attack on the fleet. It was impressive and so were the figures for operating these aircraft: our take-off times were better than any of the others and our landing intervals (time taken between one aircraft and the next) were eight seconds better than the next carrier and 34 seconds better than the slowest. I must say it was a thrill to have a small part—passing Corsairs up the deck to Little F— and watching him despatch them. Harry would have the next to go pawing the ground like a horse under the tapes, tail jerking with the revs and then lifting as his flag dropped to send the great steed tearing off—before the last was quite clear! He would turn immediately to collect another from the director behind, while the rest of the pack crept forward in cacophonous expectation.

I had expected to find it a new experience, for once having nothing to do with guns, but this was not the case. The Gunnery Officer (Lieutenant Commander Dan Duff, a most likeable fair-haired giant with a puckish sense of humour—'hands to the pumps, guns I mean' was his stock phrase in an emergency) required me to supervise a pair of 20 mm Oerlikons when aircraft were not being operated. These were on the port side abreast the island, about eight feet below the flight deck and my main duty was the same as in the *Prince of Wales*, to pick out their next target.

A good start to Iceberg 7 on May 5 was provided by the news that Hitler and his dreadful little hunchback henchman Goebbels were dead; the end in Europe could not be far off. There was one difference between this day's attack and all those going before: *KG V, Howe*, the four cruisers and some destroyers detached before first light to bombard various targets on Miyako Island—simultaneously with the bombing—leaving but one cruiser and six destroyers. We thought little of this; the poor devils had done nothing but steam about for weeks and it was time they had some employment; in fact it was more for morale purposes than anything else that Admiral Rawlings had decided on the move. He underestimated the enemy, however, who appreciated at once that the carriers were for the first time without the gun protection of the remainder.

Action stations were sounded off at 05:15. Corsairs were in front this time, then Avengers and more Corsairs which were not going off until later. As ever, they looked sinister, dark against the greenish sky. The order came to start up, drowned in staccato reports as a score of whirling propellers flickered among blue exhaust flames. The steady roar took over and we resigned ourselves to wait, the wind tugging at our trouser legs as the minutes ticked by to zero hour. To the east crimson streaks were already silhouetting the jagged black fretwork of massed planes, when a flag dropped from the yardarm and at once the stern began to slide as the rudder bit. I was aware of an avenue of faces, ghostly pale in their anti-flash gear, peering intently from each side and down from the island structure. The leading Corsair—prima ballerina of this scene that never failed to grip—was already responding to the conductor's baton. The ship steadied on her course into the wind, which was strong (how useful this was soon to prove!). By now Harry Hawkes' flag was vertical. The pilot, animal-like in his weird get-up, watched it from his shuddering cockpit with gross pentagonal eyes. His chockmen were gone, but those at the machines behind crouched as low as they could to shield their streaming faces. The audience craned forward. Down came the flag and the goofers and gun's crews ducked away from the shower of grit that whirled aft to start another operating day.

As usual the first trio of Corsairs was flying past in formation as the early Avengers started off. One of the latter lost height, banked to the right and fell into the sea, to come past our starboard side. Few saw this and we were surprised to hear the action commentator say that the crew had joined the Goldfish Club (of those who had ditched) and been picked up by *Ursa*.

Once the strike was away we moved the remaining aircraft forward and bunched them in the bows. The sun came out and hands went to breakfast, leaving only the duty defence watch closed up. The various preparations had been made and there was nothing much to do until the strike returned and the next Combat Air Patrol took off.

The Avengers got back safely, although some were well shot up. Then—it was just before 10:00—came reports from the ADR that they had a bogey at long range. *Victorious'* fighters were sent off to intercept and we went to repel aircraft stations. On arrival at the Oerlikons I found that Midshipman (S) Basedon, recently joined from *Illustrious*, had been detailed to help spot targets. He listened politely to an account of his duties and then let it pass in the course of conversation that the wing of a kamikaze had grazed *Illustrious'* funnel about ten feet from his head when employed on the same job; at which we had a good laugh.

The loudspeakers announced that *Victorious'* fighters had shot down a 'Zeke' Jap fighter 70 miles from the fleet. This almost certainly meant others somewhere and we spent an anxious time looking all over the sky, but particularly up-sun. All at once I heard, above the guns' electric motors, the sound of our own aircraft engines on the flight deck behind. Three Avengers were being moved forward. As there were enough directors there to cope I nearly did not bother but in the end hoisted myself on to the flight-deck and signed a couple past. In doing so I moved up a few yards to a position a little forward of the island on the port side.

Suddenly, without any warning, there was the fierce 'whoosh' of an aircraft passing very fast and low overhead and I looked up in time to see a fighter plane climbing away on the starboard side, having crossed the deck from aft at 50 feet. I was thinking casually what a stupid thing to do and that he was lucky not to get shot at, with a scare on, when the starboard bow Oerlikons opened up a stream of tracer at the retreating enemy. He banked steeply, showing the Japanese red blob markings, and flew down our starboard side, the focus of a huge cone of converging yellow balls as every close range weapon on that side began to hammer away. I thought he was certain to buy it and stood watching until he passed behind the island. I remember PO Lambe at this moment standing with his hands up as a sign to the Avenger he was directing to stop, about 30 feet from me.

Then the Jap came into view again from behind the island, banking hard to come in towards the ship from the starboard quarter, apparently unharmed and by now the target of fewer guns. His silhouette changed to a thin line with a lump in the middle, and he seemed to hang in the air as he dived for the ship.

I waited for no more but sprinted to a hatchway some 20 yards forward on the port side. Expecting to be blown to bits at each stride, I arrived at the hatch just after a tubby leading seaman of the AHP called

Chambers, who had homed in from another angle. He proceeded to trip down the steel ladder step by step so I launched myself at his back and we fell in a heap to the bottom. At the same moment there was a flash and a great crash shook the ship. I gave it a second or two to subside, during which the light from the rectangle of sky above turned to deep orange, and ran back up the ladder.

It was a grim sight. At first I thought the kamikaze had hit the island and those on the bridge must be killed. Fires were blazing among several piles of wreckage on deck a little aft of the bridge, flames reached right up the side of the island, and clouds of dense black smoke billowed far above the ship. Much of the smoke came from the fires on deck but as much seemed to be issuing from the funnel and this gave the impression of damage deep below decks. The bridge windows gaped like eye sockets and most of the superstructure was burnt black. The flight deck was littered with debris, much of it on fire, and there was not a soul to be seen.

I grabbed a foam generator nozzle from its stowage nearby and ran out the hose, indicating to a rather shaken turret-safety number who was lying down between the turrets of B group, to switch on the machine. Men began to pour up from the sides of the flight deck and I pushed the foam-erupting nozzle into someone else's hands, to go round the crews of the other machines who were getting to grips with the main fire. It was very fierce with occasional machine-gun bullets 'cooking off'. Smaller fires in the tow-motor park, fire-fighter headquarters and odd bits of aircraft scattered around were attacked with hand extinguishers. The AHP were pushing unburnt aircraft clear and carrying casualties below. Some enthusiast appeared from the boat deck to cause initial confusion by playing water hoses from there on to burning oil and petrol; both float and so the fires merely spread but this was dealt with. Generally speaking the foam machines—both old and new—did good work, some blistering and almost too hot to touch. Soon there were pools and mounds of foam all over the place and the pungent smell everywhere. Large reserves of manpower materialised which did sterling work under the Commander, dragging heavy lumps of scrap iron that had been aircraft to the cranes, bringing up fresh drums of foam compound, refilling hand appliances, and generally helping to clear up. With reserves in the Fleet Train we could not tie up hangar space unprofitably and whole though badly damaged aircraft were ditched without ceremony (except for a rush for the clock!). A boat deck crane would be trained over the flight deck to collect the load on a tripping hook; the crane would be swung over the sea and the hook tripped for a fine splash.

In the middle of this there was another kamikaze alarm and we all took over while two attacked the *Indomitable*. One blew up,

Two Corsairs after the second kamikaze. See page 254.

Above and Below *Clearing up after the second kamikaze.*

Above *Transferring wounded to a destroyer.*

Right *Captain Philip Ruck-Keene, CBE, DSO.*

Below *Corsairs parked beside the port after 4.5-in battery.*

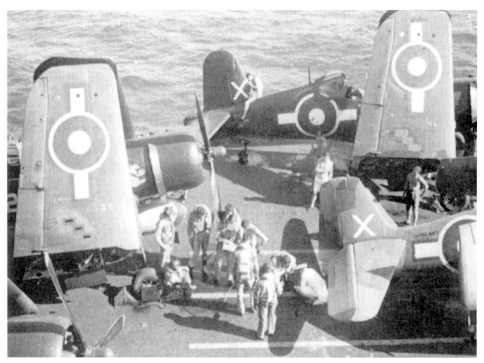

Above *Corsair pilots receive last minute instructions before a sortie.*

Below *Vice Admiral Sir Philip Vian saying goodbye to the assembled ship's company on the return of HMS* Formidable *to the UK after the Japanese surrender.*

disintegrated by pom-poms, about a hundred yards off the ship, and the other hit at such a low angle that he merely skated down the fortunately clear deck and over the side.

The kamikaze which hit us carried a 500 lb bomb and it was thought (there were no living witnesses) that the pilot released it just before he struck. By bad luck the bomb had caught the point of intersection of four armour plates, a very persistent slice about one foot by nine inches going down through several decks to come to rest in a fuel tank. On its way it wrecked the barrier operating machinery, bucked the hangar fire curtain and cut a steam pipe which filled the centre boiler room with steam. One or two valves had to be turned very quickly before the area was left to scalding steam. This one splinter had reduced our speed temporarily to 18 knots and been responsible for much of the smoke that had towered above the ship. Shipwrights were soon at work filling the hole (about two feet square with an 18-inch depression over 16 feet) with rapid hardening cement and steel plate, engineers were getting one barrier operable by hand (turret crews from the two forward groups were to haul it up and down with large tackles) and work on radar and communications damage was under way.

Considering the appearance of the deck immediately after the incident, our casualties seemed comparatively light: two officers and six men killed and 45 wounded. The Air Engineer Officer (Lieutenant Commander Knox) lost an eye and sadly the stalwart Petty Officer Lambe of the Aircraft Handling Party later died of wounds. Lieutenant Berger was killed in the Operations Room, and a steward in the Bridge Mess, which was punctured by shrapnel. A pilot was killed in an Avenger on deck. Another Avenger (the one Lambe had been directing) and the kamikaze himself were blown to smithereens, and seven more aircraft on deck burnt right out.

The Jap pilot had started his initial dive at the ship, but finding that he was overshooting the bridge decided to pull out (luckily for most of us originally on deck) and, after firing a cannon burst, had come round again. His coolness and audacity, to say nothing of skilful handling of the machine, were indicative that high class pilots were being used on suicide missions. Several bits of Jap pilot and aircraft were found. I collected a piece of tyre, cannon shell, and part of his bomb-release mechanism; someone found his hand with wristwatch still on it (though not going!); a yellow silk jacket was discovered for'ard and Guns was to be seen during the general clean-up poking bits of Jap off the funnel with a long pole.

When things had quietened down I remembered, with grim amusement, an extraordinary feeling I had experienced when running for the hatch. It was that my knees were made of water, my feet of lead and that my real self was yards ahead of my body, left floundering along behind! Actually I was probably running as fast as I ever had. (This was quite forgotten until reading Sir Roger Bannister's account of his epic four minute mile, when he described the same sensation; presumably something to do with willpower.)

We had a very popular USN Liaison Officer permanently on board, Lieutenant Commander Ben Hedges. There had been considerable discussion about the relative merits of armoured decks or the extra aircraft carried by US carriers, and when, after the hit, Hedges and the Captain were dusting themselves down, Ruckers gripped Hedges' arm and raising his other fist in a characteristic gesture said 'Well, what do you think of our bloody British flight decks now?', to which Hedges replied 'Sir, they're a honey!'

At the time the Captain made to Admiral Vian 'Little yellow bastard!' to which the Admiral replied 'Are you addressing me?', and some time later signalled 'Well done *Formidable*'.

Though she could do 24 knots by 13:00, we could not fly off any more strikes that day (the 16 Corsairs aloft when we were hit roosted temporarily elsewhere). However, life continued potentially eventful. Though *Indom*'s main radar had been put out of action her fleet fighter direction team (under Captain E.D.G. Lewin) functioned with great skill so that eight Jap aircraft were shot down in four different attacks. All the carriers had a hand and no enemy aircraft got through. Admiral Rawlings returned with the bombardment force some time before the last and highly successful sortie, when Seafires from *Indefat* 'splashed' three out of a group of four attackers and Corsairs from *Victorious* shot down their 'Gestapo' aircraft (whose job was to instruct his evil brood about which ship to dive on to). All this meant several calls to repel aircraft.

On the first occasion I found my guns deserted, no Midshipman and no guns' crews. There was a certain amount of blood about and tin hats on the deck. The nasty realisation that they were casualities and the nearness of my own escape were confirmed from the pom-pom crew nearby who said that the seamen were wounded and they thought the Midshipman was dead. (He and one other turned out to be badly wounded and the third just slightly. The latter, A.B. Fowler, continued for months to spit out bits of shrapnel as they worked into his mouth from his jaw and throat.)

I strapped myself into one of the vacated Oerlikons, and proceeded to shoot down an aircraft with my own fair hands. During a stand-to a lone fighter came in sight on the port beam, almost out of the sun, and made for us in a shallow dive. I gave him a long burst and had the immense satisfaction of seeing him dip suddenly and splash into the sea. Easing the leather straps off my shoulders I locked the gun stationary and stepped down from its platform with a sense of deep satisfaction.

Not only was it a good effort but I had almost certainly saved the ship considerable damage.

The Gunnery Officers' broadcast system clicked on to introduce its usual background hum, and I stopped to listen. Five words in Dan Duff's driest tone drained the colour from my face—'That was one of ours'. I have had some shocks in my Naval life, but for unmitigated horror, this was probably the worst, only eased when *Undaunted*, creaming to the scene to stop with a convulsion of astern power, signalled that she had picked up the pilot more or less unhurt. He proved to have been coming back for an emergency landing, on what must have been *Indomitable*, and may not have been in full control of his aircraft. I was exonerated—in fact nothing was ever said—as friendly aircraft never approached like this and in such circumstances shoot first and enquire afterwards was the thing. I resolved to go over and apologise to a pilot for the second time in my career (remembering the *Bermuda*'s catapult incident) but the opportunity did not occur until it was all rather ancient history. However, it is one of many things I wish I had done.

The Captain was able to report by 17:00 that his ship was operational and soon afterwards all but four of our absent Corsairs landed on. We felt rather pleased with ourselves as each one bumped over the 12-inch depression in the deck, followed by a roar from the Captain of Marines to his Royals to haul the battered barrier up again.

Corsairs from *Victorious* shot down a last enemy aircraft at supper time, lowering the curtain on an eventful day. Throughout it, the enemy, though not too successful with three hits and a near miss, had shown considerable ingenuity. It appeared that the kamikaze which got us had achieved surprise by flying very low (and so indetectable by radar) until quite close. But it did look as if they had shot their bolt for the time; next day, a repeat from the BPF's point of view, there was little retaliation. Our four Corsairs, still in *Victorious*, distinguished themselves when directed on to a very high 'Zeke' snooper, to splash it before returning home. The Admiral congratulated *Victorious* but she replied that those responsible were 'paying guests from *Formidable*' and added 'Nice work your flight; 40 minutes from the deck to 28,000 feet at 70 miles!' No flak came from Ishigaki, so it was presumed that the bombardment had proved effective; yet again all runways were believed unserviceable and in the evening the fleet withdrew to refuel.

It was a very busy two days for *Formidable*: improving the deck depression, plugging splinter holes, repairing equipment of all sorts, scrubbing and painting the island, in addition to replenishing ammunition, foam compound and the usual provisions. Not least was the transferring by crane, in large rigid cots, of over 30 wounded.

Operations were supposed to be resumed on May 8 but heavy rain storms and ten-tenths cloud dictated a postponement of 24 hours. A CAP was flown and I think it was this day on which, galling to relate, I notched up my third cause for apology to a pilot. It dealt my confidence a sharp, if temporary blow, though the pilot, Sub-Lieutenant A. Ewins, was very good about it. I was parking Corsairs just astern of the island, quite a delicate task as there was only a foot to spare in any direction. The last one had to go right up to a pom-pom sponson. I was inching the pilot forward—his engine roaring with propeller virtually invisible—and paying too much attention to clearance with the next wing stub when there was an ear-splitting clatter that drowned everything. The engine coughed to a stop and, as the triple blades slowed, I saw to my dismay that they had been bent back, like grotesque petals, on the now burnished sponson. The pilot laughed it off but I knew that not only would he miss the next strike but his maintenance crew would have to work all night to fit a new propeller and rectify whatever other damage had been caused by a 'bloody fish-head'. Ewins (who was to be Mentioned in Despatches) was a tall, good-natured, unassuming fellow who some time later, I think in the operations off Japan, returned with a large chunk of his wing shot away. Our excellent photographer took a picture of this, reproduced elsewhere, Ewins writing on my copy: 'Just a horrible line!'

Formidable had eight Avengers in the first strike next morning and our Corsairs flew target CAP over the two islands and fleet CAP on and off all day. Once again a Corsair's bomb that had declined to release came off on landing to bowl up the deck towards us. It caused less alarm and despondency this time but hit the after barrier—we now had both in action, still worked by hand—and wrote it off. Just before noon a snooper was sighted but not engaged. The fleet had been seen but little occurred, beyond further sighting reports, until tea-time. At 16:45 a group of five low-flying bogeys was detected to the west. Seafires went out to intercept and shot one down but were eluded by the rest who also avoided another flight of Seafires and closed the fleet at high speed.

We had been at repel aircraft stations for some time—there were fresh faces at the two Oerlikons—when the bugle went for action stations (the difference being that every man-jack in the ship closed up at his appointed place, not just those with gunnery stations). A klaxon blared from Commander (Flying's) position, 'Anti-Hawk stations! Anti-Hawk stations!' was broadcast and in case anyone was still in doubt a large red flag flickered from the island. Anti-Hawk stations, introduced after the last incident when so many people had been caught in the open, told those who could to take cover and all the unemployed squadron personnel to muster in the cross passages under the flight deck, ready to stream out and fight fires.

There was nothing to do now but watch and wait. As a terror weapon these kamikazes were unsurpassed. It was a sensation of 'the full twitch' as Air Branch slang had it, especially on a cloudy day, after perhaps ten minutes of a broadcast running commentary on the steady approach of a formation to hear the dry announcement, 'They have split up now and are too close for radar detection'. Everyone who has to stay in the open searches the sky with his neck on a swivel, light weapons traversing back and forth, up and down, in amplification of their Gunner's nerves. There is not a man, streaming with sweat under his protective clothing (flame-proof balaclava, gloves, goggles and overall suit with stockings, not to mention tin hat) whose hands have not discovered some piece of equipment that needs last minute adjustment. When at last you see him and all the guns are blazing it's not so bad, but there is still something unearthly about an approaching aircraft whose pilot is bent on diving himself right on to the ship. Wherever you are he seems to be aiming straight for you personally, and in the case of those in or near the island, that's just what he is doing.

We had been searching the sky for some minutes when gunfire broke out to port. *Victorious* was firing and even as I looked there was an explosion on her flight deck. Moments later she opened up again and there was another attacker coming in from astern. It was streaming flames but kept going and also crashed on her flight deck. More gunfire from the same direction. Both *Victorious* and *Howe*, ahead of her, were firing now and I could make out two aircraft in the distance, fairly low, flying so as to pass astern. The blue sky was full of little black puffs marking their passage towards us and tracer criss-crossed as each ship came within range. Our port after battery opened fire and then most of the port close-range guns although the distance was really too great. Both aircraft passed astern about a mile and a half away. One began to shallow dive on to *Howe* and was shot down in flames alongside her; the other, to our intense interest, banked to its left and headed straight for us, fine on the starboard quarter.

It dipped its nose and came tearing down. The air was shuddering with gunfire and again I thought it could not get through.

It was a large machine carrying either two bombs or two drop tanks and liable to make a big mess. I watched it long enough to see bits fly off its starboard wing and then retired to a prone position in the walk behind my guns, which being on the disengaged side could do nothing. At the after end of the walk was an eight-barrelled pom-pom whose size made a recess in the flight deck necessary. This gun could not bear either and the loading numbers were on their stomachs. Being plumb abreast the aiming point we could all expect 'the full'. It was a long four or five seconds.

Then a terrific detonation and a wall of flame curled down from the deck above and seemed to encircle the pom-pom mounting. I got up to run as it looked like coming my way, but a lot of smoke took its place. At the same time the sea, for perhaps hundreds of yards from the ship, was a mass of splashes, big and small, from descending objects.

With the thought that the pom-pom's crew must all be burnt I climbed on to the flight-deck to much the same sight as before. Several furiously burning piles of wreckage that had been aircraft, the island all black, smouldering debris everywhere and clouds of thick smoke welling upwards.

The kamikaze seemed to have exploded close to the pom-pom mounting at the after end of the island because the area was in considerable disarray. The gun itself was surrounded by a protective steel wall about six feet high; I ran and looked over this at a sight that stamped itself on my inner eye from that moment. The blackened body of the Gunlayer, headless, sat rigid in his elevated seat, crouched forward in the aiming attitude with hands still grasping the 'bicycle pedal' control in front. There was an aeroplane wheel on the deck beside and the brave man must have continued to fire his gun until the very last moment. The rest of the crew, who had probably ducked down in time, seemed to be all right.

Looking round I saw that, among several flaming aircraft, the immediate danger was a Corsair fitted with a drop tank in the middle of the flight deck just abaft the island, on fire and standing in a large pool of burning petrol. Nobody was doing anything about it and I noted to my fury the red skull caps of some of the fire party just showing above the flight deck each side as they awaited events with some prudence. The quickest thing to do was to shame them into action, so I ran for the mobile CO_2 machine which was housed at the fore end of the island and trundled it up to the Corsair. The latter's machine-gun bullets were cooking off with the heat, whether up the barrels or not I was unsure but took the seamanlike precaution of advancing in line with the engine. As expected the CO_2 machine was no use—being designed for confined spaces—but it had the desired effect. One or two men appeared and then we were joined by the rest, all bringing equipment to bear, mostly the new knapsack foam throwers. The fire was intense and for some time we did not seem to be making any impression. Though mostly directed aft by the wind over the deck, the flames from the burning petrol rose up every so often to envelop the drop tank and it was evident that should the wind come from the side, or worse still astern, that would be it. The Captain was probably otherwise concerned so I sent a man up to ask him not to alter course if he could help it. Eventually, as the number of appliances increased we got the upper hand; even so, as the petrol pool was extinguished in one place it would flare up in another.

My lungs filled with smoke and I had moved out of the way for air when there was a tap on my back and 'The Captain wants to see you,

Sir'. The fire was now out, the petrol under a thick blanket of creamy foam, the firefighting had eventually gone rather well and I thought 'What the hell does the old blighter want to criticise now?' A senior air officer who had been watching circumspectly from the island doorway said something rather nice as I passed but I was quite unprepared when the Captain was congratulatory fit to take my breath away. I descended to the flight deck in a rosy haze—one is only human—but behind it was a cautionary voice saying that if I had not acted at once I would have been in line for a court-martial, or at any rate had to live with a personal stigma for the rest of my life.

Meanwhile, and quite unknown to me, another kamikaze had dived on the ship but been shot down*. The rest of the flight deck was brought fairly quickly under control. Our recent experience had enabled me to improve parts of the fire-fighting organisation and at least no one sprayed water about. There were more fires because there were more aircraft to provide the fuel; the kamikaze had crashed through a deck-park of 11 Corsairs out of which we lost eight. As fires were extinguished unburnt aircraft were hauled clear. It did not help that the concussion had burst all their tyres; nor that the towing tractors had previously been destroyed, though two jeeps that must have been procured from the Fleet Train stood in quite well. Once, when busy in a corner with a hand-extinguisher, I looked up to find the whole flight deck deserted. The take-cover klaxon had gone again as another attack was expected and I had not heard it. Reaching the boat-deck down a vertical ladder in record time I knocked into Commander (Ops) who was running for a good cubby hole (presumably he had been caught like me) where I joined him. Nothing happened so we cautiously made our way up again.

All fires were out about 20 minutes after the incident. The bomb had exploded ten yards further aft than the first, without penetration, except that a rivet had been blown out, allowing burning petrol to fall through the hole to the hangar below; a nasty fire had ensued resulting in damage by flame and water spray to four Avengers and eight Corsairs. On the flight-deck we lost one Avenger as well as the eight Corsairs, with one Corsair damaged. Apart from the loss of aircraft and doubling the shrapnel holes in the island, which now resembled a giant black pepper-pot, not much harm had been done. Casualties, thanks to the new warning system, were only one killed and eight wounded. (Evidence of our second Japanese casualty was one eye, picked up by a rating with a strange sense of humour; it was put in a match-box which

* *Uganda*'s Report of Proceedings noted: 'One third of *Formidable*'s flight deck from aft appeared to be ablaze . . . Although her after gun positions were shrouded in flame and dense black smoke, the carrier's armament kept barking away at the new threat, which was blown apart in the air'.

he would suddenly push open in front of unsuspecting messmates.) We landed on a strike shortly afterwards—they had taken temporary refuge in *Victorious*—and continued much as if nothing had happened.

Admiral Vian signalled 'Well extinguished. Any foamite left?' and it was gratifying to get from *Uganda* 'Our sincerest admiration'. I hoped that Moose would have approved too.

It was surprising to find that the crew of the pom-pom that had been engulfed in flames were quite all right; anti-flash gear was made of uncomfortably hot material but it was good to have such evidence of its efficiency. Not so reassuring was the plain fact that our pom-poms and Oerlikons simply did not have sufficient physical stopping power. Both our opponents were hard hit but came on, possibly aided by the freezing of control surfaces at high speed. The new *Implacable* had a quadruple Bofors guns of larger calibre and we hoped for something similar when next in Sydney.

Ben Hedges said he thought that an American carrier would have been sunk by fire in either attack as the kamikazes would have gone straight through. One British view was that the naval constructor or whoever it was that insisted on armoured decks should be made an Admiral of the Fleet, a duke, a millionaire or anything else he preferred!* A personal comment on the action was that afterwards I realised I had kept up a steady flow, *sotto voce*, of foul language. Not normally given to this, I presume it was a curious way of letting off steam.

An event that had gone quite unnoticed on the 9th was VE-Day, the end of the war in Europe; however we spliced the mainbrace on the 10th. At home there was naturally wild rejoicing. From my mother:

Hart's Gorse
9/5/45
VE-Day

This is VE-Day at last! We have just been listening to the King broadcasting— and then Eisenhower—Tedder (bad)—Montgomery, etc . . . One can hardly believe it has at last really come . . . when we hear the Japs have thrown their hand in too, then we shall have a real V day! However, it is a wonderful thing that it's over in Europe, and at the end that it went so quickly . . . Hitler disappeared—bumped off I expect. Goebbels poisoned, Goering disappeared . . . no word of our having located that arch-swine Himmler. Lewes was festooned with flags—out of every window and across the streets and everyone wearing red, white and blue rosettes—and the girls with their hair tied up in red, white and blue ribbons! There is a procession and bonfire at Firle tonight.

*Eventually revealed as Vice Admiral Sir Reginald Henderson, Controller, in 1936. He made the decision entirely on his own initiative but sadly died of overwork before the first ships appeared (*Naval Review*, July 1965).

De Valera has finished himself and Ireland by sending condolences to the Germans on Hitler's death.

Thursday 11th

Lewes went mad in the evening and had a torchlight procession and bonfire. Everyone got drunk and you could hear the noise from here at midnight!

They have found Goering, decked out in gold lace and with many rings on his fingers, one a huge sapphire! The Pacific news say that our fleet is bombarding and bombing again—I wonder so much if you are among that lot?

'That lot' learnt at dusk on the 10th that the fleet was 'retiring to lick its wounds' since *Victorious* could only operate a few aircraft at a time due to damage to her forward lift and we had only four Avengers and 11 Corsairs serviceable. So the next morning saw us back in the fuelling area for a repeat of the last occasion. One satisfactory difference was the smaller casualty list due to the Anti-Hawk scheme. *Ursa* came alongside for transferring this and that and Robin semaphored to me 'Glad to see you all in one piece' to which I replied 'So am I'.

HMS *Formidable*
14/5/45

We are having a fairly tough time, but it's quite good fun in some ways. I saw Robin very close the other day. The weather is pleasant except when there are low clouds. I quite forgot! The wonderful news of the war in Europe being over! I'm afraid it doesn't mean much out here, at least not so much as it might. It must be lovely to have no blackouts, etc, and of course the end of hostilities. I wish I was at home for a whoopee party with you both and the Cecils and the Kellys.

I cause a good deal of amusement by varied apparel in action. Being the flight deck fire-fighting officer as well as other things I wear a red waistcoat. I came to the conclusion it didn't go well with a blue overall and yellow skull-cap so changed to a red skull cap. I now wear a white overall, red waistcoat, and red and white tin hat; I also have a red and white megaphone so the effect is pretty startling. I was complimented by the Captain and the Commander the other day (more cannot be said) which was rather gratifying, especially as the Captain is not given to compliments.

The sea is always flat calm and I haven't, touch wood, ever felt sick in *Formidable*, which makes the world of difference. I think I'd rather have the Japs than seasickness.

Iceberg 9 had taken up May 12 and 13, both without retaliation from the air. The enemy gunners remained unsubdued, however, and of course in ever better practice. An Avenger returned with only one wheel and due to our shaky barriers was directed on to *Indom*, where a comparatively safe landing was made. The other ships must have been surprised during the next replenishment period when an impromptu concert was held on our flight deck; it was to celebrate the first anniversary of the ship's present commission. An Avenger ditched on take-off during Iceberg 10 and there was a barrier prang that was potentially horrific but ended in a touch of farce. A Corsair came in too high and too fast, missed all the wires, hit the wrecked barriers full tilt, was swung right round and to starboard and careered some way up the deck, which fortunately happened to be clear. His precursor was on the port side beyond the barriers, being directed by Harry. I heard that this pilot's expression, when he saw another Corsair passing him, going backwards, was worth a month's pay. The heavy barriers were still being raised by the turrets' crews, strung out for'ard and, although treated as a bit of a lark, this was fairly hard going in the heat. Perhaps it was the sight of this bizarre amalgam of ancient and modern that prompted Admiral Rawlings to signal 'The way in which you have been able to operate after making good your damage reflects the highest credit on all concerned'.

Unfortunately, the same could not be said about a serious accident during the fuelling period that followed, though the outcome could have been far worse. An armourer inadvertently fired the guns of a Corsair in the hangar, the Avenger ahead of it exploded and a major petrol fire ensued. There were many bombs in the hangar at the time and the fire curtain (dividing it in half) still inoperative from kamikaze damage. All the hangar sprayers had to be switched on, which did not improve the electrics of the aircraft being maintained. After some anxious minutes the fire was brought under control by those in the hangar who, for a time, shut themselves in to prevent oxygen getting to the flames. I played hoses on the flight deck to cool it down but even so the water rose in steam and it was necessary to double mark time to prevent the crepe soles of my shoes from melting. It was hard lines on the Captain, after the ship's excellent start, having to report that seven Avengers and 23 Corsairs were in various degrees unserviceable. The Admiral must have sent an understanding reply (I think Vian had more than a soft spot for Ruckers—they were of the same mould) because the Captain signalled 'Your letter very much appreciated as we are feeling very low about the whole show'.

There were exchanges in a lighter vein after Vian in *Indomitable* had signalled to Rawlings that, though *Formidable* only had 16 Corsairs and two or three Avengers, her continued presence would not only provide fighter effort and a spare deck but 'it will be nice for the rest of us that there will be four targets instead of three'. *Formidable* made to *Indomitable* (personal for Captain Eccles)—'I suspect your cheerful handiwork in the last para', and then 'I believe you have some photos of the attack of May 4 on us. If so would appreciate copies to show my grandchildren', to which Captain Eccles replied 'Copies will be sent but, unless you are now, I doubt if you ever will be a grandfather!'

Two more operating days followed, in which *Formidable* provided target and fleet CAPs (bogeys were reported but there were no attacks) and then in the evening of the 21st was told to leave for Manus and Sydney to expediate repairs. We did not like vacating the field before the one more Iceberg scheduled, but could hardly pretend there were no compensations. As we parted company with two destroyers and the BPF dwindled astern, *Victorious* winked 'Don't bag all the decent Corsairs when you get to Sydney, play fair', to which Ruckers replied for most of us 'I suppose you mean girls, not Corsairs'.

Arrival at Manus marked a month at sea. When they desisted four days after we left, the remainder of the BPF had done two months, divided by eight days at Leyte. This way of operating had not been experienced in the Royal Navy since Nelson's blockade of Toulon and, all things considered, had been a success. 203 aircraft had been lost from all causes out of an original complement of 218. 93 per cent losses for 57 enemy aircraft destroyed was not a victory by that count but the object had been denial of the Sakishima airfields to the Japanese at a time when the conquest of Okinawa was proving most difficult. Eleven strike days had been completed (2,449 sorties) and all five carriers taking part had been hit by kamikazes at least once. CTF 57 (Admiral Spruance) sent Admiral Rawlings a most appreciative signal and reported to Nimitz that the BPF was experienced enough to operate closely in future operations with the American Fast Carrier Task Force.

The girls were there all right when we arrived at Woolloomooloo but almost outnumbered by dockyard mateys who swarmed on board to tackle our various defects, including the welding of bigger and better plates over the hole. This became quite famous. HRH the Duke of Gloucester, Governor General of Australia, was our first visitor and Admiral Fraser the second. Aircrews were given 14 days' leave and the rest of us four to six.

HMS *Formidable*
8/6/45

. . . I had four days. I went by train to a place called Bungendore, about 200 miles away, arriving at lunchtime. It was a little village, right in the country, a nice smallish house very old for Australia, whitewashed and woodwork. My host and hostess were a young Mr and Mrs Forbes Gordon (all the stations around there were owned by people called Gordon or Osborne). He was ex-RAAF, very quiet and nice; she was charming and in the family way.

I rode a very good horse helping him round up sheep and got an afternoon's quail shooting. We also had a large picnic lunch-cum-duck shoot with some Gordons next door, where T. was staying, and saw sheep being shorn. Lots of marvellous food, cream, etc, and plenty of sleep.

Everyone said how well I looked on return, not that I think I looked particularly bad on going . . .

These were a wonderful four days, all arranged by Nell Knox.

The ship duly received some single Bofors guns instead of the Oerlikons and six Hellcats from *Indomitable*—four night fighters and two photographic—but these additions paled into insignificance alongside the big one. This was AC1—Admiral Vian—for we were to fly his flag during the next tour of operations. In practical terms the vacating of cabins and offices to make room for the staff was the biggest bore and this, of course, occurred, but I think we were all pleased to have Vian. It was an undoubted honour that he had chosen *Formidable* (*Indom*, just relieved by *Implacable*, had retired for a refit) and, though it would sometimes be uncomfortable to have big brother right on top of us, we felt equal to anything he might require (the first thing he required was a bathroom alongside his bridge, not easy to implement). Lastly, Vian's mode of operation was stimulating, similar to the Captain's, and no doubt we felt 'in for a penny, in for a pound'. In the event there were no dramas that I remember and four weeks after arrival we were twisting out of Sydney harbour again, proudly sporting his flag.

10

Under Nimitz and Vian

Manus came and went unlamented and, on July 16, we were treated to a memorable sight, the American Third Fleet provisioning from their Fleet Train: nine heavy and six light carriers, seven battleships, 15 cruisers and 60 destroyers! Though there were more carriers but fewer battleships it reminded me of our combined Home and Med fleets congregated at Gib before the war. They filled the horizon over a wide arc, a numerical concentration of naval power that has not been matched since.

The BPF was to operate as one of the four Task Forces (TF 37 this time) of the Third Fleet, which had just begun the preliminary softening up of Japan itself, prior to invasion. In the late afternoon the whole armada moved off towards the flying position, four groups in line abreast (the BPF, on the right, the most northerly) advancing over a 45-mile front. *Formidable* launched 16 Corsairs. Joining up with seven Fireflies from *Implacable* that flew off north-west about 200 miles to carry out 'Ramrod' attacks (bombing and strafing airfields) at Sendai, Masuda and Matshushima. Tokyo was about the same distance south-west and for the first time I felt great satisfaction, though heaven knows it was second-hand. Those two ships at the bottom of the sea off Malaya with their Midshipmen in captivity, Richard Onslow and his *Hermes*, Anthony Terry and those men at the Malay School in Padang—seldom out of my thoughts—it had been good in May to feel we were doing something about them, but to be actually bombing Japan, that hitherto had seemed so far away...

Three of our Corsairs were shot down or had to ditch but all the pilots were rescued, one by an American and two by our destroyers. The next two Ramrods, provided by *Victorious* and *Implacable*, were aborted because of bad weather, but ten Corsairs from *Formidable* and 12 from *Victorious* got through successfully and attacked installations on the far coast of Japan. South of us the Americans had flown off two strikes which had been aborted and Admiral McCain, our immediate superior, cancelled further strikes for the day to leave, we felt, a feather in the British cap. This was the season of typhoons, with unsettled weather of extraordinary local variation. Strikes took off in bright sunshine to find

261

the target shrouded in low cloud and driving rain, or the reverse applied, and sudden dense fog patches made life hazardous for aircraft returning low on fuel.

After dark we flew off our night fighters in sheeting rain to provide CAP over a bombardment force which included *KG V*. This went to within 14 miles of the coast and bombarded industrial establishments, one of *KG V*'s targets being the Hitachi engineering works which received 91 rounds. Landing-on aircraft at night in pouring rain is an unpleasant business and never was I more sure that my services were going to be required. Dim lights along the edge of the flight deck provided an uncertain avenue for the pilots to aim at and Joyce's bats were illuminated. Apart from reflections in the streaming, swaying deck, this was about all the pilots could see. My admiration for them knew no bounds. All got on without trouble and when they had disappeared into the welcoming if muted glow of the hangar I turned in, thankful and tired. It had been a long 21 hours.

The next few days followed an irritating on-off pattern with bouts of bad weather allowing CAPs and an occasional strike to be fitted in. On July 24 when we were about 200 miles east of Kyushu—the southernmost of Japan's main islands—848's Avengers bombed Tokushima, one of them being lost, and all four British carriers went for a *Kaiyo* Class carrier, leaving it with a broken back and on fire. (A photograph taken showed a clean break, with the two halves sagging.) Japanese fighters claimed four victims, though none from *Formidable*. Two Ramrods followed, the second of which got lost due to the weather closing in. By the time they sighted the fleet their tanks were practically empty, one Corsair coming down in the sea before it could land and another taking the first carrier it saw and just making it. I think it was a member of this party who found himself over an American carrier and quickly obtained permission to land. Unfortunately the American landing-on signals were diametrically opposite to our own. At the first approach the pilot was waved round again; the second was as bad but he landed on somehow to heap invective on the batsman for giving him the wrong signals. The batsman defended himself stoutly and then they both realised that the pilot had been reading the signals as American while the former had been doing his best to provide the British version! It must be added that on subsequently reaching *Formidable* this Corsair finished up half over the port side, with me thankful that the pilot climbed out under his own steam and stomped off cursing.

Much the same happened to an Avenger the next day; the only one to find the allocated target, it returned with only ten gallons left. The collapsing of one wheel occurred several times. The sea had been calm for so long that perhaps it was the swell that caught some new pilots unawares (there had been some very young replacements at Sydney). The result was not particularly frightening so long as the aircraft, scraping to a halt on one wheel and the opposite wingtip, did not slew too much. One such pranger scooped up an arrestor wire with its bent propeller, the wire coming down just forward of the perspex cockpit which was probably fortunate.

Strikes continued against shipping in the Inland Sea and against Tokushima airfield. The weather worsened yet again and course was set for the next replenishment area. Enemy air activity was now increasing. A high-speed reconnaissance plane was shot down by the Americans to crash in flames inside our screen and yield two Japanese bodies to *Tenacious*. There were reports of balloons and 'window'* over the fleet and just before landing on at 19:00 one of *Formidable*'s Hellcats shot down a parachute with a black box dangling from it, thought to have been a radio homing beacon. All this spelt danger, and in fact it was only averted by the efficiency of our fighter direction team. The fighter cover of four Corsairs and four Hellcats were landing on *Formidable* when three groups of bogeys were detected and the Americans reported splashing a 'Myrt' bomber. Landing-on was accordingly stopped with two Hellcats still aloft.

The perspex display in the ADR was full of aircraft, amongst which was a group at 94 miles which Captain Lewin was sure were hostile. The American Group CIC (Combat Information Centre) officer in overall fighter direction command was sceptical but Philip O'Rorke was instructed to intercept and directed the two Hellcats on to these bogeys. Shortly after 20:00 there was an excited 'Tally ho!' from Lieutenant Atkinson who, with Sub-Lieutenant McKie, was at 20,000 feet, 30 miles from the fleet. They tore into the formation, shooting down the leader and two others and damaging a fourth. American fighters from the night fighter carrier *Bonhomme Richard* then arrived and dealt with the remainder. There were 30 Japanese 'Grace' torpedo bombers in all, none of which carried out an attack. Torpedo bombers have the advantage at night—*vide* the 'Torch' attack on *Bermuda* and *Sheffield*—it was now bright moonlight and many ships would undoubtedly have suffered if the Lewin/*Formidable* team had not lived up to their name. As can be imagined the two gladiators returned to considerable acclamation.

After two days' fuelling the BPF was back with attacks on airfields and shipyards with the usual outlandish names, and on shipping in the Inland Sea. Opposition was strong, both in the air and from flak, the fleet losing eight aircraft. Two Corsair pilots of our 1842 Squadron were forced to ditch in a harbour mouth. All dreaded falling into Japanese hands with good reason (they were briefed only on their part in any operation so as not to give much away under torture) and the two pilots

* Aluminium foil dropped to clutter radar screens.

must have felt that this was it. Their delight can be imagined when an American submarine came right in and picked them up. The American rescue service of submarines and flying boats was excellent.

Another Corsair limped back with large chunks of wood in and about its engine, having flown into the airborne remains of his predecessor's target. Though it was evident that every single one of our pilots, bomber or fighter, continued to press home their attacks as if AA fire did not exist, there was one in particular, Lieutenant R.H. 'Hammy' Gray, the senior pilot of 1842 Squadron, who was a byword for leading daring sweeps with attacks at very close range. He came up to the bridge mess for some reason that evening or the next. I had, of course, seen him about a good deal but did not really know him and was surprised at the infectious, lighthearted, self-deprecating nature of this fair-haired, rather tubby Canadian. I thought what an extremely nice chap and found it difficult to imagine him as the ice-cool killer he became when strapped into the cockpit of a fighter.

Whether or not the first strikes got off successfully, each day started with ranging aircraft at about 03:00 and continued either with aircraft operations all day or frustrating waits for the weather to clear. If there was night flying it might end any time, depending on the visibility and chance of kamikaze or torpedo attack. As described, replenishment days were little less demanding. Though we had settled into the routine and the enemy were surprisingly absent, the actual tempo of flying was greater than during the Iceberg operations, with more aircraft movements per day, and wear and tear began to take its toll. I think it was about this time that the Aircraft Handling Party became so tired (mainly ranging aircraft but with many other tasks as well) that it was only Harry Hawkes' special brand of leadership—he was to get a well earned DSC—that enabled him to ask for further effort when they had truly gone beyond their tether. Having to be literally on my toes, so as not to miss a second, as every single aircraft landed, my particular problem was the inability to relax. It began to get me down; until I hit on an odd but successful remedy. This was to imagine that each one, as it approached, was going to crash. Somehow this took the strain off—if it did crash I was not surprised, if it didn't all was well anyway. (I have since applied this in many other spheres; to expect the worst conserves much nervous energy.)

The pattern continued with replenishment periods every few days. One of these was greatly complicated by a tremendous typhoon-bred swell. To keep a safe distance between the ships, the jackstay along which we were receiving 500 lb bombs was 300 feet long, tended by a large body of men who continually hauled or rendered so as to keep it taught.

We were to have returned to the attack on August 3, the BPF's targets being in the Hiroshima area. The day dawned bright and clear but a mysterious signal cancelled operations and to the perplexity of all there was no further development for four days. Then, on August 7 the reason was made plain. A monster bomb had been dropped by the US Air Force on Hiroshima. Few if any of us knew what an atomic bomb might be, but it was obviously something very special and the first wonderings stirred as to whether the war might end sooner than we had dared to hope. The enemy's reaction was unknown and to help them make up their minds Admiral Halsey intended continued attacks.

August 9 proved to be a full and for HMS *Formidable* a tragically memorable day. Conditions, unfortunately, were good and an Avenger strike plus three Corsair Ramrods were flown. The first Ramrod and the Avenger strike caused much destruction, especially to airfields in the north of Honshu. The second, led by Hammy Gray, sank a destroyer and damaged other naval vessels; but they returned with the news that he had been shot down. With the war probably in its closing stages the Captain had told the squadron COs not to take unnecessary risks. This was duly passed on to Gray, but true to form he must have taken little note of it. Leading the others, he came in low over some hills in a high speed dive but was met by intense fire, both from the shore and five ships. Gray dropped his bombs on the destroyer *Amakusa* and was beginning his getaway run to seaward at 40 feet when his port wing erupted in flames. The aircraft banked steeply to starboard and then, both wings now ablaze, turned on its back and plunged at full power into the sea. (The others re-formed under Sub-Lieutenant Mackinnon, the next senior pilot, circled round and repeated the attack. The *Amakusa* had already sunk but two other ships were damaged.)

One of his pilots, Sub-Lieutenant A. Hughes wrote: 'It was my first raid over Japan, but Lieutenant Gray was so cheerful and inspired such confidence as a leader that my nervousness was allayed before it started . . . he was liked and respected by all and his death cast a shadow not only on the pilots but on the whole ship'. This was true; his gallant end after five years of war and within days of peace put a lasting damper on us all, which not even the eventual award of a posthumous VC (the only one earned by the Royal Navy in the Pacific Campaign) did much to lighten.

Nor was this the only blow. When Gray's men returned, one—with no hydraulics—carried out a successful belly landing but another, almost out of fuel, requested permission for an immediate landing. He was approaching normally when his engine stopped about 50 yards off the stern. The Corsair, descending fast, hit the very top of the roundown, where the flight deck curved down towards the stern. It remained there for a second and then began to run back. The batsman, powerless to do anything, took a couple of agonised steps forward as if to will it to stop. The plane gathered speed, slewed round, pointed one wing in the air as the other dropped over space, and disappeared. Moments later it could be seen in the wake, almost submerged, and then was gone. There was no sign of the pilot. It was thought he might have been knocked out by the original shock as the brakes should have held the plane until help arrived. Another five seconds of fuel would have saved him. Also a Canadian, he was due to go home, whether or not the war went on, and this second tragedy all but extinguished such euphoria as we had left on that subject.

However, two other Corsairs on CAP shot down a 'Grace' bomber over an American Task Group and the day ended with another atom bomb, this time on Nagasaki. Presumably there was an adaquate supply of these astonishing weapons and the least optimistic felt that even the Japanese could hardly go on while city after city was obliterated. This appeared to be the case when next day the enemy agreed to the terms of the Potsdam agreement (unconditional surrender) except that they stipulated that the Emperor should be left on his throne. Presumably this had to be discussed by the Allies (Russia had declared war on Japan the day before) for there was no further development. In fact both sides went at it as hard as ever. All day BPF aircraft ranged far and wide; not without cost as six aircraft did not return. One was Sub-Lieutenant Maitland's, one of the best pilots of 1841. In the spirit of Hammy Gray he was making a second strafing pass over an airfield. Though we did not know it, this was the last attack to be made by *Formidable* in the war. The enemy in their turn, as a last defiant gesture, tried all day on the 9th and 10th to get through to the ships—both kamikazes and conventional bombers—but not in massed attacks and the CAPs shot most of them down.

And then came an announcement that, foreshadowed but still unbelievable, put the sighting of land from *Djohanis* in the shade and set us slapping each other on the back.

HMS *Formidable*
14/8/45

We have just spliced the mainbrace in honour of VJ-Day, the Japs having packed in this morning. Well, it's all over now and with luck we shall be home soon, though we still don't know when. It really is incredible that it is all finished when two weeks ago it might have lasted two years. I'm glad I got out here and saw it finished I must say and rather hope we go to Singapore, though that will come under the Indies fleet I expect. We lost three pilots on the very last strikes which was very sad.

I must say it seems a long time ago when I was 19 and a Midshipman in the *Nelson*.

So the war was over. My immediate reaction was one of thankfulness that I had escaped whole. I had been prepared for sudden death but it was the idea of being badly wounded that appalled. I suppose this

266

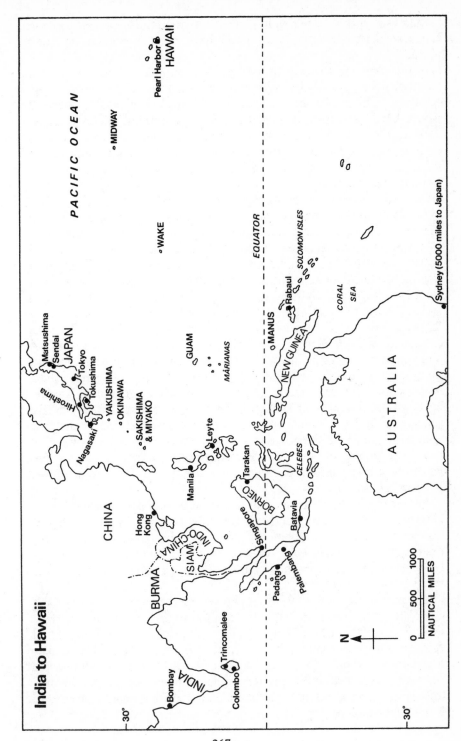

India to Hawaii

PACIFIC OCEAN

Pearl Harbor ● HAWAII

○ MIDWAY

○ WAKE

EQUATOR

Matsushima
Sendai JAPAN
Tokyo
Tokushima
Hiroshima
Nagasaki ● YAKUSHIMA
● OKINAWA
● SAKISHIMA
& MIYAKO

GUAM
MARIANAS

MANUS
○ MANUS

Rabaul ●
SOLOMON ISLES

NEW GUINEA

CORAL
SEA

Sydney (5000 miles to Japan) ●

AUSTRALIA

CHINA

Hong
Kong

BURMA

INDIA

Bombay ●

Trincomalee
Colombo ●

SIAM
INDO-CHINA

Singapore

Manila ●

Leyte ●

Tarakan ●

BORNEO

CELEBES

Batavia ●

Padang ●
Palembang ●

30°

30°

N

0   500   1000
NAUTICAL MILES

feeling was natural, if selfish in view of the thousands—such as those in Japanese prison camps—who should have been uppermost in one's mind.

It was given out that except for *KG V, Indefatigable*, two cruisers and ten destroyers, the BPF under Admiral Vian would be returning to Australia. This caused general but not universal rejoicing. Personally I would have liked to have stayed and seen something of the Japanese surrender—even from afar—but then I had not been away from home as long as most and had a vested interest in this occurrence anyway. A fortnight later *Formidable* as flagship led in through Sydney Heads to a tremendous reception that ended with a thousand individual crescendoes as we went ashore to ecstatic friends. On the 31st there was a victory march through the streets, with most ships represented and then, heavily engaged in paint ship, we fell to wondering 'what next?'

It was not known whether outlying Japanese strongholds would accept the virtually unconditional terms and a reduced BPF presence was required, for some months, in Japanese waters. Admiral Rawlings went home, relieved by Admiral Vian who transferred his flag from us to the *Implacable* and shortly returned north. He was to write in a foreword to *A Formidable Commission*: '*Formidable*, under the command of Captain Philip Ruck-Keene, CBE, DSO, proved from the moment she joined the Pacific Fleet to have a striking power second to no other ship; and her well-led and well-trained company were to show in due course that they could take knocks as well as give them. I could have wished for no finer flagship'. There is no doubt that all the five carriers of the BPF were good, with little to choose between them. Few who served in any of the others will agree, but adding to the above, hard facts like landing-on periods and strike/interception results (the ship was to earn more decorations than any other) it is difficult to deny that *Formidable* had a distinct edge.

All her aircraft had flown ashore, with of course their ground crews. No-one thought anything of this at the time, they would presumably be back in due course, but except for junketings aboard we were not to see them again. This seemed a sorry way to end things; but the speedy repatriation of the thousands of unfortunate prisoners of war was to receive justifiable priority.

Our part in this was soon foreshadowed by the receipt of a thousand camp beds, a thousand deck chairs, mountains of relevant stores— including 6,000 bottles of beer—and, to the astonishment of all except Ruckers who had organised it, 21 attractive nurses and four ditto female Red Cross workers. To cope with the sick, these were accommodated right aft in the Admiral's quarters under the aegis of Philip O'Rorke (officially Liaison Officer with the Female Staff, but soon shortened to The Chief Eunuch).

However, before getting down to this new role, there was some letting up to be done, including a few days' leave. I had a wonderful time with the Osborne family at Currandooly before the ship left Sydney, riding, swimming and eating. There was even a fox shoot but in this I hardly excelled; as my sights came up to a copper flank I saw in my mind's eye a scarlet horseman raise his cap on the skyline and fired to miss, preferring to be considered a hopeless shot rather than a madman brought up not to shoot foxes!

HMS *Formidable*
10/10/45

We are just getting into Sydney having been up to Manila to collect 1,000 Australian and 100 British prisoners of war. We didn't get ashore at Manila. We have no aircraft onboard and are doing a sort of pleasure cruise which has gone very well though quite hard work. I am in charge of the 100-odd officers and their arrangements, which has kept me busy. They are in better shape than we expected though treatment seems to have varied to extremes from one camp to another. Some of them are fit and others almost skeletons. Only a few lucky ones who could pinch food have had anything but boiled rice for four years. I heard that the POW Midshipmen from the *Exeter* (ex-*Prince of Wales*) were OK, also Colonel Warren (up to a year back), but no news of any of the people in Sumatra with me, although we are not by any means the only ship doing this.

One little man came up to me and said wasn't I the officer in charge of the ferry boat from Penang to Port Swettenham after the evacuation of Penang? We had a long talk. He was a Corporal in the RAOC. Apparently the Japs were absolutely down and out, the POWs got no less food than the civilian population, and the civilians were kind to the POWs when they could be and were very glad when the war ended. On the whole the chances of Japan being reformed seem good. I did my chair act at two concerts. The Aussies loved Uncle Atty's "Once before death and twice afterwards" story!

When the last man had eventually disappeared ashore we felt both emotionally drained and glad to have known them; what we found both noble and surprising was a lack of bitterness against the Japanese. This was an attitude which I myself found impossible to adopt when there was news of daring raids which had been carried out on Japanese shipping in Singapore harbour, secret until now. As I read I became rooted to the spot. It was all about Ivan Lyon, Lieutenant Colonel, DSO, MBE (who will be remembered, as a Captain, as having won the respect and affection of us all, though none more than me, in *Sederhana Djohanis*); one of Colonel Warren's Special Operations Executive men (the MBE had been awarded for his organisation of the Indragiri escape route), Ivan had at once started to plan a raid—using limpet mines to be stuck to hulls—on shipping in Singapore. Meanwhile his wife and little son had arrived safely in Australia (from Singapore) and he asked her to

269

join him in India. Very persuasive, he had soon obtained the ear of General Wavell and thus backed, took himself to Australia, the obvious base for the projected raid. Having countermanded his first cable to his wife he arrived, in July 1942, to find that not only had she already left but that her ship had been sunk and both of them taken prisoner by the Japanese.

With Jock Campbell (also of *Djohanis*) in charge of administration, and using an old ex-Japanese fishing vessel rechristened *Krait*, he raised, by force of personality and at the outset somewhat against Army inclination, a sort of seagoing commando force. This was mainly of Australians but included all sorts of officers and men with suitable characteristics. After months of intensive training they sailed—it was September 2 1943 by this time—from a small port on the west coast, carrying four special canoes. After many alarms they arrived unsuspected at Pohm-Pohm of all places. Earmarked earlier by Ivan, this was the next island to mine and where *Kuala* and *Tien Kuan* had been bombed with such dreadful results (they did, in fact, see the mast of one still protruding and when landing found .303 ammunition, food tins and other evidence of the last unfortunate visitors). Pohm-Pohm was to be the pick-up point a fortnight later.

The *Krait* took three of the canoes and their crews to another island nearer Singapore, landed them and withdrew. Setting off on the night of September 27, the canoes entered Keppel Harbour and all attached their mines successfully (Ivan Lyon and AB Huston were surprised in the act and actually watched by a Japanese seaman for some time). Getting away safely, though not without incident, all returned to the advance base to hear their mines explode. (Pictures of them on this island were to appear in the *Illustrated London News*. One shows Ivan nonchalantly studying Singapore shipping through a telescope; I could imagine how in a tense moment he would have been asked his opinion and the answer—'I keep an open mind'.) The *Krait* duly picked them up at Pohm-Pohm and got clean away, though the hue and cry can be imagined. She anchored whence she had came after 5,000 miles and 47 days away. Some 39,000 tons of Japanese shipping had been sunk. Lyon, Lieutenant Davidson, RANVR, and Lieutenant Page, AIF, received DSOs, three ABs DSMs and *Krait*'s crew two MMs and several Mentions in Despatches.

The following year Ivan Lyon put more ambitious plans into motion. The success of 'Jaywick', as the operation had been called, smoothed the way and this time he was given a submarine, HMS *Porpoise*, to do the infiltrating. When she sailed almost exactly a year after *Krait* had done, the object was much the same. *Porpoise* landed the canoes and retired, to return on November 8. No-one knows exactly what happened because not a man survived. Lyon, Davidson, a Lieutenant

Ross and several others died fighting one of the many Japanese parties that were scouring the area. The remaining ten were rounded up piecemeal and put in Outram gaol in Singapore. They were tried as spies because they were not wearing uniform. The story of the magnificent behaviour of this gallant, tragic little band is a saga that was never given the publicity it should have been, at least in the UK. They could have saved their lives by making degrading admissions, but none would (a Royal Marine Major, R.N. Ingleton, and Lieutenant Page, were now the leaders). After being kept in captivity for months all were beheaded on July 7 1945, only a few weeks before the Japanese capitulated. Their bearing during their last days and at the end was so good that the Japanese Commander in Chief, General Itagaki, addressing the full staff of his Army said: 'We Japanese have been proud of our bravery and courage in action, but these heroes showed us a fine example of what true bravery should be. Unless we try much harder to make ourselves better soldiers, we ought to feel ashamed of ourselves before these heroes'.

I was thankful that poor Ivan (who was, in fact, recommended for the VC) did not have to endure the last drawn-out chapter. I may be maligning it, but his regiment seems to have taken very little notice.

There was an immediate and poignant sequal to this news of Ivan.

HMS *Formidable*
Sydney, 24/10/45

. . . I also dined with the Lyons. Mrs Lyons mentioned a young woman she'd met who had just got back from a POW camp with a small boy, both of them having been caught in a liner going to India. I said it must be Mrs Lyon (wife of the Gordon Highlander in the prauw) and it was. He is now missing since November, having been doing very dangerous sabotage work against ships in Singapore. The Japs say they shot him in November and as there is no reason to disbelieve them, I'm afraid it's true. However, I contacted Mrs Lyon, who is a very pretty Frenchwoman, and gave her some prauw photographs and a copy of the story which I also told her. She is very brave but realises there is not much hope I think. He arrived in Australia *five days* after she left (in 1942). Isn't it a tragedy?

I expect you have heard my news . . . Everyone has been very nice about it. Admiral Vian congratulated us and said to me 'You certainly earned yours'. We had a cocktail party on board soon after to which I invited half a dozen friends and T. and I went out to dinner, etc, afterwards. Went for a sail with some friends of Robin's, the Parkers, and have been up to Aunt Nell often. She had a very good dance which was especially put off for me because the ship was late getting in.

We are sailing today for Rabaul, Singapore, Madras, Batavia and Sydney in that order. Taking Indian ex-POWs from Rabaul to Madras and afterwards Indian soldiers from India to Batavia. We call at Singapore to oil and I shall, of course, do my best to get ashore.

A sideboy from the Officer of the Watch had come to say that there was a lady with a small boy to see me on the quarterdeck. On the way I braced myself for the possibility of an emotional trial. I had been pretty upset about poor Ivan and goodness knows what sort of state his widow must be in. I found a charming young Frenchwoman with a delicate oval face under swept-back hair, who spoke with an attractive accent (that in fact never left her). She introduced herself and her four-year-old Clive—who clung to her hand with both of his—in an altogether calm and dignified way. I was selfishly thankful to find she knew all there was to know about her husband. She talked about him quietly and told me her future plans; her parents—her father was Governor of the Condore Islands—had been murdered by the Vichy French just before the war with Japan*; she was going to Ivan's parents in England as soon as possible. I, who should have been a help, was almost tongue-tied with the pathos of it all. She had indeed missed her husband by a hair's breath, spent over three years in a prison camp in Palembang in conditions of terrible privation and shortage of food, only to be released to hear of his death. Her son was timid and thin but did not look unwell and obviously this heroic little Amazon had done her very best for him. She was not without a sense of humour even now, and my admiration was only equalled by the frustration of being able to do very little for her as we were leaving almost at once to collect Indian soldiers at Rabaul†.

From there we doubled back round the south of New Guinea and then struck westwards between Java and Borneo. Islands were often in sight on one side or the other, long stretches of palm blending into streaks of green or dark grey depending on the direction of the sun, and sometimes steep mountains behind; the whole confection, mirrored in limpid water, certainly took me back. And so did a day at Singapore.

HMS *Formidable*
6/11/45

We are now between Singapore and Ceylon (going to Bombay), a journey I seem to remember having done before. I had an intensely interesting day at Singapore from 11 am to 10 pm. It was really like walking round in a dream seeing it all again, very little changed, and with the effect increased by the number of things seen in the short time as I certainly got about. I had a great stroke of luck as I met a Pay Lieutenant Reeve in the Naval Office, who had been the Drafting Commander's Assistant at the FSA and now in charge of the docketing of particulars of people missing, etc, as compiled by released POWs.

---

*Both were awarded the Cross of Liberation, posthumously, by De Gaulle.
†I went to see them at Farnham on return home and kept up with Gabrielle on and off until her death in 1979. Clive joined his father's regiment and then retired to a farm in Norfolk where I have the pleasure of staying with him and his charming wife (and two Lyonic sons) from time to time.

272

I found that all the people at Padang of my party were put in a camp in Sumatra. Poor Beckwith, Terry and Wood are unheard of—Beckwith almost certainly dead—in fact Terry too as he sailed from Padang (as I thought) in a ship that was torpedoed with one survivor, a Brigadier, who made Batavia and died there. Monro, the 1st Lieutenant of the *Kung Wo* (on the island with me and later went off to pilot a junk to Sumatra) was also taken prisoner (now released).

Comander Reid (who detailed me for the raid on the Jap lines) was senior officer of one of the worst camps (at Palembang, Sumatra) and is a byword for his superb courage and leadership among all POWs. Apparently whenever he heard or saw one of the POWs being beaten or roughly handled he would go and put himself between the Jap guards and the man concerned, invariably getting the beating as well himself, until in the end they began to respect him and desisted. Our (BPF) pilots who were shot down over Palembang (when I was in *Indom*) were shot.

I think I told you about Lyon. I found my own name and particulars all correct in this book, up to leaving Padang of course. Reading all those names and lists of ships sunk and accounts of horrors both of people who got away before, at the same time, and after me, it is hardly believeable that I escaped. I had hoped we'd pass close to my island but we had to take a roundabout route due to mines.

Captain X, who got away from the island in the first boat, when asked by Reeve what had happened to Monro said that the latter had been drinking and they had fallen out. If I'd had time I'd have gone round and given him a nasty interview. Perhaps we shall go back there again. Captain Atkinson (Captain of the Dockyard, Singapore) was shot by Australian soldiers when trying to stem a rush on the liner *Empire Star*. They took her by force and made the crew sail to' Batavia. Commander Livingstone (with Atkinson when I last saw them) got to Sumatra but was murdered there by natives who thought he was Dutch. Admiral Spooner and the AOC died of malaria on an island south of Singapore where they had landed after being sunk. The Sub of the *Repulse* was taken prisoner but is OK. The Surgeon Commander in the *Kung Wo* (whose car I was nearly shot for stealing) died or was killed in Sumatra, or he may have gone with Terry.

Anyhow, this chap Reeve told me where to get transport and I went in a sort of shooting brake up to the Naval Base by the Bukit Timah road (down which the Japs advanced on Singapore) I looked all over the FSA which was in good order and used as a barracks again, surprisingly the MAA by remarking that I'd spent many an uncomfortable night under his table! (His office was my passive defence HQ) and also saw the dockyard which had parts of it smashed by Super Fortress bombing. I then came back to Singapore in the evening by the old road down the centre of the island. The native lights were coming out among the trees, and what with the warm sweet smell and the chickens just escaping in time and the black driver beside me it was almost as if the last three or four years had never taken place.

I went to the Oranje Hotel and looked in my old room. The place where a shell had hit the skylight was still just boarded over!

The hotel where I had lunch was where Terry and I had an Xmas 'do' in

December '41, albeit rather a depressing one. Singapore as a whole is in very good order. All the Japs are in huge camps in Johore to the north, behaving very well. Apparently it is just as well we didn't have to take the place by storm, which I had thought would have been a very good thing, as they would have (a) razed it to the ground and (b) massacred all POWs and civilian internees. The Malays and Chinese were very pleased to see us back. It was a very full day for me and I nearly secured a Japanese sword, only the officer who dispenses same hadn't arrived at his office so I couldn't wait! Sounds like the good old story again.

One thing I had meant to do at Singapore which I forgot was to leave 'my' cowhide boots (in which I walked out of the place) at the FSA. They had belonged to a Surgeon Lieutenant Commander Schofield who I have since discovered was the *Durban*'s doctor. They ended up by serving me very well in action on the flight deck until the heat melted the soles.

As the *Formidable* nosed her way among the crowded shipping in Singapore Roads and came gingerly to anchor, the gruff monotone of running cable had sounded for me like the last notes of a very long march. Singapore—not with its Japanese defenders satisfactorily stunned from wave after wave of attacks, but anyway ours again and what was important, without loss. A slight haze hung over the sea front. The Hong Kong-Shanghai Bank, Union Buildings and the Customs House looked placid enough but I only had to close my eyes to see them silhouetted against an orange glow, with occasional pillars of flame reaching up to the pall above.

Reeve produced two books compiled by British prisoners of war, one giving the names and details of everyone killed or missing, the other stating the fates of all the ships that had left Singapore in Febuary 1942. Thirty-five vessels (from MLs to quite large ships) left on and after Febuary 13—Singapore fell on the 15th—not one getting through.

Most of the personal news was bad but among others Pool (Sub of the *Repulse*), Clark (of the operations up country) and the *Prince of Wales* Midshipmen were all right. (I was soon to run into the latter. They had withstood starvation, brutality and disease, all coming through. The spirit that clearly prevailed came out in a story one of them told me; they were working in a nickel mine in a remote part of the Celebes and beri-beri, dysentry and malaria were taking their daily toll when an *Exeter* officer, Lieutenant Mark Kerr, became critically ill. The Midshipmen were keeping watch by his side throughout the night and one of them, unable to detect any breathing, said that he thought he had died. At this Kerr opened his eyes and murmured, 'Not yet if I can help it!' I asked the narrator, 'And did he die?' 'Oh no' was the reply, 'That's him over there.')

Opposite Dick Beckwith's name were some cryptic details provided by a Stoker Farrow. I copied them down on a signal form and wrote to

Yvonne Beckwith, his wife (she had returned the picture left with her when the ship sailed and we had corresponded from time to time).

The form reads:

Beckwith R.C. Lt. R.N. (*Prince of Wales*) M.L. *Elizabeth*
Elizabeth left Singapore night 13/14-2-42. Sunk by gunfire Banka Strait 16.2.42. Passengers R.M.3, R.A.F.6, Army 2. Survivors 2 only, including Sto. Farrow (POW)
Survivors *Fanlin* report *Elizabeth* just behind *Fanlin*. Saw her ordered alongside destroyer, 20 min. later destroyer hauled off and sank her by gunfire. Fate of crew unknown.

I will now jump ten years to an RAF hospital in Germany. A tall young woman in Welfare Officer's uniform came into my room. She looked somehow familiar but I could not place her and after a little conversation asked if she could get a pen out of my reefer jacked in the wardrobe. 'Oh, you're in the Navy!' she said 'I wonder if you knew my brother, Richard Beckwith?' I said indeed I had and told her what I knew. She knew more, Yvonne presumably having contacted Stoker Farrow (who had been left to drown but picked up later) and what I learnt made me very proud just to have known Dick. The Japanese destroyer Captain had sent for him as CO of *Elizabeth* and informed him that he himself would be taken prisoner but that the ML with the rest of those onboard would be sunk. Dick replied that he would rather return to his ship. This was doubtless an understandable request to a Japanese brought up in the tradition of honourable suicide and he said all right, if he wished. Dick returned and the destroyer stood off and shelled the unfortunate *Elizabeth* with the result known. Thus came the end of a very gallant officer, a cold-blooded sacrifice that lacked the spur of any military advantage. An end to be ranked, in my opinion, with those of Sir Richard Grenville, Captain Oates, or any posthumous VC that was ever earned. There is also a tragic epilogue in that poor Yvonne Beckwith died not long after the war, virtually of a broken heart.

The Fleet Shore Accommodation appeared to be in reasonable shape. What a pity I did not have the *Sultan* badge with me—taken down from the Wardroom bulkhead with the vow to put it up again one day—but, of course, it was several fathoms down in the *Kung Wo*. New fire engines stood in Macintosh's brigade HQ (it will be remembered he was a staunch companion when on the run) the administration offices were in full swing and as I cadged a lift in a lorry to Singapore the lights came on in Captain Atkinson's old window.

Darkness gave full play to lighted kampongs and the glow of fires between palm trunks on either hand as we clattered through Sambawang and Ni Soon, the latter still a desolation where it had been burnt out by incendiaries. There were fleeting glimpses of Chinese and

Malay stalls, and white-clad Indian figures looming suddenly in the headlamps to be missed by inches. Back among Singapore's honking traffic, drifts of conversation came through the jabber, 'Vairy cheap, only 50 dollar'—'Cor, t'ain't worth a tanner!'—'Here John, this one, how much?'—'Yessir, Yessir, come in!' Singapore was getting back on its feet all right.

At Bombay I scoured the hospitals for my cousin Jack Barton; word had it that, in bad health, he had arrived from a prison camp at Palembang, but he had already been sent home. Fierce looking Indian soldiers were embarked, armed to the teeth but not without their creature comforts; the morning watchmen were surprised to be serenaded—when we sailed for Java—by cocks in trucks on the flight deck. Their owners were looking forward to quelling the trouble that had arisen in Indonesia. Having had the Japanese yoke removed, this part of the world was the first to flex its muscles against the old colonial power, a practice which, of course, spread. Landing them at Batavia, we called at Tarakan to pick up 1,300 Australian soldiers and retraced our steps to Sydney via Morotai.

Passing one small island the ship was stopped and a team of shipwrights sent ashore. For all I know the Captain had made some mental note when going the other way, but the next we knew was several enormous tree-trunks being towed back to the ship. They were hoisted on to the flight deck and secured down. Ruckers had found an architect among the RNVR officers who now got down to designing a house. Except that the tree-trunks caused worry in rough weather encountered later, that was as far as it went for the time.

All of a sudden I received a spate of wonderful letters. They were from many of the men in my party left at Padang in March 1942. Home at last after unspeakable hardships and ill treatment, they made little mention of these until pressed. Here are some:

16/11/45

My name is J.H. Hughes, Able Seaman. I was in your party that got to Sumatra by junk after Singapore fell and I was glad to hear that you got away and did not get taken prisoner like myself. It all seems so long ago. I got back about three weeks ago. I apologise for not having written before, I am very sorry. I've been a little forgetful, can't get settled yet.

What I really want to say is that I am very grateful and want to thank you for giving my mother and Dad first hand news, and making them feel easier, when you wrote in July 1942 about me.

Hoping you are in the best of health and enjoying life as much as myself.

There was one from K. Jones, 'Ordinary Seaman', who had been so imperturbable in the boat, lying off that island, when a Jap fighter came at us—

'. . . since that time I have experienced many hardships, but as you will see by the address I am now with my people.'

Of course, poor Jones was now an AB of three years standing. There was one from Able Seaman Brown, whom (with AB Witherley) I had rated up to Acting Leading Seaman; it may be remembered that they, with Macintosh and myself, had shared an ambush for two toucans.

28/10/45

I am writing to let you know how really grateful I am to you for informing my parents of my whereabouts and health. It relieved their minds somewhat and at least they knew I was still living. I sincerely hope your plucky escape across the Indian Ocean has left no serious mar on your health.

Well, Sir, I must thank you once more, and hope your relatives and friends are reunited and all as happy as we are at home. So now I will close hoping that sometime in the future I may have the good fortune to sail with you again.

I replied saying that I had felt awful leaving them in the lurch and was never certain that I had done the right thing; also I asked what had happened to him.

11/12/45

Thank you so much for your welcoming letter, and hope you are in the best of health. First of all, Sir, (this leaving us in the lurch business) I can assure you none of us think of it that way, personally I think it took guts to see it through.

Well, Sir, you asked for a brief account of what happened when you left, so here goes. The Japs came in on the 16th and on the 18th confined us to the Dutch barracks at Padang. Their first job was to send all Naval and RAF officers to Singapore . . . [there follows a description of forced labour at Padang, Medan, Mergui, Jaroy, Modmein, and Thanbyvzayat] Well, Sir, we finally reached Siam after 2½ years of downright slavery, but I suppose you have heard all the horror stories by this time so I shall not bother to relate them.

This is all for now if at any time you are in England, I would consider it a pleasure to meet you personally. Well goodbye, Sir, and the best of luck to you and the *Formidable*.'

Then I got a letter from dear old Hobbs, the Petty Officer who had been so magnificent throughout the period on the run. He had clearly had a terrible time.

6/12/45

Hoping these few lines find you, as I wish to thank you for letting my wife know I was safe in Sumatra.

All the boys were very pleased when they heard that you and others had made a break, what days, eh Sir? I often think of Mr Monro, and the Japs took him from us the first day in Camp, many others are dead now, E.R.A. Roper, you remember him, I really forget them all, most of the Naval lads were lost when we were being shipped from Medan June 25 1944, in the *Van Warywick* an old Dutch liner; we were packed in the holds, at midday, on the 26th we were tin fished, two fine shots, sure would like to know the sub's commander, roughly 300 men lost their lives, thousands more died of beri beri and starvation. I am on leave until 6.3.46 just getting over my beri beri. My eyes are very bad, but have not to wear glasses as my sight will return, hopes?

I could go on and write quite a book of our adventures from *Repulse* to the west coast of Sumatra to the east.

Well, Sir, I trust that all's well with you. I am pensioned now. Cheerio and a Merry Xmas to you and yours.

PS. Hope to hear from you, at least every time a ring goes on the Coat, or some pretty one's finger. All the best Sir.

Apparently at Padang the officers *were* separated from the men, as Colonel Warren had predicted to me. This did not always happen, however, witness Commander Philip Reid's gallant behaviour mentioned earlier.

Then came a letter which I must say I was very pleased to receive. It was from Colonel Warren himself.

Army and Navy Club
2/12/45

I have recently seen your father at the Club and he has given me your address.

I got home a month ago and should have written before. I want to thank you—on two counts. First for carrying out your part of the contract made at Padang—you got across and, later, were a contribution to 'the cause'. I congratulate you on your effort in the Pacific. Secondly for your letters to my wife and my cousin, Dorothy Hutton. So few people, I find, think of doing nice things these days that it is good to find someone who does.

I was with Commander Alexander most of our 3½ years and we flew out of Bangkok together. We were 6 months in Singapore (Changi) and 3 years in Siam. Bad in parts but we managed some fun sometimes. Jock Monro (RNR), Poole, and all nautics came through except Dickinson (MRNVR) who died. I saw Passmore yesterday, Waller in Bangkok, Campbell (now Colonel OBE!) in Ceylon. Broome and Davies have done excellently in Malaya, and will have a good story to tell no doubt. Lind rang me recently and sent me some photographs. Cox I saw in Ceylon.

Everyone seems to be flourishing. No doubt you will be home soon. I've got a lot of refreshing (!) courses to do so don't know where I'll be, but Admiralty will always get me. I'd like to see you when convenient.

England's a queer place and its not easy to adjust one's ideas to the modern outlook I find. 'Damn you Jack, I'm all right' seems to be the viewpoint, and mud-slinging by those who make cheap money writing books, seems to have been a popular pastime. However, no doubt everything will adjust itself in time.

Good luck to you, my best wishes to you always and thank you again!

Colonel Warren eventually retired to America. It is one of my greatest regrets that he came back to live at Lymington near us without my knowing and died there in the mid-'70s. I expect he saved my life.

Though not unathletic I never had a strong constitution (nine operations have been clocked up to-date) and have doubts on my surviving a Japanese prison camp. Commander Alexander had of course been last seen at Dabo (when he gave me the opium) shepherding the rest of us through. There is a nice cameo of him in *The Tragedy of Singapore*, when as the senior officer of a camp he was sent for one day (the once gold oak-leaves on his cap black with grime) by the Japanese commandant. 'You are to take over' the latter said, saluting, 'Today Japan lost the war.'

This last, satisfactory post script to my Malayan experiences arrived as we heard that the ship would be going home immediately after Christmas. Leaving Australia was a bitter-sweet affair, in fact as far as the ratings were concerned the number that elected not to leave but be 'demobbed' down under was considerable. The hospitality shown to us all had been on a different plane to anything ever encountered before. I had been lucky with my introduction to Nell Knox but there had also been many others who had treated me as one of the family. Leaving them was not unlike leaving one's family and I do not think there would have been much protest—at least among us regulars—at some postponement of our return. At the same time going home was going home and years of war had taught us not to pass up that one. It was decided to say a suitable thank you and this was done in the form of a memorable dance, or dances, first night ratings (3,500 guests) and second night officers.

HMS *Formidable*
1/1/46

You will have got my cable by now to say I am on the way home. Isn't it exciting! Did you see John Bowles got married? I must write to him. Admiral Vian came and spoke to the ship's company in glowing terms when we left Sydney and the actual departure was impressive with other ships cheering us, boats with their bands and 'chuckers up' keeping alongside, the crowds all waving from the shore. I could see Aunt Nell on her veranda through binoculars . . .

And so we sailed for Fremantle, Cape Town and home, the ship's paying off pennant (traditionally a third as long again as herself) unable to rise much in the still air.

I was in due course less than happy in the Bay of Biscay. Heavy rolling also strained the lashings of the Captain's tree trunks on the flight deck and caused concern for a short time. (Perhaps another jump into the future—some two years this time—may be permitted. Ruckers came to inspect my shore establishment—he was Director of Naval Training—and afterwards we talked. Expecting to get a life out of him I

279

asked what had happened to the tree trunks we had brought home with some difficulty. What became of the eventual house? He fixed me with the look I knew so well. It had lost nothing in the intervening period; if anything it had gained from being crowned by an Admiral's peak. 'I live in it, dammit, I live in it,' he said).

As he brought HMS *Formidable* alongside at South Railway Jetty, Portsmouth, and I picked out my parents from the sea of faces welcoming us, my mind went back eight years to when a brand new Midshipman had climbed the brow to the *Nelson* at exactly the same spot. In some ways it seemed yesterday, in others a century ago. The future was a pleasant question mark; one could look forward to a lot of things. But for me there would always be large blanks; there could be no shared delights with John, Edward or Sandy, as there used to be before the war. For the umpteenth time I wondered why I had been spared and not even one of them. A benevolent providence seemed to have been watching over me ever since I should have been on the fo'c's'le of the *Nelson* when she hit a mine; there was the shell from the *Bismarck* that lodged in the fuel tank and failed to explode; the cancellation of the raid at Singapore because the enemy chose to attack first; the motor launch I nearly left in being never seen again; the delay in Sumatra which prevented me from sharing Terry's fate; *Sederhana Djohanis*; and recently—if that kamikaze pilot had not decided to go round again . . .

Even now, 40 years on, if my luck seems to be temporarily out, I feel it is only someone redressing the balance.

Index

282

283

284

285